Jeffrey Grey

The Commonwealth armies and the Korean War

An alliance study

Manchester University Press
Manchester and New York

Distributed exclusively in the USA and Canada
by St. Martin's Press, New York

Copyright © Jeffrey Grey 1988

Published by Manchester University Press
Oxford Road, Manchester M13 9PL, UK

*Distributed exclusively in the USA and Canada
by* St. Martin's Press, Inc.,
175 Fifth Avenue, New York, NY 10010, USA

British Library cataloguing in publication data
Grey, Jeffrey
  The Commonwealth armies and the Korean
  War : an alliance study.—(War, armed
  forces and society).
  1. Korean War, 1950–53—Campaigns
  2. Commonwealth of Nations—Armed forces
  I. Title II. Series
951.9′042   D5918.8

951.904

Library of Congress cataloging in publication data
Grey, Jeffrey.
  The Commonwealth armies and the Korean War: an alliance study
  Jeffrey Grey.
      p. cm.—(War, armed forces, and society)
  Bibliography: p. 228.
  Includes index.
  ISBN 0-7190-2611-3 : $35.00 (est.)
  1. Korean War, 1950–1953—Great Britain. 2. Great Britain. Army.
Commonwealth Division, 1—History. I. Title. II. Series.
DS919.3.G73 1988
951.9′042—dc19   87-36700

7 DEC 1988

ISBN 0–7190–2611–3 *hardback*

Typeset in Great Britain by
Alan Sutton Publishing Ltd, Gloucester

Printed and bound in Great Britain by
Biddles Ltd, Guildford and King's Lynn

The Commonwealth armies and the Korean War

Allied armies come together without properly understanding what each other means; they have different interests to pursue, which they will not sufficiently explain to each other; their language is different, their manners not the same, and their discipline dissimilar.

Montecuccoli (1609–1680)

Dealing with an enemy is a simple and straightforward matter when contrasted with securing close cooperation with an ally.

Major General Fox Connor (Chief of Staff, AEF, 1917–18)

Alliances, to be sure, are good, but forces of one's own are better still.

Frederick William of Brandenburg ('The Great Elector', 1667)

Contents

Illustrations

Maps

Acknowledgements

The production of a book brings with it numerous debts to both individuals and institutions. I wish to thank my colleagues in the Department of History, University College, UNSW, at the Australian Defence Force Academy, especially Dr Peter Dennis and Lieutenant-Colonel D.M. Horner. Both read the entire manuscript in successive drafts and their comments and observations have saved me from errors of fact and interpretation. Professor Alan Gilbert has helped in more ways than he probably cares to remember. As head of the Department of History he supported my work in the midst of many other demands upon his time; his belief in the worth of younger scholars is reassuring at a time when it seems that many of us may be squeezed out of the profession by contraction in the universities. I wish to thank Dr Robin Prior, also, for reading and commenting upon the final draft of the manuscript. Responsibility for such errors as remain must reside with the author.

The Council of the Australian War Memorial and the Dean of the then Faculty of Military Studies, University of New South Wales at Duntroon, Professor Geoff Wilson, helped fund the research for the thesis on which this book is based, and I gratefully acknowledge their assistance. A large number of individuals gave generously of their time in answering letters from a total stranger, and some willingly submitted to the additional intrusion of being interviewed. A full list of these is located in the bibliography, and my indebtedness to them is evident throughout the text. Transcripts of these interviews will eventually be placed in the library of the Australian War Memorial.

For assistance with access to archival material, I wish to thank the following: Mr Chris Taylor, Australian Archives, Mitchell; Mr

Tim Bryant, Australian Archives, Brighton; Mr Michael Piggott and Mrs Helen Creagh, Australian War Memorial, Canberra; the Director and staff of the New Zealand Archives, Wellington; Dr David Smurthwaite, National Army Museum, Chelsea; the Trustees, Director and staff of the Liddell Hart Centre for Military Archives, King's College, London; the staff of the Public Record Office, Kew; Dr Peter Thwaites, Imperial War Museum, London; Mrs Jean North, Ministry of Defence, London; General Sir Anthony Farrar-Hockley, British official historian of the Korean War; Mr Dacre Cole, Historical Division, Department of External Affairs, Ottawa; Dr W.A.B. Douglas, Director, and Mr Paul Chaplin, Directorate of History, Department of National Defence, Ottawa; the staff of the Public Archives of Canada, Ottawa; Ms Sally Marks and Mr Steve Tilley, National Archives and Record Service, Washington DC; the staff of the Modern Military Field Branch, Washington National Record Centre, Suitland, Maryland; Dr Richard J. Sommers, United States Army Military History Institute.

Mention must be made of Brigadier Brian Burdett, former British Defence Attache, Seoul, and Sir William Keys, National President of the Returned Services League of Australia, who helped with arrangements during a field trip to the Republic of Korea in 1985. For typing the various drafts I wish to express my appreciation to Ms Kristina Evans, and also to Mr Paul Ballard of the Australian Defence Force Academy for drawing the maps.

Transcripts of Crown-copyright records in the Public Record Office appear by permission of the Controller of Her Majesty's Stationery Office. Excerpts from Commonwealth records held by the Australian Archives appear by permission of the Director-General.

It is customary for authors to acknowledge the contribution of their families to the completion of their work. The recognition of my debt to Gina in this regard is no less profound for being routinely expressed.

Abbreviations

ABCA	America, Britain, Canada, Australia
AIF	Australian Imperial Force
ANZAC	Australian and New Zealand Army Corps
ANZAM	Australian and New Zealand Agreement concerning the defence of the Malay barrier
ANZUS	Australia-New Zealand-United States
AWM	Australian War Memorial
BAOR	British Army of the Rhine
BCFK	British Commonwealth Forces, Korea
BCOF	British Commonwealth Occupation Force
BRINDIV	British-Indian Division
CASF	Canadian Army Special Force
CCF	Chinese Communist Forces
CGS	Chief of the General Staff
CIGS	Chief of the Imperial General Staff
C-in-C	Commander-in-Chief
CINCFE	Commander-in-Chief, Far East
CMMFE	Canadian Military Mission, Far East
CPV	Chinese People's Volunteers
CRO	Commonwealth Relations Office
CRS	Commonwealth Record Series
DEA	Department of External Affairs
D HIST	Directorate of History
EUSAK	Eighth United States Army, Korea
FARELF	Far East Landforces
FEC	Far East Command
FOO	Forward Observation Officer
GHQ	General Headquarters
GOC	General Officer Commanding

HQRA	Headquarters, Royal Artillery
IDC	Imperial Defence College
IWM	Imperial War Museum
JAPC	Joint Administrative Planning Committee
JCOSA	Joint Chiefs of Staff in Australia
JCS	Joint Chiefs of Staff
KATCOM	Koreans Attached to the Commonwealth Division
KATUSA	Korean Augmentation to the US Army
Kay-Force	[New Zealand] Korean Force
KOPA	Korean Operations Pool Account
KOSB	King's Own Scottish Borderers
KPA	Korean People's Army
NARS	National Archive and Record Service
NATO	North Atlantic Treaty Organisation
NZA	New Zealand Archives
NZEF	New Zealand Expeditionary Force
PAC	Public Archives of Canada
PPCLI	Princess Patricia's Canadian Light Infantry
PRO	Public Record Office
RAAF	Royal Australian Air Force
RAR	Royal Australian Regiment
RCR	Royal Canadian Regiment
RCT	Regimental Combat Team
RMC	Royal Military College
ROK	Republic of Korea
R22eR	Royal Vingt Deuxieme Regiment
SCAP	Supreme Commander for the Allied Powers
SHAEF	Supreme Headquarters, Allied Expeditionary Force
USAMHI	United States Army Military History Institute
UNC	United Nations Command
UNRC	United Nations Reception Centre
VCIGS	Vice-Chief of the Imperial General Staff
WNRC	Washington National Record Centre

Introduction

The Korean War is a watershed in the history of Commonwealth defence cooperation. It marks a period where the national interests of the old Commonwealth had diverged, while its armies had reached a high level of standardisation, compatibility, and inter-allied effectiveness. At a time when Commonwealth unity, so far as it ever existed, had begun to decline in form as well as in substance the Commonwealth armies could point to a general level of inter-allied operational and administrative cooperation that few wartime alliances have matched and none surpassed.

Any examination of the experience of Commonwealth military forces in the Korean War reveals both this high level of cooperation and a great deal of friction, at virtually every level. The forces contributed to the United Nations Command by Australia, Britain, Canada, New Zealand and India drew upon a common military heritage and organisational and operational methods derived from British practice to form a highly proficient, multi-national division. As might be expected in such circumstances, relations were not trouble free. The further up the chain of command one proceeded, the greater the potential for disharmony and the harder the officers and officials present had to work to ensure the continuing smooth functioning of the Commonwealth organisation. The issues of financing and supply caused immense problems, some of which were not resolved until a decade after the fighting in Korea ceased. The question of command responsibility was also vexatious, and even when the matter was supposedly resolved in late 1950 it was raised again on a number of other occasions. At the level of strategic planning, disagreement arose not so much from differing strategic conceptions on the part of the various Commonwealth governments, for this was an American-run war from beginning to end, as through efforts on the part of the British, in particular, to return to that level of influence with the Americans in the conduct of the war that they had enjoyed in the Second World War, and to do so while denying the Dominions any such advantage.

This book is principally concerned to show the pattern of relations between the Commonwealth forces within the context of the Korean War, and at certain levels only. No attempt has been made to present every aspect of Commonwealth involvement, nor to provide a continuous operational narrative. The former would be beyond the scope of a single volume while accounts of operations, of varying quality, are generally available. The participation of Commonwealth air and naval units is not touched upon, either. The major reason for doing this is that Korea was overwhelmingly a ground war, to be won or lost by ground combat. This is in contrast to the war in the Pacific, where naval units were of prime importance. The ground force effort was also much larger in terms of men and resources, and for these reasons occupied much more time and attention than did air or naval units. Some preliminary examination indicates that study of Commonwealth air and naval units does not raise any substantive issue of Commonwealth relations or policy not already posed by consideration of the ground forces. While the air and naval units concerned may well have experienced difficulties, and are worthy of study in their own right, the type of roles assigned to Commonwealth units suggests that these were more narrowly operational.[1]

As with most studies of war-time alliances, the diplomatic and grand strategic aspects of the Korean War have received considerable scholarly attention while the interaction of allied forces, in many ways the bottom line of success or failure for any coalition, has been generally neglected. I have concentrated therefore upon this level of alliance relations by examining command, the combat effectiveness of forces, questions of supply and finance and, where appropriate, strategic and other government policies. In terms of intra-Commonwealth relations this last aspect most frequently manifested itself in the form of manpower and equipment policies, and these will be discussed and examined at some length.

The decisions to commit forces, what size they would be and whether to field them together highlighted both current concerns and older issues. The importance of the non-operational control and administration of the forces brought to the surface the disputes between Britain and Australia over the latter's desire for a role in Pacific affairs that had re-appeared in the last year of the war with Japan. Examination of the combat effectiveness of Commonwealth units reveals not only a consistently high level of performance, but also disagreements with both each other and the Americans on matters of doctrine and organisation. It also demonstrates the problems inherent in reliance upon the main power in a theatre when that power's approach to war differs considerably from that of the forces dependent upon it. Brief comparisons are drawn with the experiences of other, non-Commonwealth, UN units, and these indicate that the outcome is usually either the absorption of the smaller force by the larger, with subsequent risk of the loss of national identity, or an uneasy compromise where the lesser force is generally left alone to conduct its operations in its own way while suffering from shortages that cannot be made up readily from its own resources. Neither outcome is wholly desirable.

Particular attention has been paid to the unfashionable and neglected subject of administration. As Lord Wavell pointed out fifty years ago, 'in most military books strategy and tactics are emphasised at the expense of the administrative factors . . . there are ten military students who can tell you how Blenheim was won for one who has any knowledge at all of the administrative preparations that made the march to Blenheim possible.'[2] Tactical matters are not ignored though. I share some of the reservations recently expressed about the thrust of the 'new military history', and agree that it may explain 'possibly less of what actually happened than do the neglected subjects of military organisation and military decision-making.'[3] The themes of this book are somewhat disparate, for that is the nature of the subject, and I have made no attempt to impose cohesion upon events where none in fact existed.

Marshal of the Royal Air Force Lord Tedder, a great exponent of allied cooperation while deputy to Eisenhower at SHAEF, observed that the British tend to draw lessons from the later stages of a war, concentrating upon periods of relative success when resources are often in abundance, and neglecting the early stages with all their attendant difficulties.[4] This is clearly a dangerous prescription for the study of coalition warfare, for in the later stages the component national parts have had time to shake down, become aware of each other's peculiarities and idiosyncrasies, and make adjustments

accordingly. It is the process by which this adaptation is achieved
that is important. Writing of the British army of 1939, General Sir
David Fraser acknowledged that 'unless arrangements have been
far-sighted and loyalty to alliance nurtured in time of peace, Allied
cooperation is defective, command systems ambiguous.'[5] The
western alliance that fought in Korea was still developing, not yet in
its modern, largely NATO-based, form, but no longer the coalition
that had beaten Hitler. This book looks at the way in which some
parts of that alliance operated in a war in which arrangements were
sometimes short-sighted, cooperation defective, and command at
times ambiguous. It concentrates on the disagreements and the
difficulties, upon the frictions of war, for no wartime alliance was
ever wrecked because the parties were in perfect agreement.

Chapter 1
The background

The twentieth century has been the great age of alliance warfare
and the search for allies, and the difficulties experienced in dealing
with them, has been an important theme in modern military
historiography. The two world wars, of course, are the most
obvious examples of great alliances in conflict, but many 'lower-
level' wars have demonstrated the same features. One thinks of the
array of Arab states ranged against the Israelis, of the Axis powers'
support of Franco, of Anglo-French cooperation at Suez, and of
Lyndon Johnson's search for 'more flags' in Vietnam. This book is
principally concerned with the interaction between the forces of
Britain and the Dominions, but of necessity also examines relations
between those forces and the Americans, who dominated the
United Nations Command and ran the war.

The problems associated with fighting as part of a coalition are
not new and are certainly not confined to the wars of the present
century. Marlborough's difficulties with his Dutch allies are well
known, moving the Duke of Wellington to observe a century later
that, by comparison, his own considerable problems with the
Spanish and Portuguese were far less onerous. In the Crimea, the
British Commander-in-Chief and veteran of Waterloo, Lord
Raglan, 'covered his staff with confusion by forgetting that the
French were now his allies and invariably [spoke] of "the French"
when he meant "the enemy".'[1] (The effect this produced on his
French allies is not recorded.) The price of Bavarian military
cooperation with Prussia in 1870–71 was the maintenance of the
Bavarian organisational and command structure. The Prussians
gained an important political advantage, but only by conceding the
principle of standardisation within the army of the new German
state. It is the modern industrial wars of the twentieth century,

however, which have most to teach us about the problems of alliance warfare, not only because they are closer to us in time but because it is these wars which have provoked the most study of specifically coalition problems.

There are five basic operational features of coalition warfare, and agreement must be reached in these areas, or the potential for differences and conflict minimised, if the coalition concerned is to function efficiently in bringing about the desired defeat of the common enemy. These areas are strategic policy, the command of the forces in the field, the combat effectiveness of those forces, their supply, and the financing of the military effort. The partners within a coalition are rarely, if ever, completely equal, and the balance of reliance upon one or more partner by the others will vary in each of the categories listed. It is when the balance shifts decisively in favour of one party in the majority of these areas that alliances break down as a result of the development of more than the normal and accepted level of friction. Clausewitz observed that in those cases where the states involved in a coalition do not possess an independent interest and independent forces with which to prosecute a war where, in effect, there is one amongst them on whose interests and forces those of the others lean for support, then the easier it is to look upon the different parties as comprising but one enemy.[2] While this may prove so from the point of view of an opponent, it does nothing to disguise the often deep-seated differences at various levels which continue to disrupt the smooth flow of inter-allied relations.

Strategic policy at the operational level must be distinguished from 'grand strategy', that level of planning and decision-making that is concerned with the higher direction of war. This is particularly true of limited wars, but has a general application even in the world wars of the 20th century. Its sharpest influence upon alliance relations at the operational level is generally felt in questions of resource allocation and priorities. Thus the decision of the British government to husband scarce resources and not send any more fighter squadrons to aid the French in May 1940 affected the ability of the French to maintain local air superiority and soured relations between French and British forces. It was a strategic, though not a grand strategic, decision which nonetheless had an important and direct effect upon the alliance at the operational level. In Korea the policy decisions which most frequently affected relations between the various Commonwealth forces were those concerning manpower, and these led to disputes with the Americans over operational questions such as the length of front or type of mission to be assigned to Commonwealth units.

The command of forces in the field is clearly important to any consideration of inter-allied relations, and the problems presented are not necessarily, or even generally, resolved by the simple expedient of assigning overall command of forces to the nation which provides the greatest proportion of those forces. Following the mutinies which wracked the French armies in 1917, the Imperial and Dominion forces under Haig's command on the Western Front carried the brunt of the fighting for the rest of the war until Germany's defeat in November 1918. In addition, French industry was kept solvent by the injection of sizeable quantities of British capital. But it was a Frenchman, Foch, who was appointed overall Commander-in-Chief in March 1918. This did not necessarily ensure smooth relations between the allies, since the British were carrying a disproportionate share of the burden while decisions regarding operations, of necessity, could not be based on this fact alone.[3] In Korea, command problems arose through the differences between Commonwealth and American tactical assumptions and practices. Difficulties were also experienced in the higher command levels because, within the Commonwealth organisation itself, the principle of linking command positions to the proportion of forces supplied was not always followed and the British, in particular, had difficulty dealing with an Australian Commander-in-Chief who held his position by virtue of his role in the occupation of Japan and not because of the size of the Australian force contributed.

Harmonious relations in the field depend to a considerable extent upon the perception that the component parts of the alliance are 'pulling their weight', and combat effectiveness is an obvious and important element of this. Although short-lived, the failure of American forces at Kasserine and the Fondouk Gap in the Tunisian campaign in early 1943 produced criticism from British and French commanders and disparagement and ridicule from their troops.[4] Dominion soldiers in the Dardanelles campaign in 1915 regarded the military qualities of the British New Army formations with little more than contempt, and this attitude was carried over to their experiences in France and undoubtedly contributed to their critical view, not only of British officers, but of the British army generally.[5] In Korea it was US Army units which attracted the most criticism for failure in combat and which led to the smaller formations from the Commonwealth and other UN forces continually being placed in dangerous tactical situations above and beyond that which they should have been called upon to face. Criticism of Canadian practices in the static phase of the war also led to a reordering of operational requirements in the interests of defusing tensions rather than in response to strict operational necessity.

Logistic questions are particularly important in a coalition when one ally is dependent upon another for the supply of equipment or material. The greater the level of dependence, the greater the potential for discord. This was not a serious problem for the Commonwealth during the Korean War, for they supplied most of their own requirements and the Americans were generous in making good any deficiencies. The United States Army did find itself equipping and supplying all other UN units in the United Nations Command, but this was not a major undertaking because of the relatively small size of the units involved, and certainly does not bear comparison with the effort required to re-equip the French forces in North Africa and Britain in 1942–43. Financial questions are linked to those of supply. Although incurred during hostilities, the resolution of war debts is generally left until after the successful outcome of the war. The British war debt to the United States after the Great War strained Anglo-American relations in the aftermath of the war, and indeed thereafter with the memory of the onerous settlement insisted upon by the American Treasury in 1923.[6] Lend-Lease was an unusual response to unusual circumstances, but even this scheme did not prevent considerable post-war indebtedness after 1945. The reimbursement of the Americans by the Commonwealth after the Korean War was the subject of negotiations which dragged on into the early 1960s, and as with the experience in previous wars suggests that allies should not merely plan ahead to ensure effective cooperation in wartime, but should also plan for the amicable resolution of problems which arise as a result of that same wartime cooperation after the hostilities have ended.

Before turning to deal with the Commonwealth inter-allied experience in Korea and examining the above factors at work there, it is necessary to look at certain aspects of coalitions in the Second

World War and at the development of defence cooperation between Britain and the Dominions in the inter-war period and immediately after 1945. There are two reasons for doing this. The Anglo-American alliance between 1941–45 influenced the pattern of events after the war, as well as defining the terms of the 'special relationship' to which the British were anxious to return in the early 1950s and which they sought to emulate, unsuccesfully, during the Korean War. The inter-war years saw a continuing effort to bring about standardisation and cooperation between the forces of Britain and the Dominions which was realised imperfectly, however, during the Second World War. The failure of imperial defence during the war influenced Dominion attitudes towards attempts to revive Commonwealth defence cooperation immediately after 1945, and these obviously influenced Anglo-Dominion military relations in the context of joint operations during the Korean War. It is these two areas which must now be examined.

Inequalities between allies within the western alliances were particularly marked in the Second World War. In 1940 the French disposed of the major force in the alliance, and the British Expeditionary Force (BEF) found itself part of a French chain of command, but also with the complicating factor of being a subordinate but distinctly national component within that command structure.[7] These inequalities led to gross inefficiencies in the coalition relationship, and have prompted the observation by Paul Kennedy that although the Second World War demonstrated the efficacy of coalition warfare (one presumes on one side only), this was not evident in the early stages.[8] The campaign of 1940 revealed an allied army much less able to withstand a German strike westwards than its predecessor in 1918. Coordination between the armies was frequently non-existent. The British liaison teams attached to the French army at various levels were small and often poorly selected, some members not being able even to speak French.[9] Montgomery, then commanding the 3rd Division in the British II Corps, recalled that communications and intelligence between the allies broke down immediately and that in the previous nine months of the 'phoney war', between September 1939 and May 1940, the allies 'had never conducted any exercises, either with or without troops [although] an indoor exercise on the model could easily have been held.' The result was that 'there was no co-ordination between the operations of the Belgians, the BEF, and the French First Army' on whose left flank the British were to operate.[10] The armies operated separately with no integrated staff at any functional level to coordinate planning, training or supply.

The strains imposed by the six week campaign which began on 10 May 1940 showed up the glaring weaknesses of the alliance and led to its rapid collapse. The end in the north came with the evacuation of Dunkirk and the French claim that the British were deserting them.[11] In the south the chaos was exacerbated by a disorganised command structure which saw British forces under the command of no fewer than four separate French headquarters, and no appointment of an overall British commander. The British writer Basil Karslake, in passing judgement on an abortive attack in this sector on 4 June, summed up the whole dismal episode. 'Every detail', he wrote, 'was mistimed or miscarried. There appears to have been a complete lack of liaison between the units engaged where those units were of a different nationality.'[12]

In this short campaign the allies ignored or failed to agree upon all those factors which govern the success of a coalition. Strategic planning before the war had been inadequate at best, with the possibility of a renewed Continental commitment ignored or wished away by successive British governments. There was no agreed-upon strategic or operational doctrine in British service circles, and both British and French officers remained in general ignorance of the prevailing assumptions which characterised each other's forces.[13] Command organisation was also seriously at fault, with the Commander-in-Chief of the BEF, Lord Gort, answering to three different levels of French command simultaneously.[14] The British themselves had compounded the error by reshuffling the highest command positions in the British army immediately *after* the outbreak of war. The combat effectiveness of the forces was mixed, and had not been helped by two decades of fiscal restriction and governmental neglect, nor by the lack of coordination between arms and services. It was a recipe for disaster, and disaster duly followed.

If the Anglo-French alliance in 1940 represents the nadir of successful inter-allied cooperation, the Anglo-American alliance provided 'the really splendid example of coalition warfare'.[15] Once again, however, it was not an alliance between equals, just as the wider coalition against the Axis powers was marked by inequality, and by disagreement. The smaller allies, in particular, dealt with their partners from a position of weakness and although some might attempt to assert a greater role for themselves by various means, British and American authorities never conceded a significant role to the lesser powers outside the field of combat.

Inter-allied cooperation betwen the two major Western allies was successfully implemented through the military structure set up to prosecute the war. At the top stood the Combined Chiefs of Staff Committee. Beneath them functioned the theatre and service commanders-in-chief who were responsible for implementing the allied strategy arrived at by the heads of government and the Combined Chiefs. Within theatres, joint allied operations were commanded and controlled by integrated command and staff echelons. Good examples of these are provided by Eisenhower's headquarters in North Africa in 1942–43, and SHAEF in 1944–45. At lower levels, of course, there was much less of this, with infrequent integration of British and American tactical formations. For both the British and US armies the corps was the lowest formation in which integration of units (divisions) was practiced generally. In Italy in 1944 the New Zealand corps comprised one New Zealand and one Indian division, while XIII corps in the Western Desert in late 1940 was made up of an Australian and a British division. No attempt was made to combine brigades of different national forces into composite divisions except in the British Indian army, which was a special case.

Any assessment of the Anglo-American alliance reveals a shift in the balance of the relationship during the course of the war. This change may be seen most clearly at the level of strategic planning. The 'Germany First' decision, taken at the ABC-1 talks in January 1941, confirmed at the ARCADIA conference in Washington at the end of that year and never deviated from, is a case in point. American planning in the aftermath of the Great War had been principally concerned with the possibility of war with Japan (Plan ORANGE), or of war between Britain and Japan (Plan RED-ORANGE).[16] Developments in world affairs in the 1930s, such as the signing of the Anti-Comintern Pact, led to revision of American strategic assumptions, especially after 1938 when ORANGE was extensively revised to take account of a simultaneous conflict in the Atlantic while nonetheless maintaining an offensive strategy in the Pacific.[17] As was to be the case during the war itself, the US Navy continued to emphasise the Pacific while the Army planners became more aware of the dangers posed in Europe. In 1939 the Joint Board, through the Joint Planning Committee, drew up a new series of plans – RAINBOW – to cater for a comprehensive range of strategic situations. Only the most wide-ranging of these, RAINBOW 5, assumed American action in concert with Britain and France against both Germany and Japan.[18]

German victories in 1939–40 changed the attitudes of American military planners, but not those of the President. Roosevelt was not inclined to accept the view that the United States 'should take no action involving possible military commitments outside the Western Hemisphere' following the fall of France.[19] The planners believed that Britain could not long remain an active belligerent, an assumption the President did not share. As Morton has argued, it was the President's view, not those of the planners, which increasingly shaped American policy in the second half of 1940.[20] By November 1940 the Chief of Naval Operations, Admiral Stark, was arguing in Plan DOG that 'if Britain wins decisively against Germany we could win everywhere; but that if she loses the problems confronting us would be very great; and while we might not *lose everywhere*, we might, possibly, not *win* everywhere'.[21] American security, it appeared, rested upon the fate of Britain.

Despite the fact that the United States entered the war as a result of Japanese, not German, aggression and despite the weight given by the service planners over several decades to the Japanese threat in the Pacific, the decision was made to remain on the strategic defensive in the Far East while concentrating upon Europe and the Atlantic first. The assumption that Germany was the main enemy was of obvious importance in this decision. Of equal importance was the assumption that American security was linked to the fate of the United Kingdom. The latter, therefore, stood in a strong position in the decision-making councils of the coalition.

This would not remain the case forever, as Churchill and others recognised. Inevitably, the Americans would come to field the preponderance of combat forces, and with such dominance would go the weight of decision-making. This was reflected at the major mid-war conferences at Cairo and Tehran at the end of 1943 in the debate over the future of strategy in Europe; in particular between OVERLORD, the cross-channel invasion of Europe, and continued major activity in the Mediterranean with the possibility of expanding operations in the eastern Mediterranean.[22] American desires to limit sharply the liability in this theatre were accepted grudgingly and the invasion of France, postponed in 1943 at least in part to accommodate the allied invasions of Sicily and Italy, together with its strategic consequences, became the main plank of allied strategy for the remainder of the war in Europe. While it may be true that the commonly-accepted picture of fundamentally opposed national strategies is little more than caricature,[23] and that the final form of OVERLORD was more in accordance with British than American desires,[24] it is irrefutable that in 1944–45 the balance within the Anglo-American alliance had swung firmly in the Americans' favour. This was reflected in the decision not to attempt to take Berlin, and in some of the positions taken at the Yalta conference; in the immediate post-war years the imbalance persisted.

After September 1944 the Americans fielded the greater proportion of forces. In the Pacific this was always the case, the only major British effort against the Japanese being the 14th Army's campaign in Burma. Elsewhere in the Pacific the Royal Navy was involved only in a minor capacity, and the British Chiefs of Staff often were not consulted directly on the conduct of the war. Attempts to change this situation at Potsdam were rebuffed.[25]

In other aspects of the alliance the story was similar. The British war effort was financed largely by the Americans through measures such as Lend-Lease, while in certain areas the British relied increasingly upon supplies and equipment of American provenance. The command organisation has already been alluded to. Generally it worked successfully, but differences between the two sides persisted and at times impinged upon operations, particularly during the break-out phase of the battle for Normandy and in the debate over the advance into Germany.[26] The combat effectiveness of both nation's forces varied, as one would expect, with the British exercising increasing tactical caution in the last six months of the war in Europe as the lack of reserves and general manpower crisis made itself felt. As noted earlier, there was little integration of tactical units.

The Anglo-American alliance has been discussed at some length because the coalition experience in the Second World War influenced events and behaviour in the post-war years. For most of the war the British retained a position of approximate equality in strategic decision-making. This rapidly ceased to be so after 1945, and glimmerings of the new order may be seen in the Americans' virtual exclusion of the British from the final acts of the Pacific War, and in Truman's decision in 1946 to stop the exchange of atomic technological information, contrary to the Hyde Park agreement of 1944.[27] With involvement in Korea, Britain attempted to reassert the role she had played previously in the higher conduct of operations, without success. The pattern of economic dependence remained unchanged, while questions of supply, command, and operational effectiveness all had to be resolved. Their resolution forms part of this book.

Britain did not act alone in Korea, just as she had not faced the Germans alone before the advent into the war of the United States in December 1941. The resources of the Empire had sustained Britain in both world wars, but the Second World War especially had seen a change in relations between Britain and the Dominions of what was increasingly being referred to as the Commonwealth.

The Commonwealth military relationship has been the subject of insufficient historical enquiry. As Richard Preston observed twenty years ago, too much attention has been paid 'to imperial defence planning and too little to military and naval developments in the colonies themselves.'[28] The existence of a Commonwealth military system has often been assumed, despite the fact that little has been done to establish the existence, or otherwise, of such a system, especially in the important inter-war period.

Imperial defence certainly exercised the minds of contemporaries. In 1926 a future commander of Canadian forces in Italy and North-West Europe, Lieutenant-Colonel (later Lieutenant-General) H.D.G. Crerar, identified the three essentials of successful Empire defence cooperation as being identity of organisation and equipment, identity of doctrine and training, and thorough mutual understanding and confidence.[29] The first two were relatively easily arrived at, for most features of the Dominion armies were derivative, from officer selection and education through to the standardisation of equipment types. There was, for example, no repetition in the Second World War of the Ross rifle fiasco which had hampered the Canadian Expeditionary Force in 1914–15. Empire preference in trade and the non-convertibility of sterling also ensured that Britain remained the principal source of supply for Dominion equipment procurement.

Attaining a high level of mutual understanding and confidence was much more difficult and relied essentially upon close and continuous contact between Dominion forces. This was easier said than done, for fiscal constraints and the geographic expanse of Empire did not permit of such things as joint army manoeuvres. Contact was therefore confined to officers and senior public servants, and to a tightly circumscribed group even at this level. The principal means employed were exchange or attachment, attendance at service schools and staff colleges, and service by Dominion officers in the Imperial and Indian armies.

The last mentioned was frequently a product of contraction, especially during the depression years. The young John Wilton, (later General Sir John Wilton and Chairman of the Australian Chiefs of Staff Committee between 1966 and 1970), graduated in a class of just twelve from RMC Duntroon in 1930, and with three of his fellow-graduates transferred to the British Army because there were not sufficient vacancies in the Australian Army.[30] He transferred back in 1939 when war seemed imminent, but between 1914 and 1946 twenty-seven Australian and five New Zealand graduates of Duntroon transferred to the British or Indian armies, and most stayed there. In Canada, four places at RMC Kingston were reserved each year for Canadians taking up appointments in the British Army.[31]

Between 1918 and 1938, all graduates of Duntroon did a year's attachment with British or Indian army units. Because of financial stringency, New Zealanders were not sent to Duntroon between 1922 and 1934, but from 1919 to 1921, and again in 1938, New Zealand graduates also served a year's attachment with British or Indian units.[32] In 1914 there were 37 Canadian officers in Britain, either on courses of instruction or having attended the 1913 army manoeuvers, while in 1925 there were five either on exchange or attachment and a further thirteen on courses.[33]

Probably the most important area for developing intra-Commonwealth understanding was at the level of the staff colleges and in attendance at the Imperial Defence College. Originally it had been proposed to establish staff colleges in each of the Dominions along the lines of the Staff College at Quetta but, as the Canadians had pointed out in 1909, the small establishments of the Dominion forces made this impracticable. Until the Second World War, therefore, Quetta remained the only staff college outside the United

Kingdom.[34] In the inter-war years the Dominions were allotted each two positions annually at Camberley and most, if not all, of the senior and middle-ranking Dominion officers of the Second World War generation were graduates of one or other college.

There has been subsequent disagreement as to the value of Dominion attendance at the staff colleges. Writing of Australian involvement in inter-war Imperial defence, John McCarthy has argued that the courses at Camberley and the Imperial Defence College were concerned with battle-field tours of France and Flanders, refighting the First World War. He cites Lieutenant General Sir John Northcott's year at the IDC, in 1935, in support of this.[35] Robin Higham likewise has stated that the British army's chief interest lay in 'returning to the status quo of 1914'[36] In referring to the IDC, Higham criticises it on the grounds that few of its graduates went from attendance at the college to positions of influence, and that overall the students and instructors at both institutions came from the same closed group.[37]

In examining the role of Australia in the allied effort during the Second World War, D.M. Horner took issue with both McCarthy and Higham in seeking to ameliorate this view. He pointed out that most IDC graduates eventually did attain positions of influence and that, in Australia's case at least, graduates almost immediately reached such positions.[38] He also stressed the value of personal contact and interaction that came with attendance at these institutions. In Northcott's year at the IDC the directing staff included three future Chiefs of the Imperial General Staff, Dill, Brooke and Montgomery, while with him on the course were the future British generals O'Connor, Martel and Percival. A future Australian Chief of the General Staff, Rowell, also commented favourably upon this aspect. It was preferable, he thought, 'to know one's associates in advance than learn their good or not so good points from bitter experience.'[39]

This position is supported by Preston, who thought that senior officers of the Commonwealth benefited from the IDC because they 'came to know well the men with whom they were destined to work between 1939 and 1945.'[40] The 1935 course at the IDC did indeed tour the French battlefields as part of a study of the advance to the Aisne in 1914, just as Northcott's class at Camberley in 1925 had toured the field at Le Cateau. In both cases, however, these studies were concerned not only with a consideration of the mobile operations of 1914 (and not, as McCarthy implies, trench warfare), but also with theoretical operations over the same ground in the *next* ten years.[41] It may well be that the assumptions which underlay some aspects of the course were flawed, particularly as regards the Singapore strategy.[42] That is not the same thing as condemning the courses as irrelevant on the grounds of being backward-looking and outmoded.

The truth lies somewhere in between these two positions. Another Australian, General Sir Frank Berryman, commented that as a result of attendance at Camberley he and a fellow Australian staff officer, Vasey, knew most of the key officers in the British and Indian forces serving alongside them in North Africa in the early years of the war.[43] At the level of the divisional staff on which they were serving at the time this was undoubtedly helpful and advantageous. Problems of supply, maintenance, or the provision of low-level intelligence, for example, were easily sorted-out on the informal basis encouraged by personal contact. At a higher level, when faced with the predelection of British commanders-in-chief to regard Dominion units as interchangeable with Imperial ones and to thus ignore sensitive questions concerning the national integrity of those units, it made not the slightest difference. As Preston again has observed, 'misunderstanding of the nature of the Commonwealth as a voluntary cooperation of independent national units [was] still to be found in high quarters in Britain.'[44] Both Wavell and Auchinleck could not or would not recognise that the Australian government, and that government's military representatives, had the right of control over the forces they had put into the field or, where they did recognise it, consistently failed to act upon it. The treatment by British officers of Canadian troops at Hong Kong became a major source of discord and mistrust, even years after the event.[45] Such incidents illustrate that a *Commonwealth* military 'system' did not, in fact, exist – at least, not from the point of view of the Dominions.

If the experience of command arrangements in the Second World War was unsatisfactory from a dominion viewpoint, so too was strategic planning. The Dominions were not included in the decision-making councils of the major allies even in situations where they deployed the majority of troops in an operation, as was the case with the Australians and New Zealanders in Greece and Crete in 1941. Only one Prime Ministers' Conference was held during the war, in London in May 1944. The Australian Prime Minister, John Curtin, had come with proposals for empire cooperation, both in defeating the Japanese and in the post-war ordering of affairs in the Pacific. The proposals got nowhere, partly because the Pacific theatre was under American control, and partly because Churchill was not interested.[46] As so often, there was no agreed Dominion position on this, or anything else. The Canadian Prime Minister, Mackenzie King, was always suspicious of the centralising tendency of Whitehall and throughout his long career was hostile to anything which in his view sacrificed Canadian interests to those of the crown or empire.[47] This applied as truly in 1944 as it had during the Chanak Crisis in 1922.

The Dominion experience in other areas of inter-allied relations in some ways mirrored the Anglo-American relationship. There was little formal integration of combat units and only limited integration of personnel in the field or in higher headquarters. The Americans extended the provisions of Lend-Lease to the rest of the Commonwealth, and became the chief source of supply for certain items which the traditional source, Britain, was no longer able to meet. The extent to which this occured varied from dominion to dominion, but all were affected,

Commonwealth defence cooperation in the immediate post-war period was further complicated by the emergence of the United States as the predominant power in the non-communist world. The notion that the Commonwealth might comprise some sort of 'third force' with the superpowers, while it continued to appeal to romantics like Churchill,[48] had no chance of realisation even if the superpowers were prepared to accommodate it. At the 1946 and 1948 Prime Ministers' Conferences the Australians again came equipped with proposals for Commonwealth cooperation, particularly with regard to the defence of the South-West Pacific Area and South-East Asia, which this time resulted in agreement with Britain and New Zealand over the ANZAM area, covering the defence of the Malayan region.[49]

The establishment of formal Commonwealth defence cooperation failed, primarily because of Canadian objections. By the end of the war Mackenzie King was already retreating 'to his pre-war isolationism', and it was not until his replacement in November 1948 by Louis St Laurent that Canadian affairs were again conducted with 'an internationalist view of Canada's external responsibilities.'[50] As noted, the agenda of the 1944 Prime Ministers' Conference had included 'Defence cooperation within the Commonwealth' as an item for discussion. King spoke at length on the dangers posed to the Dominions by having matters 'always settled in London'. Where Curtin and the New Zealand Prime Minister, Peter Fraser, supported the adoption of a common foreign policy between Britain and the Dominions, King would agree only to a statement of common *policies*. He also ensured that the final communique made no reference at all to the problem of Commonwealth defence by flatly refusing to discuss it.[51] His view of the Anglo-Dominions relationship was stated succinctly in the Canadian House of Commons, on 4 August 1944, when he observed that 'in the British Commonwealth there has evolved a unique alliance of a peculiarly tough and enduring kind whose members act together not because they are under any strict obligation to do so but because they have the will to act together.'[52] Observers might be forgiven for thinking that at times the Canadian Prime Minister was more interested in demonstrating the lack of obligation.

The same thing happened at the 1946 Conference. The new government of Clement Attlee had wished to revive the old system of Imperial Conferences, but this also foundered on Canadian objections. The agenda once more listed Commonwealth defence cooperation for discussion. The Foreign Secretary, Bevin, drew attention to the heavy fiscal and manpower burden faced by the British, and expressed the desire that the Dominions would assume formal responsibility for the defence of their respective regions. King once again declined. The Canadians favoured coordination at most, not centralisation and all they would agree to was the exchange of service liaison officers for this purpose.[53] Agreement might have been reached with regard to the ANZAM region, but any wider system responding to centralised direction had no chance of acceptance. This undoubtedly explains the failure of the proposal, also made at the 1946 Conference, to decentralise stocks of military equipment and training establishments throughout the Empire.[54]

Attempts were made to revive the concept of an Imperial General Staff but this had no more chance of success in 1946 than it had had when first attempted in 1909. Although the Chief of the Imperial General Staff was to retain the 'Imperial' in his title until the defence reorganisation in the late 1960s, the increasingly independent stances of Commonwealth governments in the post-war world robbed it of any meaning.[55] A further indication of the changed situation for the British was the signing of the Basic Agreement on Standardisation in 1947. Discussions between Montgomery, then CIGS and Eisenhower, then US Army Chief of Staff, on wartime difficulties between the two armies led to Britain, Canada and the United States all becoming signatories to an agreement which was confirmed and further widened in 1950 and 1954.[56] This obviously held future implications for the supply of weapons and equipment to the forces concerned. It also marked Britain's declining status as a leading military power and emphasised the changing relationship between Britain, the dominions, and the United States.

Chapter 2
The Korean War – an overview

The Korean War began in the early hours of 25 June 1950 when powerful forces of the 223,000 strong Korean Peoples Army (KPA) rolled across the 38th parallel and attacked the lightly-equipped army of the Republic of Korea (ROK). The origins of the war lay in the unsatisfactory settlement of Korean affairs following the end of the Second World War. Korea had been incorporated into the Japanese empire in 1910, and the country had been run for the benefit of the Imperial power. 'Summing up the Japanese impact', wrote Peter Lowe, 'it may be said that efficient but harsh administration was provided; economic progress was promoted yet in a distorted way, designed to benefit the colonial master.'[1]

The defeat of Japan brought an end to colonial rule in Korea, but it was unclear what would take its place. Little was known about Korea in 1945, especially in the West, and this was reflected also in wartime planning by the allies. Roosevelt envisaged some form of trusteeship for Korea, to last as long as forty years if necessary, while at the Cairo conference in 1943 it was agreed that the country should receive independence at some point. The Tehran conference confirmed a period of trusteeship for Korea, and the war ended with Korea's future status unclear. Japan was required to surrender all colonial possessions acquired since 1895 and Korea was to attain independence, but not immediately and with the interim arrangements not yet clarified.[2]

The peaceful resolution of the Korean problem was a victim of the deteriorating relations between the wartime allies and the onset of the Cold War. Disagreement between the Russians and Americans over trusteeship for Korea led to the continued division of the country along the 38th parallel and the development of the two occupied zones into two separate countries. Some attempt was made to hand the problem over to the fledgling United Nations, most particularly through the establishment of the United Nations Temporary Commission on Korea (UNTCOK) in November 1947. This body was intended to supervise elections in the country as a whole if that was possible, or in the south alone if it was not. UNTCOK was replaced by UNCOK in December 1948, but the new organisation proved no more effective than its predecessor in resolving the impasse within Korea and bringing about the peaceful unification of the two zones.

The murderous animosities which existed between the right-wing nationalists in the south, led by Syngman Rhee, and the communists in the north, under Kim Il Sung, led to persistent attempts by the two sides to destabilise each other through violent incursions across the parallel. Aided and abetted by their patrons, the Soviets and Americans, the two sides waged a vicious civil war through guerrilla activity which killed 100,000 people before the first shots were officially fired. The tensions in the Korean peninsula were not reduced by the withdrawal of Russian and American occupying forces in December 1948 and June 1949 respectively. Both sides left military advisory missions behind, and the Russians equipped the KPA with armoured vehicles, heavy weapons and combat aircraft. While the American's Korean Military Advisory Group (KMAG) reorganised and trained the ROK army, the latter was smaller than the KPA and lacked the range and quality of equipment acquired by the north from the Russians. In particular, the ROK lacked an air force and possessed no armour.

Thus when the north launched its invasion of the south the forces opposing it were hopelessly outclassed. Some of the ROK troops fought bravely, as demonstrated by the fact that it took the North Koreans three days to capture Seoul, but many units collapsed or ran. The evacuation of the capital, and the loss of much military equipment when the only bridge over the Han river was blown early, led to further rapid deterioration in the South Korean forces. By the time large numbers of American troops began arriving in Korea the ROK army, having suffered sixty per cent casualties, was largely ineffective, although this condition proved temporary.

One set of revisionist thinking has tried to show that the war was in fact the result of a southern attack upon the north to which the KPA responded by wholesale pursuit and invasion of the south.[3] Without in any way downplaying the provocations offered by

Rhee's regime in the period after 1948, this is unconvincing. A major assault of eight divisions is a complex military operation requiring considerable logistical and other planning. It is not launched spontaneously on a half hour's notice. Bruce Cumings has produced evidence to show that North Korean aircraft were being readied for operations in the days immediately prior to the outbreak of war,[4] and the Australian military observers attached to UNCOK, Lieutenant Colonel F.S.B. Peach and Squadron Leader R.J. Rankin, saw no evidence of ROK preparations for offensive action along the parallel during the same crucial period. But even had there been a small ROK incursion northwards that morning, the response was so massive as to indicate that the KPA had been preparing to invade the south regardless.

It is now generally conceded that Kim Il Sung launched his war of conquest and reunification on his own initiative and not as part of a centrally directed Kremlin atempt at world domination. Equally, he probably had Stalin's general agreement for an invasion at some stage. At the time, following Soviet provocations over Berlin and Czechoslovakia and the extension of Soviet control over Eastern Europe, it seemed otherwise to Western observers. The distinguishing feature of American policy towards Korea between 1945 and 1950 was unwillingness to see the country fall to the communists, although the Truman administration was reluctant to make assistance to the ROK a priority, a tendency highlighted by the Secretary of State's famous speech to the National Press Club in January 1950. Once the potential threat had become a full-scale war, however, the Americans acted quickly.

The United Nations Security Council passed a resolution on 25 June urging a cessation of hostilities and branding the North Korean action a breach of the peace. It was assisted in this, as in all its other moves in the first month of the crisis, by the absence of the Russians (and their veto). The latter were boycotting proceedings in protest at the continued represenation of China by delegates of the Kuomintang regime on Formosa. President Truman met with his senior military and political advisers, and began preparing the ground for the commitment of US combat forces to Korea. On 27 June the Security Council passed a further resolution calling on member states to 'furnish such assistance to the Republic of Korea as may be necessary to repel the armed attack and to restore international peace and security to the area'. On 29 June General

Douglas MacArthur was ordered to deploy the air and naval forces of his Far East Command (FEC) in Japan in support of ROK forces. The next day, following a pessimistic situation report from Mac-Arthur, the Joint Chiefs of Staff (JCS) lifted all restrictions on the use of American ground forces in Korea.[5]

Ultimately this decision ensured that the North Koreans would not prevail. Initially, however, the course of the fighting favoured them. The battered remnants of the ROK army, reinforced by American ground troops from Japan and Okinawa, were pushed down the peninsula until they held a perimeter along the Naktong river around the southern port city of Pusan. Fears were expressed that even this line would be overrun and the defenders pushed into the sea. But despite pressure from the KPA along the perimeter, the North's offensive was running out of steam as lengthening lines of communication and heavy aerial interdiction from American and Australian aircraft caused serious logistical problems. When Mac-Arthur staged his highly successful amphibious landing at Inchon well to the rear of the enemy's positions, the North Koreans began to retreat and then to collapse.

The war now proceeded in see-saw fashion, with MacArthur's forces harrying the KPA across the 38th parallel. The policy of resisting aggression in Korea was transformed into one of 'roll-back' – pushing back the tide of communist expansion by uniting the whole of the Korean peninsula under non-Communist, Southern rule. But the recently victorious Chinese communists in Peking could not regard such a prospect with equanimity, especially since their industrial base in north-east Manchuria relied heavily upon the hydro-electric power grid located in the north of the DPRK. The United Nations was warned, through the Indian ambassador to Peking, that the Chinese would intervene if UN forces threatened China's border along the Yalu river. MacArthur belittled and ignored all cautions, and launched his forces, both US and ROK, toward the border, despite being instructed by his superiors in Washington to use only ROK troops close to the Yalu in the hope that such 'restraint' would placate the Chinese. In October and November the Chinese infiltrated at least eighteen divisions of Chinese Peoples Volunteers into North Korea[6] and through a massive intelligence failure on the part of the UNC, which failed to see them, laid the basis for 'an ambush on the grand scale'.[7]

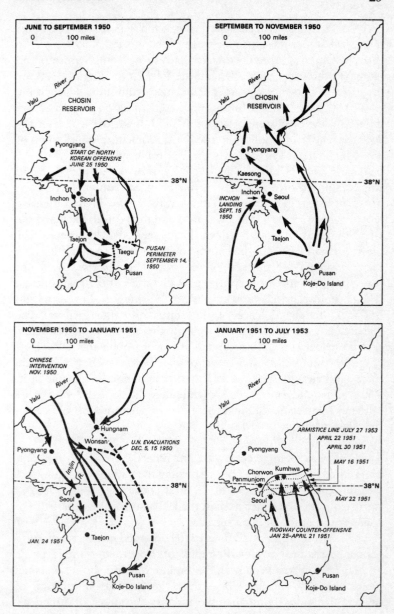

Course and progress of the Korean War, 1950–53

If MacArthur's strategic conception at Inchon ranks as one of his most brilliant strokes, his placing the unsupported X Corps on the eastern flank of the northwards advance from Wonsan and Hungnam was strategic folly, and the 1st Marine division paid the price at the Chosin reservoir. The balance again tipped against the UNC and MacArthur's forces, now containing contingents from other UN member states, again retreated down the length of the country. The front finally stabilised again some forty miles south of Seoul in January 1951. Slowly the UN forces pushed back up the peninsula as the Chinese offensive in its turn ran its course. Seoul was recaptured on 15 March, having changed hands four times in less than a year. The Chinese launched their Fifth Phase Offensive in April–May 1951, but this was held and then driven back and the UNC resumed its slow northwards advance. By November 1951 the front had re-established itself roughly along the parallel, and there it stayed for the rest of the war. The Chinese could not overcome the superior firepower and air forces of their opponents, while a political decision was made in Washington to revert from 'rollback' to the defence of the status quo ante bellum. The Americans were not prepared to incur the heavy casualties necessary to defeat the Chinese and North Koreans in the field. They opted instead to find a substitute for victory, and spent two years in truce talks first at Kaesong and then Panmunjom in pursuit of it. The war ground on mercilessly while they did so, exhibiting many of the characteristics familiar to an earlier generation of soldiers on the Western Front in 1916–17.

The UNC was set up to cope with, and reflect, a broadly representative United Nations force. Before turning to examine the Commonwealth experience in Korea in detail, it is useful to look briefly at the organisation and structure of the UNC and at the experience of some of the other UN contingents.

The UN resolution of 27 June 1950 had urged member nations to furnish assistance to the Republic of Korea, and the Truman administration was keen both that military action should be taken under the aegis of the UN – thus avoiding the impression of unilateral action – and that the military resources of America's allies should be utilised in the fight. On 7 July a further resolution was passed by the Security Council making Truman the executive agent of the Council in carrying out United Nations action in

Korea. Contributing nations were to furnish forces to a unified command under the United States. The commander was to be an American, and Truman designated the Joint Chiefs of Staff his agents for Korea. The JCS recommended that MacArthur be placed in command, a recommendation which Truman accepted. As the bulk of the fighting was to involve ground combat forces, the Department of the Army was responsible to the JCS for planning and directing the military operations of UN forces.

MacArthur established the UNC on 24 July. General Headquarters was located in Tokyo, for in effect MacArthur merely converted his Far East Command into the United Nations Command. At no time during the war did the UN seek to interfere in operations in Korea, and as MacArthur later testified to Congress, his links with the world organisation were nominal.[8] Within a month of the North Korean invasion, the higher command relationships and overwhelmingly American character of the UNC had been established, and these were not to alter during the course of the Korean War.

The JCS decided at the outset that the most important criterion governing the acceptance of offers of assistance was military effectiveness. Thus the offer of 33,000 Nationalist Chinese troops was rejected on the grounds that their training was poor and their equipment inadequate. By 23 August seven offers of ground forces had been accepted by the JCS, while a further four had been made by 5 September. With the acceptance of foreign contingents came the need to ensure efficient and effective use of these troops.

GHQ in Tokyo drew up a policy covering the integration of forces into the United Nations Command, covering important considerations such as command relationships and the employment of forces, the training and staging of units, logistics, discipline, and administration.[9] While in theory this should have ensured the smooth processing and integration of non-American combat units into the theatre, in practice much of this careful planning proved a waste of time and effort because many of the units despatched to Korea did not conform to the requirements laid down by MacArthur and the JCS. MacArthur had stipulated that units should be of at least a reinforced battalion in strength with organic artillery, while service units were to be of a size and integrity as would make them immediately usable. The headquarters planners in Tokyo had further specified that units were to arrive completely equipped and capable of being maintained from US sources, especially with regard to weapons which needed to be compatible with American ammunition. They were also to arrive accompanied by a minimum of 60 days of maintenance supplies and equipment. In the majority of cases this simply did not happen, putting considerable strain on an already overburdened logistic and administrative network.

Other than the Turkish and British Commonwealth contingents, the UN forces contributed were of battalion size and hence incapable of independent tactical deployment. No attempt was made to form a composite United Nations division out of this disparate material, and the units were attached to US Army regiments as an extra battalion or, in the case of brigade groups, to US Army divisions as an additional regimental combat team (RCT).[10] The attachment was semi-permanent, since this enabled the two sides to become familiar with each other's 'peculiarities' and develop good working relationships. Eventually all US divisions had UN units attached in this manner.

The Filipino battalion did not function well, and was not used extensively in heavy combat; some initial problems were experienced with the Thais and Ethiopians also. Overall, and despite the difficulties of different languages, organisation and tactical concepts, the UN units generally integrated successfully and fought hard and well. Their battlefield performance was often out of proportion to their small size although this could be a disadvantage since high casualties suffering during periods of intense action could render them temporarily ineffective as units. They suffered from a lack of some items of equipment, such as artillery or modern signals equipment, which had to be made up by the Americans, and the great distance from countries of origin, particularly from Europe, meant that reinforcement and rotation of personnel was often slow and inefficient.

Of all the difficulties faced, those posed by the differing conceptions of operations were the least easily resolved. The French battalion, for example, was commanded by a much-decorated and often-wounded Foreign Legionnaire who had taken a reduction in rank from general to colonel in order to command in Korea. He used the *nom de guerre* 'Monclar', seemed to have little notion of indirect fire, did not hold with the American concept of massed fire support, and was vehemently opposed to night attacks. The Belgians were not used to concentrating such a wide variety of weapons in their rifle companies as were standard American units, and most UN units seem to have varied in their use of air-ground support.[11]

The Turks used 'a mixture of British training and Turkish practicality'. Like the British they favoured the high ground, since it gave them good observation and enabled them to bring sweeping and plunging fire to bear which kept the enemy well back from their defensive positions. They disliked overhead cover on their trenches and bunkers, and tended to break off patrols as soon as the enemy's position had been established. They also considered reconnaissance in force and combat patrols wasteful in casualties without a compensatory gain in ground while, like the French, they were not at all averse to the use of the bayonet charge where their American ally would have used firepower.

General Matthew B. Ridgway, Commander of the Eighth Army from December 1950, approved of the aggressive tactics employed by the best of the UN contingents, and in attempting to rebuild American morale after the Chinese intervention he held up Turkish or French successes as inspirational examples. After praising the French bayonet charge at Wonju on 10 January 1951, he noted that 'the only other reported use of the bayonet of which I have knowledge was not by US infantry, but Turkish. Conduct was said to have been equally gallant and results equally good.'[12] He also conceded, however, that their insistence upon doing things in their own way could make them 'a hair shirt many times' to their American commanders.[13] One commanding general of the US 2nd Infantry division likewise thought that the Dutch troops 'had a mind of their own. If they thought their assignment (either attack or defense) made good sense they were superb – otherwise they sometimes did what they thought appropriate.'[14] As a number of senior American officers attempted to tell Monclar, his approach to operational problems was not always appropriate or appreciated, and sometimes led to the French taking heavier casualties than necessary.[15] This could cause problems for the US command, because national governments would certainly demand explanations should their contingents suffer inordinate losses. Overall, the British observer Air Vice Marshal Bouchier thought that 'the way [the] European Contingents as represented by the British, Turks, Greeks, French and Dutch have demonstrated their fine fighting qualities is very heartening for us and most enlightening for the Americans.'[16]

Seventeen countries contributed a total of four infantry brigades, nine infantry battalions, one medical ambulance company, one evacuation hospital, and one mobile surgical hospital to Korea. In addition, Iran offered two ambulance units, Pakistan an infantry regiment and Lebanon a reinforced infantry battalion, but these were never sent. By 9 July 1951 military forces from other member countries of the UN constituted 6.3 per cent of the total forces opposing the North Koreans and Chinese. United States forces comprised 70.4 per cent, with the ROK army accounting for the remaining 23.3 per cent.[17] There was some criticism of this in the US Congress and the press, but this was not shared by the Truman administration which recognised that the UN contingents made an important strategic and diplomatic contribution to the American cause in Korea. Some made an important tactical contribution as well. In any case, it is not clear that the over-stretched resources of the US Army could have coped with any further demands from even larger or more varied UN forces in 1950–51.

The other UN forces in Korea were smaller than the Commonwealth formations, and were absorbed more readily by the Americans both because often they were generally patterned on American models and because they were more nearly totally dependent upon US resources. In practice, there were two major military systems within the UNC, one American and the other essentially British. The latter derived from the experience of two world wars and had not yet been dwarfed by the disengagement from empire and the rise of the superpower blocs. This placed the Commonwealth units in a quite different position from the smaller UN forces and from the Koreans themselves. All were integrated into the United Nations Command, however, and all had to deal with the American way in war.

Chapter 3
The Commonwealth commitment to Korea, 1950

The indecision over the commitment of forces to Korea highlights the unexpected nature of the conflict. The problems in manning and fielding units and formations for service with the United Nations Command clearly illustrates the extent to which the forces of the Commonwealth had been allowed to run-down in the short period since the end of the Second World War. Only Britain, with its considerable overseas commitments, can be excused for this, but even then only partially because of the poor quality of decision-making over the use of national servicemen. Other than the small force in Japan, already being wound-up in June 1950, Australia's other main commitment, in the Middle East, was theoretical rather than actual. The same is true for New Zealand while Canada, although obliged to station forces (one brigade group) in Germany under the new North Atlantic Treaty, had yet actually to do so. The poverty of Commonwealth defence thinking in the intervening years since 1945 is in no way better illustrated.

In committing ground forces to the Korean War the governments of the Commonwealth nations concerned were confronted with two problems. Firstly, they had to raise and organise the troops who would constitute the means by which they discharged their obligations under the United Nations resolutions. It is these considerations which will be examined in this chapter. Of equal importance was ensuring the correct utilization of the forces so committed, and this will be discussed in Chapter 5 when we examine the performance and experience of the individual brigades in Korea.

The sudden requirement to field forces in Korea caught all countries unprepared, and each responded differently to the task of raising those forces. Much of the pressure which was placed upon the various service headquarters originated with the Americans, who from the first were having a very hard time of it in Korea as much of the ROK army disintegrated around them and their own under-trained, under-equipped forces, hurriedly despatched from occupation duties in Japan, proved unequal to the task assigned them. In a desperate bid to get troops into the line, MacArthur took spare units from wherever he could find them, including stripping detachments from the Okinawa garrison. Apart from American forces the only other body of ground troops on hand in Japan was the remaining Australian battalion of the British Commonwealth Occupation Force (BCOF), 3 RAR. Only two weeks after the outbreak of war, Lieutenant General Sir Horace Robertson, Commander-in-Chief, BCOF, cabled his superiors in Australia concerning demands for the use of this unit. He had been approached by correspondents in Japan concerning its possible use, and he reported that he had shown

some of the more responsible ones how useless such a small component would be and how embarrassing it would be even to the Americans . . . I have even offered to Gen[eral] Walker commanding Eighth Army some detachments to relieve in Japan troops whom he might need to send to Korea in order that I may anchor the battalion in Japan.[1]

He cautioned, however, that it would be difficult to prevent a request being made.

It would be difficult indeed, for MacArthur was desperate for trained soldiers. He had already raised the prospect of employing Nationalist Chinese forces from Taiwan, though whether he was serious in this, or merely attempting to exert pressure on his and other governments, is perhaps debatable.[2] Neither the Australian nor the New Zealand governments were keen to be drawn into a commitment in Korea, since the armed forces of both were woefully run-down, and both were in the throes of introducing national service schemes. Additionally, strategic assumptions at that time geared both countries to a major deployment to the Middle East in the event of a general or world war. This contribution to Empire defence was unquestioned, and the British government was keen that it should remain so. Against these considerations, however, had to be balanced the effect upon the Americans of any attempt to withdraw the remaining Australian battalion from Japan at this particular moment.[3]

The British were not eager to get involved either, and initially at least the British Chiefs of Staff did not contemplate providing forces for Korea since, in their view, American resources were sufficient to meet the contingency which they put 'at a tentative figure of three to four divisions to drive Northern Korean forces out of Southern Korea.'[4] The Foreign Office recognised the need to 'line up the Commonwealth as far as possible, particularly Canada and Australia', since collectively they might then 'have a real influence upon the Americans'. They went on to note that American attitudes would be

highly charged with emotion so long as they are suffering casualties and so long as they are being driven back. It may be that our only hope of acquiring a status in the matter which they will respect will be to provide some ground troops to fight alongside theirs. This is clearly a most unpalatable proposition, and it would be right to consider it only if it were felt that it was our only way of influencing American policy in a vital matter.[5]

It was not Korea that was 'a vital matter', however, but the propect of influencing American policy and of further cementing the 'special relationship.'

Any hopes the British entertained concerning a principal role for themselves with the Americans had to take congnizance of the Australian Minister for External Affairs, Percy Spender, and his ambitions in creating a similar role for Australia. His desire to succeed in negotiating a Pacific Pact with the United States, where his Labor predecessor, Dr H.V. Evatt, had failed and in opposition to the wishes of his Prime Minister, R.G. Menzies, is fairly well-known and has been dealt with fully by Robert O'Neill.[6] Of interest here is the manner in which this commitment of Australian forces was made within the context both of decisions in other Commonwealth capitals, and of American wishes in the matter.

The Secretary-General of the United Nations, Trygve Lie, was causing embarrassment to member governments through his public appeals for material support for Korea.[7] It was one thing to support the call for aid in resisting Communist aggression, quite another to be requested to back it with troops. On 18 July the Canadian Chiefs of Staff Committee met to consider Lie's appeal, and quickly agreed that 'Lie's appeal for aid . . . was not authoritative insofar as the Chiefs of Staff Committee was concerned', and further that 'the imminence of the Korean problem should not be allowed to obscure the more important matter of general military preparedness on a longer term basis and in light of the whole panorama.'[8]

In a statement the next day the Canadian Prime Minister announced therefore that the despatch of Canadian army units was not warranted.[9] Canadian disinclination to act, however, was subject to some questioning within the Commonwealth and particularly from New Zealand, whose government had been concerned for some time that Canada was gradually withdrawing from the Commonwealth and about the implications which this carried for Empire defence cooperation.[10] For its part, the New Zealand government professed itself at a loss to know how to reply to Lie's appeal, since it claimed to have no trained personnel in the army other than instructors.

The British were torn between a desire to assuage the demands of American public opinion, already critical of the absence of any allied forces in what was purportedly a United Nations operation, with their apparent inability to spare any forces which would have any appreciable military impact upon the campaign.[11] The question of sending some force, however token, was now under active consideration as pressure to commit troops mounted. General Sir Neil Ritchie, Head of the British Joint Services Mission in Washington, wrote to the CIGS that although the Joint Chiefs of Staff fully appreciated the extent of British global commitment, the American public was less understanding, having been somewhat shaken by the initial reverses in Korea. He reported that the Army Chief of Staff, General J. Lawton Collins, thought that from a military point of view 'a British land force could [not] assist much.'[12]

It is difficult to reconcile this apparently self-satisfied American viewpoint, as reported, with the fact that a week earlier MacArthur had been informed by Washington that he should sound out the Australians about the use of BCOF ground troops in Korea.[13] In truth, the military situation in Korea was more serious than the above exchanges suggested and, in the short term at least, there were sound military reasons for employing trained combat forces from any country with anything to offer. In the long term, of course, American resources were more than sufficient to fight the Korean War, but the demobilisation and run-down of the US Army after 1945 meant that it would take time to marshal those resources. In other words, although the political reasons for presenting an allied front to the rest of the world were always important, on two occasions in the Korean War, July-September 1950 and November 1950–March 1951, there existed a real military need for trained men with rifles from whatever source.[14] It seems probable that US authorities were playing off various members of the Commonwealth against each other, and the rapid reversal of British policy at the end of July seems to bear this out.

The last week of July 1950 was a busy one for Commonwealth officials. On 25 July MacArthur's chief of staff, Major-General Edward M. Almond, advised Robertson that SCAP desired the operational deployment of 3 RAR to Korea 'at the earliest practicable date.'[15] Robertson, who had forecast this possibility for several weeks, requested a quick decision from his superiors. As O'Neill has shown, the Australian government was now confronted with an important choice, one made all the more urgent by advice that the British government had suddenly changed its mind about a troop commitment, and would make a public announcement at 8 pm, Australian time, on 26 July. By manipulation of the time zone differences, Australia was able to announce its own commitment of ground troops an hour before the British, doing so largely at Spender's instigation.[16] The New Zealand Prime Minister also announced a ground force commitment that same night, beating both the British *and* the Australians.[17]

The Canadians were forced now to re-examine their policy, and not only because they were under pressure from the New Zealand government to participate in any Commonwealth action in Korea.[18] The Canadian Prime Minister earlier had made it clear that committal of forces would be undertaken only after the Canadian parliament had had the opportunity to discuss the matter, and with an eye to Francophone Canada's possible reactions. In this former attitude, St Laurent harked back to the stand taken by Mackenzie King during the Chanak crisis in 1922, and indeed thereafter, while the need to acknowledge French Canadian views had been demonstrated in both world wars and was yet another factor limiting the choices facing any Canadian government.[19] The Chiefs of Staff Committee now met again to review Canada's position in the light of recent events. All they concluded was that forces could be sent if required, but that for the present the Chief of the General Staff should do no more than 'plan on a precautionary basis towards a possible decision to dispatch . . . ground forces.'[20] They clearly were not enthusiastic.

Britain, Australia and New Zealand had all undertaken troop commitments to Korea. They had now to find the men to meet these undertakings. At the time of the offer of ground troops, the strength of 3 RAR in Japan was between 500–550 men. The war establishment of the battalion was 960.[21] Under the terms of the Defence Act, Australian soldiers had to volunteer for overseas duty in a specific area. These men had volunteered for service in Japan, and were now required to volunteer for service in Korea. Most did so without hesitation. There was a further complication, however, in that the policy governing overseas service in an operational zone required a soldier to have reached the age of twenty-two. In August 1950 this meant that 125 men in 3 RAR were unable to proceed to Korea. Rowell attempted to revert to the rule as it had applied in the Second World War, where nineteen was the age limit, but with only partial success. A Cabinet submission by the Minister for the Army, Josiah Francis, lifted the limitation for those already in the Australian Regular Army or serving with BCOF, but retained lower and upper age limits of twenty and forty years of age respectively for all further special enlistments for Korean service.[22] By way of comparison, in the US Army a volunteer accepted for service could be sent anywhere, while those called up under the selective service scheme became eligible at nineteen.

The New Zealand government decided to raise a field artillery regiment for Korea entirely by special enlistment. With the exception of a handful of officers and NCOs, New Zealand did not send regular soldiers to Korea, a decision which some regulars regarded later as a mistake because it denied the New Zealand army valuable operational experience. Recruiting was confined to New Zealand citizens of European or Maori descent between the ages of twenty-one and thirty-two. Officers and ex-officers were accepted up to forty years of age, NCOs, and ex-NCOs up to thirty-eight.[23] No difficulty was experienced in obtaining the required number of volunteers.

British policy was different again. The minimum age for enlistment in the British army was seventeen and a half, with eligibility for general service world-wide at nineteen. National servicemen were called up at eighteen years and three months with active service eligibility also set at nineteen. The period of obligation under the national service scheme was set at eighteen months, but pressure from the Army to increase the period to two years was resisted by the government. While perhaps understandable from the domestic political viewpoint, this had serious consequences for manpower planning. There was no point in sending national servicemen to Korea for, by the time they were old enough to be sent on active service, they would have only six months of their enlistment left to run. Since it was envisaged that units would rotate in the theatre every twelve months, the whole proposition became totally impractical.

The period of conscription had been reduced from eighteen months to twelve in April 1947 as a result of pressure from the Labour backbench. This was done in the face of strong opposition from the chiefs of staff and against the inclinations of leading members of the government. The move arose out of factional disputes within the parliamentary party, and proved short-lived. As one historian of the Attlee administration has written, 'the revolt over conscription, which later went up to eighteen months after all, and later still to two years, was henceforth easily contained. On balance, such rebellions . . . were dealt with firmly by Attlee and his colleagues, with little danger to their authority.'[24] Fear of a strong negative reaction in 1950 seems curiously misplaced.

It was proposed to send the 29th Infantry Brigade Group, part of the strategic reserve, as Britain's contribution to Korea. All national servicemen within its ranks would have to be withdrawn and replaced. 29th Brigade had an establishment of 417 officers and 7,955 other ranks. The decision concerning national servicemen meant that the army had to find a further 202 officers and 6,124 other ranks with yet a further requirement for another 126 officers and 2,117 other ranks as first reinforcements spread over the first year. This was a massive and, it must be said, unnecessary task entirely imposed by domestic political constraints which did not in fact exist, as subsequent changes to the scheme soon after demonstrated. An army already under severe pressure for manpower had therefore to review further the options open to it.[25]

A number of measures were taken. 369 regulars whose engagements were shortly due to expire were retained. Consideration was given to the withdrawal of regulars from other units, but this was largely discounted by the planners on two grounds. The time-factor would not permit the concentration in England of regulars drawn from units in the Middle and Far East, while regular strengths in units based in Britain and Germany averaged 250 per battalion. As

Lt-Gen Sir Horace Robertson inspecting soldiers of the Royal Northumberland Fusiliers, 29th British Infantry Brigade, 1950

the planners noted, 'withdrawals on the scale required for this commitment would be crippling', especially since the units in BAOR were required to maintain standards of operational efficiency. It was hoped that some national servicemen might enlist as regulars, known either as type C or type K volunteers, but this was regarded as 'a possible bonus' only.[26] That left only the reservists.

There were other problems with this option, and even here the War Office found that it had to differentiate between classes of reservists. The 'Z' and 'W' reservists were not considered for recall, because these classes comprised national servicemen called up between 1939–46 or 1947–48. It was considered politically impossible to recall released national servicemen to do what serving national servicemen were not required to do. This meant that the army would have to rely on the 'A' and 'B' sections of the Regular Reserve. Reliance upon this source would cause structural problems within the Reserve, since it contained a high proportion of NCOs, many of whom would find themselves filling private soldier vacancies. The Infantry Group system for drawing replacements would have to be abandoned for the purpose of the exercise, and the overall balance of the system would be upset, since a high proportion of the total would have to be drawn off.[27] The consequences were serious in human terms also. The men recalled to the colours had served through the Second World War, and many had only a short period of reserve obligation left when they were recalled. They were by definition likely to be settled family men with jobs or businesses to run, and their resentment at this disruption to their lives can be imagined, especially when large numbers of young national servicemen without their personal and family obligations were not being required to go to Korea. To compound this situation, some of these men were then taken prisoner in the chaotic fighting of late 1950 and early 1951, and spent between two and two and a half years rotting in Chinese prison camps, if indeed they survived at all.[28] It was a wasteful, sometimes tragic, and unfair system with little to commend it.

It might be argued that a mobilization system should be fair, but must be effective even at the cost of equity. Had the British national service scheme been as half-hearted and ineffective as its Australian and New Zealand counterparts proved to be, then the decision to recall reservists in 1950 would be unarguable. This was not the case. National servicemen were fighting at that time against the Communist insurrection in Malaya, and proved as good as soldiers later in Korea as their regular and reservist counterparts. Notions of military effectiveness had little or nothing to do with this decision.

The need to maintain a regular military establishment adequate to the demands made upon it was a realisation facing others. The Australian CGS, Rowell, had informed the British unofficially that he favoured Australia sending a brigade group in its own right, and that in his opinion such a move would enhance rather than endanger the defence preparations of the Australian government. The Australian government took the latter view, however, and it must be judged a realistic one, since they later experienced some occasional difficulty in maintaining the small force they did commit. Moves were also made to obtain forces from India, Pakistan, and South Africa. These efforts came to little, for India was attempting to buttress its position as leader of the undeveloped countries, especially in the United Nations, Pakistan was not prepared to send forces while engaged in deadlock with India over the demilitarisation of Kashmir, and South Africa, consistent with her intentions in the Second World War, would not deploy ground forces outside the African continent.[29] The Commonwealth military effort would have to be confined to Britain and the remaining 'old' Dominions, although India did contribute a non-combatant medical unit, the 60th Indian (Parachute) Field Ambulance.

The Canadians now began to consider not simply whether they would commit forces, but what form such a force should take. In a memorandum of 1 August prepared for the Cabinet, the options open to the government were reviewed and recommendations made. A single battalion could be sent, to serve in a larger, almost certainly American, formation. Canada could field a regular regimental combat team, or alternatively send a mixed brigade of volunteers for service in an 'international division ... with other forces made available to the United Nations by countries other than the United States.'[30] While requesting details from the Australian government concerning the basis on which the latter had agreed to commit troops, and the controls on their use that they intended to maintain, St Laurent announced on 7 August that recruiting would begin for a special brigade of infantry for service in Korea.[31]

Canada was in fact to end up following parts of all three of the options presented in this paper.

As both Wood and Stairs have recounted, the Canadian recruiting programme was severely mis-managed. In a chapter euphemistically entitled 'Growing Pains', Wood quotes the report made by the Defence Research Board on the recruiting campaign. This report noted that 'the precipitate manner in which this special mobilization was initiated, the mandate that all who applied should be forthwith processed, the speedy clearing of applicants which was demanded . . . were regrettable features to be avoided in any similar programme hereafter.'[32] This was in part a result of the decision to recruit a special force from the civilian population. But as Stairs has noted, the undue haste in raising the force was mainly to blame for the initial difficulties. In the first seven months of the life of the force, to March 1951, twenty-five percent of the total numbers enlisted had either been discharged as unfit for whatever reason, or had simply deserted.[33] It was not a good beginning, and as a result it was to be some time before the Canadian Army Special Force took the field.

Problems in Korea would not wait for the Canadian difficulties to resolve themselves. August was a critical month on the Naktong perimeter, with the North Koreans maintaining pressure upon the enclave around Pusan and the assault at Inchon still in the planning stage. Forces were needed, and needed urgently, but with the complicating factor, for the Australians at least, that single battalions by themselves were of limited operational value. As Robertson informed Rowell, an individual battalion without supporting arms 'might in an emergency be attached to an American RCT but is more likely to be employed guarding L[ines] of C[ommunication] and rear areas against guerrillas. If used alone without supporting arms it is more likely to bring disaster on us than credit.'[34] He concluded that those who advocated an independent role for 3 RAR should show 'how we can be separate and distinct and still get a soldier into the firing line as I am unable to see it myself.' Australia's strong advocacy of a unified Commonwealth force, discussed in more detail in chapter 6, stemmed from the fact that unlike Britain or Canada the force she fielded was always too small for independent action.

One option facing the Australians was to attach the battalion to an American RCT, most of which were operating on a two battalion rather than full three battalion establishment. This in fact was the offer made to Robertson by the commanding general of Eighth Army, General Walton Walker.[35] A practical alternative was not far off, for the Australians were not the only ones being importuned to dispatch their forces quickly. The VCIGS was strongly opposed to detouring troops from Hong Kong or Malaya ahead of the departure of the 29th Brigade,[36] but the truth of the matter was that the British were really left with little option in the face of the denuding of American garrisons in Okinawa, Hawaii, Puerto Rico and Panama.

Two things happened. The British government bowed to pressure from the army and increased national service to two years, but not immediately and with the age requirement for active service kept at nineteen.[37] On 16 August Brigadier Basil Coad was briefed to prepare two battalions of his 27th Infantry Brigade in Hong Kong for service in Korea. The sort of pressure brought to bear is well illustrated by Lord Tedder's signal to London on the same day in which he reported that

from a military point of view they are in desperate need of reinforcements; from the morale point of view the GIs in Korea are having a very unpleasant time, are feeling very lonely and would be immensely heartened by the visible presence of British troops; from the political point of view people are beginning to ask when are United Nations promises going to be implemented in the form of men with rifles in Korea.[38]

The situation could not wait for the arrival of the 29th Brigade, at that stage scheduled for November.

And so the 1st Battalion, Argyll and Sutherland Highlanders, and the 1st Battalion, The Middlesex Regiment, were hurriedly prepared for active service. The Argyll's strength stood at 640, of whom 110 were national servicemen, while the Middlesex could muster 580 all ranks, of whom 280 were national servicemen. Neither had complete support companies, and approximately 1300 reinforcements were needed to bring the battalions up to war establishment plus first reinforcements.[39] They were eventually made up to a strength of around 600 each, with officers being drafted in from wherever they could be found. In several cases, platoon commanders were taken from the Royal Army Ordnance Corps.

This turn of events solved the problem of how to field the

Australian battalion, and the acting Prime Minister, Fadden, announced that 3 RAR would operate with the 27th Brigade, although he neglected to reach prior agreement on this with the British government.[40] The matter was amicably sorted out, with the brigade arriving in Pusan on 29 August and soon after going straight into the line. 3 RAR arrived on 28 September after completing unit training. In recognition of this, the brigade was renamed the 27th Commonwealth Infantry Brigade. The inclusion of the Australian battalion, by now at full establishment, added much-needed weight to the brigade which was still, however, reliant upon the Americans for all supporting arms and most services. It was intended that when the 29th Brigade reached Korea it would relieve the 27th Brigade, and the Australian battalion would then be attached to it.[41]

Before turning in the next chapter to consider the resolution of the command and control problem something remains to be said of British manpower policy, and in particular of the fate of those reservists recalled to the colours at the outbreak of hostilities. This necessitates dealing with events well into 1951, but as an important concern of this chapter has been the effect of manpower upon the commitment of forces, we shall complete this discussion of the matter here.

In settling the manpower question it was important to determine the length of a tour of duty in Korea, since the turnover rate in the combat zone would obviously dictate the rate at which replacements were required and hence the number of men. As the Adjutant-General noted, 'all the recalled reservists are serving in Korea, where they provide a high proportion of our total force, and in particular of the Infantry.'[42] Fifty-six per cent of the 29th Brigade were non-regulars, and although this group comprised some national servicemen and type K volunteers, the overwhelming majority were reservists. Within the brigade itself, the proportion of non-regulars varied from seventy percent in the infantry and artillery units to just thirty-eight percent in the Royal Engineers. Because of the expiration of their service dates, the Army was faced with the prospect of withdrawing and replacing some sixty-six percent of the force by the end of 1951. It therefore became necessary to set the length of a tour for regulars at 'not more than eighteen months.'[43]

Replacement of units was good both for morale, given the

Table 3.1 Strength of forces, June 1951

	Actual	Authorised
28 Brigade	2,993	3,056
29 Brigade	6,305	7,146
Total	9,298	10,202

Note: The total strength of all UN forces at this time, excluding US and ROK troops, was 24,128.
Source: WO 281/164.

rigours of the Korean climate, and experience. As the CIGS noted in early 1951, it was 'not a bad thing to let a lot of units have 9 mths [sic] or a year in Korea.'[44] The situation was helped by the fact that by March 1951 the American divisions had finally attained something approaching their correct establishment of 16,000 men, with a further 10,000 replacements in transit.[45] The crisis period had practically passed. By June 1951, the strength of the two British brigades stood as shown in table 3.1. The disparity in strength between the brigades is obvious, even more so when it is remembered that the figures for the 28th Brigade include the Australians and New Zealanders as well.

In January 1951 the decision was taken to begin a phased withdrawal of reservists from September the same year, and the War Office estimated that all such men would be released from the army by February 1952. The army did not plan to recall any other reservists in the period 1952–55. Those time-expired regulars who had been retained would also be released gradually, from a total of 26,900 at 1 April 1952 to nil by 1 September the following year. To make up the short-fall in the army's manpower programme, the call-up age for national servicemen would be reduced to eighteen years.[46]

Thus all those men who had been forced by the international situation to return to the army, when they might reasonably have expected this role to be filled by others, were finally quit of their obligations. This would have been small comfort to the families of those killed, or to those captured and languishing in Chinese prison camps in North Korea. The contortions of British manpower policy at this time hold some important, albeit largely negative, lessons for future defence planners. The disinclination on the part of the government to mobilise the Territorial Army, because of the disruption it would cause and the political implications inherent in such action, is understandable. Little consideration seems to have been given to the disruption caused to the lives of reservists hurriedly recalled for service in Korea.

The decisions concerning the use of national servicemen that were finally forced on the government should have been taken from the beginning. Preparing the 29th Brigade for Korean service on short notice was quite difficult enough without the administrative and organisational chaos caused by withdrawing and replacing two-thirds of the force simply because they were national servicemen. With their national service scheme firmly in place the British were in a better position than either the Canadians or New Zealanders to place their trained forces in the field at short notice. One is moved to wonder whether the British might not have avoided depleting the Hong Kong garrison in August 1950 if they had not fashioned this additional impediment to the speedy despatch of the 29th Brigade.

Australia never faced any serious difficulty in getting 3 RAR into Korea for, although the army was run-down it could, at a pinch, support a single battalion in the field. By opting for specially-enlisted forces rather than the use of regular units, the Canadians and New Zealanders experienced greater delays in raising and training their forces, which did not in fact reach Korea until the first half of 1951. It was never likely that any other member of the Commonwealth would offer ground forces for Korea.[47]

Chapter 4
Resolving the command and control problem

In the early days of British Commonwealth involvement in Korea the deployment and operations of Commonwealth forces were characterised by a great deal of improvisation. This was equally true of the command and control of these forces. A fresh commitment in north-east Asia had not been expected and so had not been planned for. As a result, the administration of the forces hurriedly despatched in August and September 1950 was also marked by confusion and a certain amount of 'ad hocery'. That the situation did not end in disaster was owed in large measure to the existence in Japan of remnants of the British Commonwealth Occupation Force (BCOF). This organisation was to provide the foundation upon which a regular administrative and logistic machinery was erected, while in the short-term it provided the back-up needed by the small Commonwealth units operating under the command of the UNC, and met those needs which the Americans, for reasons that will be examined later, were unable to satisfy.

Few forces in recent history can lay greater claim to that over-used label 'the forgotten army' than can BCOF. While a great deal of research has been done on the allied occupation of Germany, studies of the occupation of Japan have focused almost exclusively upon the American role in post-war Japan. The Americans were the largest occupying force, the Commonwealth fielding 36,154 men in an initial total force of around 250,000, and MacArthur was the Supreme Commander for the Allied Powers (SCAP).[1]

This is not the place for a history of BCOF, though such a work is overdue.[2] Certain aspects of the occupation force must be understood, however, in order to make sense of the role it was to play during the Korean War. Additionally, many of the personalities were carried over from the first period into the second, and this continuity explains a great deal both about the success of the system and about the conflicts which arose within the Commonwealth organisation.

A Commonwealth role in the occupation of Japan came about from the Commonwealth, and especially British, desire to play a part in the finale of the Pacific War, thus strengthening its voice in the decision-making councils of the allies in the Far East. Economic considerations were important, as was the need to re-establish European prestige in Asia. Victory over the Japanese had been overwhelmingly an American victory, and the British wanted to assert strongly the Commonwealth's right to a part in the post-conquest settlement.

British aspirations ran into difficulties almost immediately. Attlee had suggested to the Commonwealth Prime Ministers that the force should consist of five brigade groups, one each furnished by Australia, Britain, Canada and New Zealand, a British/Indian brigade, and a tactical air force component. Australia insisted on sending an independent Australian force under an Australian commander who would be directly answerable only to SCAP and his own government. Canada was not interested and never formed part of the occupation force, a decision which was to cause problems for the Canadian forces during the early part of the Korean War. The decision, however, was in keeping with Canada's historic lack of interest or involvement in Asia and the Pacific. The difficulty with Australia was of a quite different order and was far more serious in its implications.

Australian attitudes had advanced considerably since 1939, or even 1941, and Australian feeling towards the Japanese in 1945 was grim, in large part because of the Japanese treatment of Allied prisoners of war. As D.M. Horner has shown, by 1945 the Australians wished to be regarded as a principal Pacific power, through measures such as membership of the Allied Council for Japan, and looked for recognition as a major belligerent of the Japanese, something which they felt had not been sufficiently acknowledged by the other major powers.[3] As was widely realised in military circles in both Britain and Australia, the proposal for a separate Australian force had damaging implications for the future of Commonwealth unity and defence cooperation. Major-General S.F. Rowell, a future Australian Chief of the General Staff at that time attached to the War Office in London, went so far as to say that as a result 'any question of Imperial defence cooperation can be put in the background forever. This business of posing as a great power is just too ludicrous for words . . . '[4] More immediately, a small Australian force such as was proposed would inevitably be swamped by the large American organisation surrounding it, and there were other benefits in being part of a larger Commonwealth force. This argument was the same one that was later to be used to rally the waverers over the decision to form the Commonwealth division in 1951.

It was in this context that Attlee agreed to the appointment of an Australian as commander-in-chief of the occupation force in order to head off the Australian proposal for an independent contribution. This was a more momentous concession than might now appear to be the case. Throughout the Second World War the refusal of the British to place their troops under Dominion generals had been a source of bitterness on the part of those officers passed over for command in favour of men who were frequently more junior, and less experienced, simply because the latter were British. The manifest absurdity of the principle had been well illustrated in the discussions concerning a Commonwealth force for the planned assault upon Japan itself, in which the British had proposed giving command of the ground element to a relatively junior British corps commander with no experience whatsoever of fighting the Japanese. Buckley explains that in order to avoid 'the embarrassment of possibly two Commonwealth forces it appeared to be wise to concede ultimate responsibility to Australia in the expectation that Australia would swallow the bait and return to the Commonwealth fold.'[5] Baiting the hook, however, must have been very galling for some sections of Whitehall.

Kenneth Morgan has stated that the Attlee administration was sensitive to 'the new pressures for Commonwealth and colonial independence coursing through the British imperial domain, from republicans in Australia to nationalists in the Gold Coast, with renewed force after 1945.'[6] It is tempting to see Attlee's agreement to an Australian commander-in-chief in this light. It should be remembered, however, that the Labour Party was as strongly pro-Empire as the Conservatives at this stage, and that even if the leading figures in the government sympathised with the aspirations of the dominions, this attitude was not necesarily shared by the leading figures in the armed forces or the Foreign Office.

Since executive authority now resided with Australia, it was left to the Australian commander-designate, Lieutenant-General John Northcott, to negotiate the role and tasks of BCOF with the Americans, specifically with MacArthur. Out of this process arose the Northcott-MacArthur agreement of 18 December 1945. BCOF was assigned responsibility for Hiroshima prefecture, although this was soon expanded to include Yamaguchi and Shimane prefectures as well. The ground force consisted of a corps of two divisions with the commander-in-chief as corps commander and under the operational control of the US Eighth Army, while the air component would be under the control of the US Fifth Air Force. The commander-in-chief was responsible for the administration and maintenance of the force as a whole, and importantly, had the right of direct access to MacArthur. In administrative matters the commander-in-chief reported to the Joint Chiefs of Staff in Australia (JCOSA). This was a short-lived and substantially unsuccessful precursor to the Australian Higher Defence Machinery which fulfilled this same role during the Korean War.

The Northcott-MacArthur agreement was not greeted with much enthusiasm by either the British or Indian representatives on the JCOSA, since they felt that the command relations set out in it raised questions about the maintenance of sovereignty over the forces contributed. (Lieutenant-General Robertson, Northcott's successor in mid-1946, also considered it a 'very hard bargain'.) In addition the British were unhappy because they felt that the Americans were deliberately relegating them to an outlying and largely rural area, whereas they had hoped for a renewed British presence in Kobe and/or Osaka where they had had considerable economic interests before the war. Buckley cites this British dissatisfaction as contributing to Northcott's recall and replacement by Robertson, but offers no evidence for this assertion, which must therefore be treated sceptically.[7] The truth is that the military functions of an occupation force, such as they were, had been completed within weeks of the end of the war. There was no pressing military need for a Commonwealth contribution to the occupation forces, and therefore they lacked negotiating strength. The Americans were in any case using Kobe and Osaka as major ports for the supply of their own forces.

Advance units began arriving in Japan on 8 February 1946. By late [northern] spring BCOF headquarters was based at Etajima, the base port was at Kure, and the force held airfields at Iwakuni, Bofu and Ozuki. The 34th Australian Infantry Brigade was responsible for Hiroshima prefecture, the 9th New Zealand Infantry Brigade for Yamaguchi, while the British Indian Division (BRINDIV), by far the largest formation, controlled a further seven prefectures throughout the Chungoku and Shikoku regions (see map 2).

As noted, Northcott did not command the force for long, and in the context of BCOF's role in the Korean War nothing more need be said about him. This is not true of his successor. Lieutenant-General Sir Horace Clement Hugh Robertson was fifty-two when he took command of BCOF. A regular officer, he saw service in the Great War with the 10th Light Horse at Gallipoli and in staff positions in Palestine and Egypt. He held various positions during the stagnant inter-war years, and when war broke out again he was given command of the 19th Infantry Brigade destined for service with the 6th Division in North Africa. He took part in the highly successful advance from Bardia to Benghazi in January and February 1941, and was promoted and returned to Australia in January 1942 to command the 1st Australian Armoured Division, the only AIF division not to see service outside Australia. He ended the war as a lieutenant-general commanding First Australian Army in New Guinea.[8]

Although a highly successful commander, Robertson only commanded on active service for about 55 days, spending most of the war on the sidelines. His relegation to essentially inactive positions can be explained largely in terms of personality. O'Neill has written that he was 'undoubtedly charismatic, exerting a strong, individual style of leadership and he always strove to achieve recognition for his particular command as the best in the army. At times he aroused antagonism, particularly among his superiors and contemporaries, for his undisguised egotism, self-assertion and occasional vulgarity.'

Contemporaries shared these views. 'There was no bushel large enough to hide [his] light. If one had been found he would have been astonished and dismayed . . . Vain, self-centred and arrogant, he looked and acted the part which he had written for himself', wrote one. 'At the right military moment, vanity such as Robbie's could be a virtue, but divorced from such circumstances vanity could become tiresome. At no time did Robbie set a ceiling on his

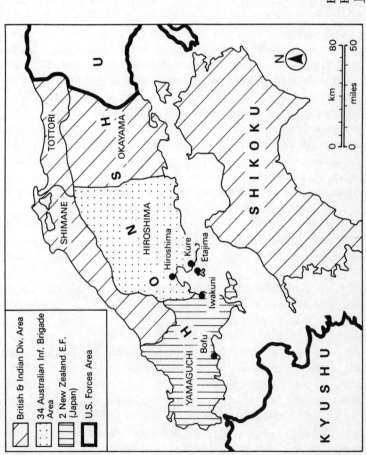

British Commonwealth Occupation
Force, area of responsibility,
Japan, 1946–50

British & Indian Div. Area

34 Australian Inf. Brigade
Area

2 New Zealand E.F.
(Japan)

U.S. Forces Area

TOTTORI

SHIMANE

HONSHU

OKAYAMA

HIROSHIMA

Hiroshima

Kure

Etajima

Iwakuni

YAMAGUCHI

Bofu

KYUSHU

SHIKOKU

N

km
0   80

miles
0   50

own military, sporting or business ability', said another.[9] No-one doubted his ability, however, which was considerable. In March 1942 Robertson had moved to have himself appointed commander-in-chief of the Australian army in place of Blamey, so it can hardly be wondered at if Blamey kept his subordinate at arms length for the rest of the war. As will be noted later, Robertson was to resist being recalled to Australia from Japan in 1951 when he would once again be subordinated to others. In this context it was also significant that he had not been preferred for the appointment as the first Duntroon graduate to be Chief of the General Staff, the job having gone to Rowell.

Although essentially non-military in nature, the problems facing BCOF were formidable and by any standards Robertson did an exceptional job as commander-in-chief. Two of the most taxing tasks were to avoid antagonising the Americans and to maintain smooth relations between Commonwealth components. Relations with the Americans were not a serious problem, for MacArthur had ensured that BCOF would operate in Japan on his terms when he had negotiated the agreement in late 1945. In addition, BCOF played a minor role in the political administrative task in Japan, since most of these tasks were fulfilled by American Military Government teams. As Buckley notes, this was a good thing for the Japanese, because the Commonwealth was generally much less sympathetic to the job of reconstruction than was MacArthur. 'A British Commonwealth-run occupation would probably have been largely unconstructive',[10] and this is certainly well illustrated by the different attitudes to 'fraternisation', with the Commonwealth initially forbidding contact between its soldiers and Japanese civilians. Robertson, however, seems to have enjoyed excellent relations with MacArthur and this, combined with his right of direct access to the Supreme Commander, went a long way to ensuring smooth relations.

The same could not be said of relations within the force. Many of the pressures that influenced decision-making during the Korean War were present already in the immediate post-war period. Thus, for example, global imperial military commitments placed severe pressure upon British Army manpower, a pressure that was heightened in 1947 when the proposed length of service in the National Service Act had to be cut from eighteen months to twelve.[11] Britain began withdrawing ground forces in February 1947, sending the

5th Infantry Brigade to Malaya. Nehru declined to leave Indian forces in Japan after independence and partition in August 1947, and these too were withdrawn. These withdrawals also brought about the dissolution of the JCOSA, since it was no longer required. As the 9th New Zealand Infantry Brigade was still in Japan, the New Zealand Liaison Officer in Melbourne was invited to attend meetings of the Australian Defence Comittee and the Chiefs of Staff Committee whenever BCOF matters were discussed.[12] In October 1948 New Zealand withdrew both her ground and air forces from Japan, and thereafter BCOF was an Australian organisation.

The Foreign Office had never been in favour of BCOF, and was a strong advocate of early withdrawal. This position was connected to the diplomats' dislike of military men having too great a say in the running of foreign relations as was the case in Japan, particularly with the appointment of General Sir Charles Gairdner as the British Prime Minister's personal representative to SCAP. Gairdner's position was also resented by Robertson, who considered that the former 'worked constantly for UK's individual interests only in direct opposition to any question of British Commonwealth co-operation.'[13] Much of the friction revolved around Robertson's insistence upon the rights and prerogatives of the commander-in-chief being observed against Gairdner's, and others', attempts to ignore him. Robertson's position was consistent and correct. As commander-in-chief during a period of military occupation he out-ranked and took precedence before all other Commonwealth officials, civil or military. Since there had been no peace treaty proclaimed there were no ambassadors as such, only heads of mission, and while he recognised men such as Gascoigne, head of the United Kingdom mission, as being senior to all other civilian officials of lesser rank, these men were still under Robertson's legal authority. Gairdner also tried to insist that Robertson had no command responsibility for the British Commonwealth Air Component, which was under the command of the British Air Vice Marshal Bouchier, but since Robertson's instructions specified that he commanded *all* Commonwealth forces in Japan, this attempted usurpation of authority proved short-lived.

Overall Robertson's relations with senior British figures in Japan were characterised by back-biting and pettiness. Soon after arriving in Japan Robertson had had similar difficulties with Major-General

D.T. Cowan, commanding BRINDIV, largely, it would seem, because Cowan had expected to be appointed commander-in-chief after Northcott's departure. These feuds prompted Robertson to observe later that he had

made the mistake of imagining that other members of the force were [as] anxious as I was to have British Commonwealth co-operation, and it did not occur to me that officers of the British and Indian army looked upon us from Australia and New Zealand as they looked upon the Indians, and were prepared to do anything to avoid being publicly commanded by us.[14]

The Indian official historian wrote that such problems arose in BCOF because of a failure to lay down precise rules of 'precedence and command' and to 'define responsibilities and channels of communication from the very beginning'.[15] This need seems childish, and in some ways perhaps it is. But the unanimity of purpose between allies, sustained in difficult conditions during war, frequently breaks down quickly in the aftermath of peace. Relations between British and Australian civilian officials in Japan were also poor, leading Buckley to note that 'most of the senior Australian figures in the occupation were to feel aggrieved by British behaviour towards its Pacific ally.' He has characterised Anglo-Australian relations in Japan as 'generally a disaster'.[16] With the end of the war in the Pacific and the appointment of a commander-in-chief for the occupation force, Gairdner's position should not have been persisted with, since he no longer fulfilled any function and therefore spent his time trying to displace both Robertson and Gascoigne. The British had agreed to the appointment of the commander-in-chief and to the arrangements for JCOSA, and then tried to circumvent both. Robertson may have lacked seniority in terms of command on active service, but British actions were dictated rather by considerations of internal Whitehall politics and, for some, irritation at being forced to serve under a 'colonial' officer. The New Zealanders, who probably felt themselves being taken for granted by all sides, had much stronger grounds for disatisfaction.[17] Buckley has concluded, however, that 'Australia was the only Commonwealth nation that could look back on the BCOF scheme with a measure of pride. By its commitment it demonstrated a new maturity in its Pacific foreign policy. The presence of Australian troops supported Australia's claims to be taken seriously as a regional power.[18] And that, after all, had been the motivation behind Australian participation all along.

On 24 May 1950 it was announced that BCOF was to be withdrawn at last. Under the Northcott-MacArthur agreement, six months notice of the intention to withdraw forces was required, and the Australian Prime Minister, R.G. Menzies, stated that some time was expected to elapse before the movement of men and stores would commence. The reason given for the decision to withdraw was that BCOF placed a considerable drain on limited resources and that the addition of these resources to the newly-announced national service scheme would assist in the success of that programme. Before anything further happened, however, the Korean War broke out.

By this time BCOF was but a shadow of its former self. Not only was the Australian element the only one left, but this force itself had declined considerably in numbers. The ground force had fallen from a brigade to a single, half-strength, battalion, while the air element now comprised only No 77 (Fighter) Squadron. Significantly, and fortuitously for the role that BCOF would be called upon to fill, most of the BCOF Base Organisation was still intact, although it too was understrength and like the rest of BCOF packing up to go home.

Soon after war broke out, hard intelligence of any sort became difficult to obtain and BCOF's first function was to act as a channel of information, not as an administrative unit. On 29 June the Defence Committee had instructed Robertson that his headquarters was not to 'make provision for the support (logistically or otherwise) of any Empire commitment or establishment' including the civil liaision missions. The decision to withdraw BCOF had not yet been rescinded, and the Chiefs of Staff Committee still saw a role for BCOF while it did remain, instructing the Commander-in-Chief to 'despatch . . . a situation report daily (or more often if necessary)'.[19] By 14 July, the decision had been made to 'hold in abeyance' the plans for the return of BCOF to Australia.[20]

This decision was not made, as might have been expected, simply in order to supply the RAAF's No 77 Squadron, by then in action over Korea. Robertson had acted as the channel for MacArthur's request for the use of the squadron although, as is now well known, MacArthur had ensured that the request was leaked to the press in order to intensify pressure on the Australian government. But both the Chiefs of Staff Committee and the Defence Committee noted that the commitment of 77 Squadron 'would involve using United States lines of supply', and that 'the only solution to supply problems is for it to be completely controlled and maintained by 5th Air Force [and] except for a small range of clothing items and major aircraft maintenance provided by Iwakuni it would be impracticable and most uneconomical for BCOF to attempt supply action under existing organisation'.[21] Rather, the decision seems to have resulted from a general sense of caution and desire to await possible developments.

These were not long in coming. Having committed air and naval units Australia, along with other member states of the United Nations, came under pressure to commit ground forces also. In Australia's case, of course, the pressure was greater because of the presence of the infantry battalion still on occupation duties in Japan. Robertson drew attention to this possibility in a message to the Chiefs of Staff on 17 July. In his view MacArthur had been forced to take considerable risks in order to save what ROK forces remained, and he felt 'that a major disaster to his forces cannot be ruled out'. SCAP was gathering troops from anywhere he could, including stripping the Okinawa garrison, and Robertson foresaw that 'an urgent call may be made to anyone who has anything to offer ... I know that SCAP would like Australians and would reason that if he got some he could expect more following his wartime experience.'[22]

MacArthur got his ground forces, not only from Australia but from Britain as well, and this had major implications for the future of BCOF. The most important of these arose out of the terms of the occupation. Countries that did not have forces involved in the occupation were not permitted to stage troops in Japan before committing them to Korea. For this reason, all the non-Commonwealth UN forces underwent training and re-equipping at the UN Reception Centre at Taegu in Korea. The Canadians also ran into this difficulty when they wanted to act independently of the Commonwealth organisation in late 1950. Although BCOF was an Australian operation by 1950, it was still a Commonwealth force in name, and Commonwealth forces were therefore able to base themselves in Japan perfectly in keeping with occupation conditions. The ability to use Japan was important for three reasons.

Firstly, the Commonwealth fielded a large force that eventually fought as a separate division. Secondly, Commonwealth and US supplies were different, necessitating separate, though parallel, lines of communication. Thirdly, Japan was much better able to meet the needs of the force than was Korea, seriously ravaged by fighting. Robertson recognised this clearly and quickly and, as usual, left his superiors in no doubt concerning his views. 'Whatever happens', he wrote,

a base here is necessary and this implies a chain of supply right forward to the front line including some advanced base in Korea . . . Any suggestion that each portion of the Empire should be separate and distinct must mean a large overhead to each with the establishment of separate bases. The waste of effort in having all these separate bases and separate units appears to me to have nothing to commend it. . . . Unless we are to just hand over individual units to the Americans using American arms, ammunition and equipment, it appears to me quite impracticable for the British Commonwealth to do anything other than have one force with one organisation and one chain of supply.[23]

Unity of forces within the Commonwealth was to be one of his most oft-repeated themes.

The virtues of Commonwealth co-operation were not immediately apparent in all quarters, and some of the issues and problems of the early period of the occupation reappeared in the early period of the Korean War. The purely Australian organisation in Japan was once again to become a Commonwealth one with responsibilities for troops other than Australians, and earlier antagonisms over the responsibility for these forces surfaced yet again. It was, at times, an unedifying display of Commonwealth disunity.

In a bid to gain kudos with the Americans, the Australians had pre-empted the British by one hour in their announcement of the commitment of 3 RAR for service in Korea. The British, however, were in a position physically to commit troops earlier than the Australians by stripping the garrison of Hong Kong and despatching a weak brigade of two understrength battalions. This formation could in no way be likened to a US regimental combat team, capable of independent operation and largely self-sustaining, because it completely lacked all heavy equipment, transport, and organic artillery. The situation arose largely as a result of the tensions in the Commonwealth organisation, and these will be examined below.

During the latter part of the war against Japan, Churchill had maintained a personal representative on MacArthur's headquarters. At the end of the war this position was being filled by Lieutenant-General Gairdner, who continued in the role well after the Japanese surrender and, as we have seen, became a considerable nuisance to Robertson in the early days of BCOF. These circumstances were now repeated with the appointment of Air Vice Marshal Bouchier as the personal representative of the United Kingdom Chiefs of Staff on MacArthur's headquarters.

Cecil Arthur Bouchier was born in 1895 and like Robertson saw service in the Great War. He served with the Royal Flying Corps and Royal Air Force in the Middle East and, in 1918–19, with the British intervention forces in North Russia. Between the wars he formed and commanded the first squadron of the Royal Indian Air Force. He took part in the Battle of Britain, and was in command of the fighter aircraft forces on D-Day in 1944. Between 1945 and 1948 he was Air Officer Commanding British Commonwealth Air Forces, Japan and thus served directly under Robertson as his principal Air Force officer. Their relationship at this time was cordial, and Bouchier acted in Robertson's place when the latter visited Australia and New Zealand for consultations in early 1948. He retired in 1949, but was reinstated in 1950 and sent to Japan. He retired again in 1953, and died in 1979.

The question of representation on SCAP's headquarters was being considered by the British in early July, at a time when they were still debating whether or not to despatch troops to Korea. Bouchier's appointment seems to have been made quickly, with little consultation within British government circles, and absolutely none with other Commonwealth governments. Alvery Gascoigne, head of the United Kingdom Liaison Mission in Japan, recommended against appointing Bouchier, since 'General Robertson will . . . be likely to resent an appointment of this nature, and it might be unwise to send out Bouchier who has recently served under him.'[24] His suggestion that Gairdner be re-appointed instead was scarcely helpful.

Robertson had never been popular with Whitehall. He was too independent and too ready to assert the rights of the Dominions. The Foreign Office and, to a lesser extent, the War Office now attempted to undermine and isolate him and, in the process, demonstrated that the inability to recognise the sovereign rights of the dominions which had characterised British attitudes during the Second World War had not changed.

Commenting on Gascoigne's message, the Foreign Office minuted Attlee that it was indeed possible.

> that General Robertson . . . may resent the appointment, especially if the holder of it were to be someone who has recently served under him. General Robertson is a particularly 'touchy' individual and we have had a good many difficulties with him in the past . . . The Canadian, Australian and New Zealand governments are all concerned as they have already sent [sic] forces to Korea: it would . . . be sufficient if we were to inform them officially as soon as United States approval for the appointment is obtained.[25]

Attlee noted that he would 'speak to Menzies on this.'

Bouchier's appointment may be explained in terms of a desire to humiliate Robertson and make his task more difficult. There is no evidence, nor was there every any suggestion, that Robertson as Commander-in-Chief, or the Australian Chiefs of Staff, had ever failed to keep the British fully informed on matters in Japan of significance to the Commonwealth. The appointment of an airman to the position is equally difficult to justify. Bouchier's career had been a gallant one, but his considerable experience with fighter aircraft in no way qualified him for command in or comment upon operations which were pre-eminently army ones. As will be seen below this was to have serious consequences early in the Korean War. The only other basis upon which the appointment could be justified was previous good relations with MacArthur.

There is no evidence that Bouchier enjoyed any great level of contact with SCAP during his time in BCOF. Many people in Japan claimed to enjoy warm relations with the Supreme Commander; few in fact did so. There is no doubt that Bouchier had a certain level of access to MacArthur *after* he was appointed as the Chiefs of Staff representative. This access was based on the position he occupied then, and not on any previous association. The only grounds on which the appointment could be justified, therefore, previous failure of communicaion, particular operational expertise, or closeness to MacArthur, did not in fact exist.

As Robertson noted, both at the time and subsequenty, his own position was invidious. Unlike earlier relations with Gairdner, however, there was no personal animosity, and

> although the position was difficult I treated him [Bouchier] as I had always done, as a friend, and endeavoured to do what I could to help although I pointed out that his position would seriously embarrass me ... [A]s a result of his presence I did not hear as much as I should have heard of what was going on and UN command were never quite sure who they should refer to on British Commonwealth matters.[26]

The difficulties arose as soon as the British decided to send troops from Hong Kong to Korea and illustrate perfectly Robertson's concerns. Although the British had been beaten by the Australians in being the first to announce the sending of troops to Korea they intended to be the first to commit them physically, and to this end Bouchier successfully urged that the Hong Kong battalions be despatched without delay, and without their transport or heavy equipment either. Bouchier was confident that the Americans would provide these, demonstrating by this his ignorance of the true situation facing the Americans in both Korea and Japan. He also proposed that all other logistic support would be conducted through American channels. Robertson was not informed until after these recomendations had been accepted in London.

Robertson was kept briefed on developments, however, by the Commander-in-Chief, Far East Land Forces (FARELF) in Singapore, Lieutenant-General Sir John Harding, under whose overall command the Hong Kong garrison came. Harding sent one of his senior staff officers to Japan, a Lieutenant-Colonel Williams, to co-ordinate matters with Robertson since, like Robertson, Harding appreciated the difficulties facing the 27th Brigade. Robertson recommended that the brigade should bring its transport with it, with which Williams concurred, but Bouchier insisted that the troops sail as ordered. The result was that the brigade sat on the wharfs at Pusan for a week waiting for their transport to catch them up.

The major thrust of Robertson's criticism, however, related to the apparent expectation that BCOF would provide certain services to the brigade that the Americans could not, and on a demand basis. Robertson knew that an agreement concerning the combining of Australian, New Zealand and British forces had been reached in Melbourne on 8 August and told Williams of it, adding that this was the only basis on which BCOF could act in support of British forces. He delivered his judgement on the situaiton in a cable to his superiors in Melbourne with characteristic directness.

I feel that we are just being made use of on the one hand and being insulted and slighted on the other. . . The Americans also are somewhat bewildered and both their Signals and Medical branches cannot understand why the whole of this is not done through BCOF. If UK is desirous of acting independently with her forces being maintained by the Americans then I consider this should apply to all her forces . . . [We can] then make very considerable reductions in BCOF and take some steps towards the withdrawal from occupation which appears likely in view of the persistent statements that a state of peace is to be given to the Japanese in the near future.[27]

He followed this with a further message to the CGS a few days later, in which he noted that BCOF was having still further demands placed upon it, 'in spite of their insistence that the military force they have sent . . . [is] no concern of BCOF'. He requested that the matter be placed on a regular footing quickly.[28]

Rowell needed no further prompting. On 31 August he addressed a long, polite and very hard-nosed signal to the Chief of the Imperial General Staff, Field Marshal Sir William Slim. His opening shot was a succinct comment on much that had characterised the Empire military relationship since the beginning of the Second World War. 'We always talk very glibly about the way we cooperate but when it actually comes to the practical test we have a special facility for doing the opposite. I suggest in the present circumstances the more or less complete sidetracking of BCOF is a case in point.' Rowell went on to ask whether, for political reasons, the British had decided to deal through the Americans or whether simple dislike of Robertson had led them to consider setting up a separate channel of their own. The end result, he felt, was that British troops would suffer from the failure to reach agreement on the use of BCOF facilities.

As things stand today Commander-in-Chief BCOF is under no obligation whatever to afford British troops any facilities. In actual fact your people are compelled to use our signals and cipher staff and I have no doubt that very soon Bouchier or Coad will be asking for . . . hospital accommodation and the like. Under no circumstances would we refuse these facilities but we would very much prefer to have their use planned for . . . particularly as any increase in the existing base facilities will have to be met from here. I suggest to you that it is not too late to put this business on the right basis and so prevent what can only become a quote buggers muddle unquote in which the only people to suffer will be the soldiers.[29]

Slim responded promptly. He assured the Australian CGS that there was no intention of cutting out Robertson or BCOF and that, on the contrary, 'our intention is that the maximum maintenance for the British force in Korea that . . . BCOF in Japan can possibly undertake should . . . be undertaken.' He expressed himself 'in complete agreement with everything you say.'[30] Bouchier's independence of action was about to come to an end.

In an attempt to preserve his position, or perhaps merely in an attempt to have it defined, Bouchier had requested the United Kingdom Chiefs of Staff to make it clear to Harding in Singapore 'and anyone else concerned . . . that I am your representative here and Senior British Military Liaison Officer . . . Therefore it is correct for all concerned to address communications personally to me.'[31] He was particularly aggrieved that Harding was communicating directly with Robertson, thereby implicitly recognising Robertson as the senior British officer. The British force for Korea, he wrote, 'is purely [a] United Kingdom Force and therefore no concern of Robertson except by courtesy. He should be kept informed of events through me . . . General Robertson can be dangerous and such interference may not end [here]'. He then accused the Commander-in-Chief, BCOF, of openly representing the British force as 'a brigade less one battalion', which it was, and of suggesting to MacArthur that the Australian battalion destined for Korea should be joined to it in order to strengthen the force. He rather undermined his own claims that the brigade was not deficient by then conceding that it would need time for re-equipping and training with unit transport and heavy weapons, precisely those items which he had recommended be left in Hong Kong.

It was inevitable that Robertson would win any jurisdictional quarrel with Bouchier, for most of the cards fell his way. (He even attempted to mobilize Foreign Office opinion in his favour through the head of the United Kingdom Liaison Mission, Sir Alvery Gascoigne.[32]) Bouchier's inability to act effectively in the role he wished to write for himself is nowhere better illustrated than by the fact that his entire 'mission' consisted of himself and one NCO. Bouchier even had to type and encode his own daily reports. In addition, he had no powerful advocate in Whitehall; the CIGS was not interested in provoking a breach with the Australians, and the Foreign Office, while happy to use his information for their own purposes, privately expressed no faith in him.[33] Significantly, he represented the United Kingdom Chiefs of Staff, whereas Gairdner had been the representative of the British Prime Minister. Since Slim declined to support him, he probably owed his appointment to the Minister for Defence, Emmanuel Shinwell, whose position was a much less powerful one than would later be the case after the abolition of the separate service ministries. This would certainly explain Bouchier's lack of influence.

While the disagreements between Commonwealth officials unfolded, the Australian Defence Committee had been working on the question of a base organisation in Japan. At its meeting on 17 August it instructed Robertson to consult with SCAP over the size and form of the base organisation, and also ordered the Joint Administrative Planning Committee (JAPC) to examine the supply arrangements necessary to sustain the proposed British Commonwealth land force.[34] The report of the JAPC recommended that so long as the force committed remained small and its period of service short, the establishment of an advanced base at Pusan together with some facilities, such as the BCOF General Hospital, at Kure would suffice. It might even be possible to recommence the winding-up of BCOF, since this would take approximately nine months.[35] The Australians were also informed by Robertson that the British had already begun to implement the base organisation at Pusan, and had appointed a commander with effect from 1 September 1950.[36]

The JAPC report suggested a very limited and attenuated role for BCOF, indeed almost no role at all, and was scarcely in keeping with Robertson's vision. But the situation now changed again. After receiving the report, Rowell had circulated it to the New Zealand CGS and the War Office for comment. Somewhat to his surprise, the War Office responded that the original agreement on 8 August, which foresaw a large role for BCOF and which, it will be recalled, Robertson had used to defend his position against Bouchier, was in fact the correct solution. While Rowell thought the new proposal to be 'the proper answer', he acknowledged that 'it would appear to be difficult to insist on a change of the policy which we ourselves proposed and endorsed.'[37] Rowell concluded that the August decision should stand, but expressed the hope that the manpower commitment could be kept down.

BCOF began to regularise the previously informal administrative arrangements almost at once.[38] Robertson, not surprisingly, was very pleased. Bouchier put on a brave front, writing to the War Office that, with BCOF taking over responsibility for the brigades, he would now 'have more time to devote to the special duties of my appointment.'[39] He was clearly disappointed, however, for in a report later that month he noted that the period during which he had been responsible for the force in Korea

has been one of the proudest and happiest experiences for me. Under pressure from the War Office and General Harding however and conscious of overall considerations of Commonwealth relations and need to keep the peace with General Robertson I have this day with feelings of deep personal sadness handed over to Robertson and BCOF these responsibilities for . . . this Brigade.[40]

It was now clear that a considerable Commonwealth effort would be required in Korea and Japan for some time to come, and it was important therefore to put all the arrangements concerning command and control on a regular footing. This was to be accomplished in the form of a directive to Robertson as Commander-in-Chief setting out his duties and responsibilities with regard to the various Commonwealth forces and their controlling bodies. Robertson had been subject to control by directive ever since taking command of BCOF, but the changes in the composition of the force and the demise of JCOSA as the controlling body in 1947 had led to various amendments, some of them substantial, so that by 1950 his current directive covered little more than his responsibility for Australian forces and his answering for them to the Chiefs of Staff in Melbourne. This clearly did not cover his new responsibilities, and a new directive was therefore required.

The Australian Defence Committee had recommended the adoption of a draft directive as early as 13 October.[41] It had to be circulated to other Commonwealth governments for approval, and here it ran into objections from the British. In particular, they would not agree to Robertson being the representative of the British Chiefs of Staff in dealing with the Americans. They insisted that this should continue to be Bouchier and that they would amend his orders to reflect the fact that he was to have no direct administrative interest in the British forces in Korea.[42] The Australians were not happy with this, considering that such a dual appointment 'was not in harmony with the established principles for co-operation in British Commonwealth Defence.'[43] Indeed, they resented it quite strongly. Major-General Cassels, as the British representative on the Defence Committee, pointed out that Attlee had discussed the matter with Menzies, and that in similar circumstances the Australian chiefs would want a representative of their own on the spot. The Australians countered that Menzies had not mentioned this to anyone, and that in the past 'they had frequently *not* had such a representative.' Parallels were drawn with 'the anomaly of Gairder'.[44] The meeting was amicable, but the disagreement was deep and it was with considerable reluctance that the committee accepted the amendment.

In the course of this meeting Cassels had suggested that, but for Robertson, there would have been no trouble and he reported to London that this was greeted with a 'general nodding of heads'. This was hardly fair to Robertson, for the only way friction would have been avoided would have been to appoint a British commander-in-chief. Having won agreement on the use of the existing BCOF organisation, however, Rowell, who was not well-disposed towards Robertson, was quite prepared to sacrifice him in the furtherance of smooth relations. Having conceded the appointment of Bouchier, however unwillingly, Rowell gave an undertaking to remove Robertson by the end of 1950.[45]

This remarkable saga of personality politics did not end here. The early draft of the directive nominating the commander-in-chief as the representative of the British Chiefs of Staff had been forwarded to Robertson, probably in error. Robertson had immediately spoken to Gascoigne and stated that the position of Bouchier had to be clarified. Later the same day Robertson received a cable from the Australian Chiefs of Staff stating that unless Bouchier was withdrawn or made subordinate to Robertson they would recommend to the Australian government that Robertson himself be withdrawn. Meanwhile the Foreign Office warned that 'this sort of ill feeling on the part of Robertson, though to some extent no doubt inevitable in view of his temperament, is very unfortunate and could conceivably do harm to our relations with Australia.'[46]

The British High Commissioner to Australia, E.J. Williams, raised the matter with Menzies, but got small satisfaction. The

Australian Prime Minister thought the matter little more than a clash of temperament, and surprised Williams by asking *him* for a copy of Robertson's directive.[47] Beyond stating their concern, however, there was little more that the Foreign Office could do, for Robertson had one considerable advantage in his favour. In so far as any individual in an organisation is indispensable, Robertson was just that. Gascoigne had made it clear to his superiors in London that it would be a calamity for Robertson to be withdrawn at that stage because of his good relations with the Americans and understanding of local conditions. Even E.J. Williams, whose attitude towards Robertson was, at best, lukewarm, was moved to say that although they were 'dealing with an inflated ego who has been a source of continuous embarassment on the personal level everyone seems to agree . . . that he has done an excellent job in Japan and we do not at this stage want him displaced.'[48] He also noted that most of the British liaison officials in Tokyo could not understand the reason for Bouchier's appointment.

The end result generally pleased no-one. Robertson remained as commander-in-chief and retained non-operational control and administrative responsibility for British Commonwealth forces in Korea. Bouchier remained as personal representative of the British Chiefs of Staff on the Supreme Commander's headquarters, even after MacArthur was removed by Truman and the major justification for his presence completely disappeared. The Australians had successfully defended the principle that an officer from the Dominions could command British troops, and had done no harm to the wider argument that favoured Australian leadership of the Commonwealth in Pacific affairs either. The Foreign Office continued to dislike Robertson, the latter continued to resent Bouchier's encroachment upon his authority, and Bouchier continued to discharge his only remaining function, daily reporting to the British Chiefs of Staff. The British and Australian Chiefs of Staff, meanwhile, laboured successfully to ensure that the logistic and administrative organisation in Japan functioned efficiently for the benefit of the troops in the line.

Much of the credit for this success could in fact be ascribed to Robertson himself. Even his most critical opponents could not detract from his considerable achievements in Japan. He had insisted, in the face of strong pressure, that the existing BCOF organisation could and should provide the back-up for Commonwealth forces in the area, and had correctly argued that it was unwise to assume or expect that the thinly-stretched American system had the capacity to support the Commonwealth. In the space of three months his organisation had been transformed from a force of one battalion and supporting services readying itself to return to Australia, to an expanding base organisation supporting one brigade already in the field, preparing to support a second, and planning to support a third should it be despatched from Canada. On top of all this he had maintained communication with Mac-Arthur who once the Korean War began, and especially after the Inchon landings, was out of Tokyo as often as he was present. He had also kept the Commonwealth governments informed of the progress towards a peace treaty with Japan, although increasingly this work was being taken over by the civilian liaison missions in Tokyo.

The transformation of his command from one involving a small mononational force to one requiring the successful direction of troops and staff from four different countries was not helped by the attitudes of some sections of Whitehall. The Foreign Office had attempted to undermine him in 1946–47, and tried to do so again in 1950. This attitude was shared by some in British military circles. The Australian historian T.B. Millar has commented that, had BCOF 'been a wartime operational command, the C-in-C would not have been an Australian.'[49] The position had become a wartime command in 1950, and British authorities had reacted accordingly. This should not be ascribed to simple arrogance or even paranoia on Robertson's part, for Hopkins has described how the War Office had earlier attempted to avoid recommending Robertson for a knighthood, an honour bestowed on commanders-in-chief of British forces by long-established custom and practice.[50] British troops arrived in Korea in September 1950, and were joined with Australian soldiers the following month to form a Commonwealth force for which Robertson once again carried responsibility. The antagonisms evident in 1946–47, dormant from then until the outbreak of the Korean War and hinted at again with the appointment of Bouchier, were now to be exacerbated further as once again a Dominion general had command of Britsh troops. Generally speaking, the troops themselves were to find such an arrangement much less objectionable than did their government.

Chapter 5

British Commonwealth forces in Korea, August 1950 – July 1951

The fighting in the first year of the Korean War was characterised by confusion, chaos, and a succession of debilitating reversals and stunning successes. The ROK Army had never been equipped with heavy weapons or armoured vehicles, and not surprisingly it initially proved no match for the aggressive armoured thrusts of the Soviet-equipped and trained Korean People's Army. American formations rushed to Korea from occupation duties in Japan were under-strength, inadequately trained, and hopelessly unfit for combat after the idle years of occupation duty. As the commanding general of the 24th Infantry Division, Major-General William Dean, later recalled,

the battle-trained veterans of the early occupation days had been whittled down by time and reassignment until they made up only about fifteen per cent of the men and officers now on duty. The division strength was down to about two-thirds of its war-time total. Infantry regiments had only two battalions each; artillery battalions only two batteries . . . Equipment was all of World War II vintage . . . We were training, but our programme was greatly hampered by the fact that the division was scattered all over southern Japan.[1]

In the circumstances, it is remarkable that the Americans managed to stabilise the situation at all, nor is it to be wondered at that this was only achieved on the line of the Naktong river in the south-east corner of the peninsula around the port of Pusan. Much of the credit for this must be given to the Eighth Army commander, General Walton Walker. Walker had earlier earned distinction as the commander of XX Corps in Patton's Third Army in 1944–45. His untimely death in an accident on 23 December 1950, and the succession of Ridgway to the command of Eighth Army, has generally served to eclipse his reputation. The credit for saving American arms from disaster early in the war belongs firmly to this tough and pugnacious little man.

It is against this background of events that the forces of the Commonwealth found themselves in Korea. The 27th Brigade arrived in Pusan on 28 August, and then sat down to wait for its transport to catch it up as a result of Air Vice Marshal Bouchier's interference in ordering that it be left in Hong Kong. A brigade without transport or heavy weapons is largely immobile and of limited usefulness even in conditions of static defence, and Walker had agreed with the brigade commander, Brigadier Basil Coad, that the brigade would not be operational until then. Within a couple of days, however, the KPA launched an offensive all along the Naktong bridgehead, and Coad found himself holding a front of 18,000 yards with his two weak battalions, and with a gap of between 4,000 and 9,000 yards between his left flank and the neighbouring American formation. It was an uncomfortable situation.[2]

Fortunately for Coad it did not last long, and was brought to an end by the first of a succession of remarkable reversals of fortune, Operation CHROMITE, the Inchon landings. These went in on 15 September, catching the KPA in flank and rear with their lines of communication strung out over several hundred miles. In coordination with this operation, the forces behind the Naktong perimeter assaulted across the river on 16 September. After several days of hard fighting, the UN forces in the south began to make significant progress against KPA forces, and by 23 September the enemy cordon had been broken.[3] The two British battalions were involved in some of this heavy fighting towards the end of the breakout phase of operations, on 22–23 September.

It was during these operations that the 27th Brigade was given its first taste of American methods, and it was not a happy experience. At the time, at least in public, the disputes and differences between the British and Commonwealth forces and their American allies were glossed over and simply not alluded to. At times this must have been very difficult to sustain, especially when British casualties resulted from American actions and errors. Although the tone of Coad's public pronouncements in 1951 was conciliatory and concerned to stress the positive features of the relationship, his confidential report to his superiors was devastating in its criticisms.

As will be seen, he was not the only British Commonwealth official to criticise American performance in the first six months of the war, but he was almost certainly one of the best placed and most professionally competent. His report was never published, and is not officially available among the War Office papers in the Public Record Office.

American forces within the perimeter had shown clear signs of being unfit for combat. Staff officers rarely left their headquarters to visit lower formations, and in Coad's experience never came to visit the ground over which they were ordering offensive operations. Their defensive positions had frequently been inadequate, 'indifferent and ineffective, usually consisting of two strands of barbed wire.' The brigade was attached at this time to the US 24th Infantry Division, and although Coad arranged with divisional headquarters for American artillery and tank officers to speak to the British on their methods of cooperation and coordination, 'none of these arrangements in fact materialised.' The practical difficulties this situation could create were brought home during the brigade's first action on 22 September, when a company of the Middlesex Regiment was unable to leave its forming-up place because the objective was being shelled by a battery of American 155 mm guns which the Forward Observation Officers with brigade headquarters were unable to control, much less stop. This was not an isolated incident, Coad noting that they were 'to experience this at other times later.'[4]

They were to experience it again the very next day, 23 September, and in a particularly tragic form. The Argylls assaulted enemy positions on Hill 282, early in the morning, but at 0945 hours the American artillery battalion firing in support of the operation was pulled out without notice. A protest was made to divisional headquarters and alternative artillery support was promised, but never materialised.[5] The enemy now counter-attacked the Argylls in their hastily-dug positions atop the hill, and without fire support the latter were gradually pushed back. 'As the guns had gone', wrote Coad, 'an air strike was called for on point 388 [adjacent to hill 282] . . . and at 1200 hours it was delivered on our own troops.'[6] The napalming of the Argylls by American aircraft further reduced the strength of the two companies holding the hill to about forty effectives, and they lost possession of the feature. Their casualties totalled 17 killed and 76 wounded, and it was only with a further counter-attack incurring more casualties, in which the battalion second-in-command was killed, that the position was retaken, although it was not held.

It would be easy to dismiss this incident, as some writers have done, as 'fortunes of war'. Such incidents do occur and it is impossible to prevent them entirely, but well-trained and disciplined troops will generally keep such occurrences to an absolute minimum. The point, however, is that this was not an isolated incident, and the causes of it lay much deeper than simple miscalculation under stress of combat, Clausewitz's 'friction'.

The provision of tactical air support to the Army by the United States Air Force was hotly debated during the Second World War, before, indeed, the USAF had even gained an identity as a separate service, and was closely linked to this fact. During Operation COBRA in Normandy in July 1944, 8th Army Air Force had bombed their own positions causing several hundred casualties and intense ill-feeling on the part of the ground troops. They did it again in early August during Operation TOTALISE, this time inflicting casualties on their British and Canadian allies, while British aircraft of Bomber Command repeated the effort in mid-August during Operation TRACTABLE. There were two fundamental problems. The first was a belief that the proper role of the air force was strategic, not tactical. The second arose because of lack of coordination between the two services when the 'strategic' bombers were ordered into a close support role. This extended even to the Tactical Air Command, whose specific mission was close air support.

A mixture of conflicting personalities – the leitmotif of SHAEF – and inability on the part of the armies and air forces to reach agreement meant that in 1944, in the words of General Omar Bradley, the allies invaded Europe 'almost totally untrained in air-ground cooperation.'[7] In spite of the efforts of some air force officers, such as Major-General Elwood R. Quesada of the American IXth Tactical Air Command, the general level of air-ground support remained uneven and unsatisfactory. It was Quesada who introduced the practice of linking aircraft and ground units by radio, and of designating specially-trained army officers to act as Forward Air Controllers. The Royal Air Force, on the other hand, jealously maintained this function in Air Force hands.

As with other aspects of American military performance, even these innovations had been forgotten by the time the Korean War began, just five years later. In part, the general American belief, developed in the late 1940s, that future conflicts would be marked by massive retaliation and not limited aims is responsible for this. As one commentator has recently noted, '[t]he promise was made to the Army to maintain the close air support mission. Yet the air force was oriented toward the strategic mission with its equipment . . . and its procurement.'[8] The Air Force in Korea spent an immense effort in attempting to seal off the supply routes across the Yalu from China, without success. The doctrine for close air support may have existed, but as Quesada himself has remarked in commenting on air operations in Korea, 'You can have all the doctrine you want, but unless you have the people, commanders, to implement those doctrines, you might as well throw those doctrines away.'[9] Air-ground coordination in Korea did improve later, helped no doubt by the change in the nature of the fighting from highly mobile operations to static warfare. But in the first year of the war there seems little doubt that the tactical air support was wanting. There were several reasons for this, including the fact that the aircraft were often based in Japan and so denied extended time over their targets. A contributing factor, as one senior Army officer later described, was that the USAF insisted on using air force ground controllers to bring planes over the target, and these officers at times were deficient in their knowledge and experience of ground combat. The army had competent ground controllers of their own, but the air force would not permit their use in controlling air force planes.[10]

Two further points are worth noting. The Marine Air Wing, brought in to provide support to the 1st Marine Division, generally did not suffer from these shortcomings. This was because Marines on the ground controlled Marines in the air, and because aircraft type and mission were devoted entirely to the ground support role. The Marines were not involved in jet fighter-interception or strategic bombing. That these problems of air-ground coordination were not merely the product of the panicky early days of the war is illustrated by the American Air Force's napalming of Australian positions at Kapyong in late April 1951, i.e. almost a year after the war had begun. In terms of casualties, this incident was much less serious than the bombing of the Argylls in September the previous year. Both incidents, and others like them, were the product of doctrinal confusion and failure to apply hard-learnt lessons from the Second World War. These may be failings common to many armed forces, but they are rather more than simply 'the misfortunes of war'. It is also worth noting that army dissatisfaction with the level and quality of ground support provided by the air force led directly to the establishment of large-scale, helicopter-based army aviation, the airmobility concept, that was to dominate army thinking in the 1960s and beyond.[11]

Returning to the 27th Brigade, Coad complained vehemently about the lack of fire support, and this went all the way up to the Army commander, Walker. It was the latter, and not the divisional commander, Major-General John Church, who eventually provided an anti-aircraft artillery battalion to support the brigade. To be fair, Church had nothing to give, but the brigade was to find itself in this situation for the rest of 1950, never sure of whether, or for how long, it could rely on fire support from American sources. This most unsatisfactory state of affairs was resolved only when 16th Field Regiment, Royal New Zealand Artillery, was attached to the brigade in January 1951. It also emphasises the risks that the British took in sending Coad's force in the shape and manner they did. As Coad was always aware, his understrength command could easily take enough casualties to render it operationally ineffective.

Strictly speaking, this possibility remained even after the Australian battalion joined the brigade at the end of September, although the addition of this up-to-strength unit provided much needed weight and balance, as the brigade war diary was quick to note. '[It] has not been a sound tactical force and has had to make the best with what it had. This has caused many problems and worries in certain situations. . . . Now, with a third battalion, the tasks allotted to the Brigade will be met and carried out with every confidence.'[12]

Pressed between the forces breaking out along the line of the Naktong and the American and ROK forces making south from Seoul to link-up with them, the KPA began to withdraw and then to collapse. UN forces linked-up near Suwon, south of Seoul, on 27 September, an operation in which the 27th Brigade played no part. As the war moved from the breakthrough to the pursuit, however, the Commonwealth brigade became actively involved. The KPA had failed to deliver a knock-out blow to the ROK forces, had failed to push the defenders of Pusan into the sea, and their diplomatic allies in the United Nations had been unable to prevent

Soldiers of the Royal Australian Regiment slogging up a hillside, 1951

the UN sanctioning of US actions and hence of a UN forces build-up in Korea. They were now to reap the consequences of their inadequacies.

The decision had been made to take the war to the enemy and cross the 38th parallel, and on 6 October the brigade was air-lifted to Kimpo airfield outside Seoul. As Robertson told his superiors in Melbourne, the intention was to use troops from as many United Nations forces as possible and 27th Brigade, now operating under the US 1st Cavalry Division, was to push into North Korea along the road from Seoul by way of Kaesong, Yumchon, Sariwon and on to the capital, Pyongyang.[13]

The key to operations at this time was mobility, and in this the 27th Brigade was at a disadvantage because it never seemed to have enough vehicles, and those it did have were often inadequate. The roads were primitive at best, and the need for four wheel drive vehicles clearly demonstrated. Many of the brigade's vehicles were two wheel drive, and in all but the best conditions required assistance in order to keep moving.[14] The motor-cycles which were standard issue on the British establishment were totally unsuitable in the heavy conditions, and had to be replaced with jeeps, as did the old Universal carriers. The long chase up the Korean peninsula proved hard going on vehicles which were not new in the first place, and many vehicles had to be returned to the rear as 'beyond local repair', thus further reducing the number available.[15]

There simply was never enough to go round, and transport shortages were a constant theme in the battalion and brigade war diaries. Nor could the Americans necessarily be relied upon to make up the shortfall. On 14 October the brigade war diary noted that another move was impending, and that

the problem of sufficient transport for lifting the brigade arises again as all Divisional transport will be required to lift the other regiments in the Division. Consequently plans are being made to make the maximum use of transport of American units in direct support of the Brigade . . . including tanks, gun towing trucks and half tracks and any other vehicle which still has some room for a full load or an even bigger load.[16]

Similar problems were reported in November. Coad noted in his report that US sources could never provide transport sufficient for more than a two battalion lift, while the war diary of the Argylls observed that 'it is appropriate at this stage to record that our transport was in very poor shape. It had already done many miles in Hong Kong and had only had a superficial overhaul before coming to Korea where it had been worked very hard with very little time for maintenance.'[17]

The brigade could not function indefinitely under this sort of stress, and by December 1950 serious concern was expressed, at several levels, over the brigade's continued fitness for action. Coad informed Robertson that the brigade was 'now reduced to daily movement of maximum 30 miles and mobile operations [were] impossible'. Part of the problem, he felt, lay in the 'willingness of all ranks to try and comply fully and promptly with orders received [which] blinds US commander and staff to our approaching mechanical collapse.'[18] Coad was sufficiently worried about his situation to contemplate the use of his directive, giving him the right of appeal to Robertson and his own government against further operational orders. This development horrified his superiors, since the prospect of dissention in the UN ranks so soon after the advent of the Chinese into the war might have had disastrous effects.[19]

By herculean endeavours, Robertson managed to scrape together enough replacement equipment and spares to keep the battalions going. The lack of transport was even more serious now than it had been in October, for as Robertson laconically informed the War Office 'where withdrawals are concerned it is not pleasant to be in a British brigade which has to rely on its feet.'[20] Coad's other serious problem, manpower, was even less amenable to solution. Far East Landforces had nothing to spare, and the strength of 600 men per battalion 'conforms with no known establishment' and made it difficult 'to undertake the tasks given by [its] US commanders.'[21]

Robertson's solution was to propose the temporary amalgamation of the two British battalions into a single unit, 'which would give us a lot of spare transport and enable us to eliminate a lot of cracks.'[22] Although in some ways a logical proposition, it had absolutely no chance of being accepted, since British infantry regiments would not stand for having their identities subsumed by hybrid amalgamation. This attitude is readily justified, for high morale is frequently held in place by such matters as unit identification. At this particular moment in the Korean War, the maintenance of morale among the British units was paramount, for they were among the few reliable troops in Korea.

For most of 1950, the entire British Commonwealth ground effort lay with the 27th Brigade. Following the outstanding success of Operation CHROMITE and the advance across the 38th parallel towards the Yalu it became unclear whether in fact the British 29th Brigade, Canadian 25th Brigade, or New Zealand 16th Field Regiment, all still being prepared in their countries of origin, would be needed at all. There was a widespread feeling that the war would, in fact, be over by Christmas. In order to capitalise upon the political benefits of participation, the Canadians made the decision to send the 2nd Battalion, Princess Patricia's Canadian Light Infantry ahead of the rest of the brigade. It departed on 25 November, by which time the Chinese had come into the war, ensuring that the rest of the brigade would be sent also.

None of the Canadian battalions had completed their training, but the Princess Pats was to be the most advanced of the brigade's three battalions and its commanding officer, Lieutenant-Colonel J.R. Stone, was felt to be the most suitable officer to work in an independent role, subordinate to British and American officers and far from Canada.[23] Like other units of the brigade, the battalion's training had undergone several interruptions and in its commanding officer's opinion it was not ready to go into the line without a further ten weeks battalion training in Korea. This meant that the battalion would not actually take the field until early February 1951, and Stone came under considerable pressure to compress his schedule.[24]

The Americans pointed to the fact that they were throwing in battalions with as much, or even less, training time as the Canadians but Stone, under strict instructions from his government, refused to budge and continued to train at Suwon, south of Seoul. The spectre of the Hong Kong debacle in 1941 once again influenced Canadian decision-making, and Stone and his superiors held firm.[25] This applied as much to the rest of the brigade as it did to the detached battalion. Rockingham recalled that

the largest area of discussion [with the Minister for Defence and the CGS] was in how short a time the Force could be trained. Many yardsticks were tried by the staff in an attempt to prevent any repetition of the Hong Kong incident but none of them were completely satisfactory and [I] was finally told that when [I] was ready to go to Korea, [I] was to say so.[26]

As a result, the Canadian brigade did not reach Korea until May 1951.

Similar doubts had been expressed about whether the 29th British Infantry Brigade Group would arrive in time to see much action, but in this case the urgent British desire to replace and withdraw the 27th Brigade ensured that the 29th Brigade would at least be sent. It arrived in Korea in mid-November, just in time to be thrown into the headlong retreat of the UN forces before the onslaught of the Chinese Peoples Volunteers. In contrast to the 27th Brigade, this brigade was large and well-equipped, with its own artillery, armour and field engineers. In Bouchier's words, these were 'the hardest and most dependable troops in Korea' at that time, not least because of the large proportion of reservists in the ranks.[27]

The failure of American intelligence surrounding the Chinese entry into the war, and MacArthur's entirely unfounded belief that any such entry would be quickly and easily dealt with, led to one of the great disasters of American arms, in many ways far more serious than the earlier reversals suffered at the hands of the KPA.[28] The loss of confidence among American soldiers was severe and widespread, and for a time threatened to undermine the entire UN military effort in Korea. It was certainly an experience which severely undermined allied confidence in the American's capabilities.

The members of 27th Brigade had been wary of American Army units even during the advance to the Yalu, but once the retreat began the situation deteriorated rapidly.[29] The brigade found itself acting as rearguard for American and ROK divisions, a situation in which the 29th Brigade too was frequently placed. US Army units were becoming increasingly nervous and disinclined to stand their ground, and Coad noted angrily that impossible demands were being placed upon his brigade as American staff work broke down and defeatism began to set in at higher headquarters. His report for the period from November 1950 to early January 1951 makes extremely depressing reading.

A few examples will suffice to make the point, and may be considered representative of the experiences of both brigades. On 1 November he was summoned to divisional headquarters to be told melodramatically, 'Coad, the Chinese are in, World War III has started'. The headquarters was in uproar, and 'I had as usual the greatest difficulty to discover what the situation was'. On 25 November, a warning order was received that we might be required in IX Corps area, they refused however to give us any notice – another example of inept staff work. This day and the succeeding ones were extremely difficult for the Brigade staff as a succession of pretty impossible tasks were handed out by Corps HQ, which required a good deal of diplomatic arguing to avoid the brigade being hopelessly committed.[30]

The low point was undoubtedly reached on 30 November. The US 2nd Infantry Division was attempting to break southwards through Chinese encirclement, and the brigade was acting in support of this effort by keeping the escape routes open. About mid-day

a continuous stream of 2 Div and ROK forces came through . . . very many were wounded, and some [were] in an hysterical condition; their withdrawal did not appear to be an organised military action and strongly resembled a rout.[31]

Despite being informed that they were in friendly territory, the American troops continued to fire randomly as they passed, wounding and killing a number of the Middlesex. As the brigade war diary reported, 'all vestige of control and leadership . . . appeared to have been lost.'[32]

Reports of these incidents quickly filtered back to Tokyo, and from there to the various Commonwealth governments. All these reports considered that the major factor in the rout of the UN forces was 'the low calibre of United States Army troops (as opposed to Marines) engaged in Korea'. An Australian observer thought that the 'US Marines, the British Brigades and the Turks has shown up the morale and the fighting ability of the US Army troops engaged in an unfavourable light.'[33] British officials also identified the Marines, Turks and British Brigades as the only 'brilliant exceptions' to a situation in which 'the fighting value of the United Nations forces has been reduced . . . to the point where it is questionable whether the force is capable of effective resistance to continued offensive action by a determined enemy.'[34]

The situation remained serious throughout January 1951, with the 27th and 29th Brigades acting as rear-guards for retreating American divisions, and taking casualties in heavy fighting as the Chinese strove, with varying degrees of success, to maintain the momentum of their offensive.[35] Both the Turks and British began increasingly to protest American decisions to withdraw in the face of insufficient enemy activity, or after actions in which the local advantage had passed to them. It was reported that the Turks, French, Dutch and Greek contingents had requested to be placed under British, rather than American, command.[36] Even Coad was beginning to make his feelings obvious. After being called upon to perform two rear-guards in three days, he recorded an exchange he had with two American commanders.

The 24th Divisional Commander naively told me that he liked the British troops to do this, as they were a steadying influence on the American soldiers. A nice compliment, but a repetition of anything becomes tiring. Another American commander who passed through us told me his troops would not liked to have been left behind in Seoul as we were and seemed quite surprised when told we did not particularly relish it either.[37]

This situation could not last much longer, and in fact even as things appeared desperate in January 1951 the recovery had already begun. Two factors accounted principally for this. Firstly, the example of the other UN forces 'is said to have been an eye-opener for other [US] troops in Korea', with the French and Dutch battalions singled out as having 'put on an amazingly good show which has been in marked contrast to the performance of the American troops.'[38] In Bouchier's words,

The Americans have learned the Chinese are easy to kill if only they will stand fast and that the more they sit tight in their trenches and fox holes when under Chinese attack the greater number of Chinese can be killed with greater safety to themselves.[39]

This new confidence was allied to the fact that manpower replacements were now flowing freely, with the badly mauled 1st Marine Division being brought up to a strength of 21,000 by the middle of January.

Crucial to the turnaround in UN fortunes, however, was the arrival of the new commanding general of the Eighth Army, Matthew B. Ridgway. Ridgway made a number of command changes at lower levels, bringing out fresh commanders for weary American formations. He toured the front areas constantly, and in a short time 'very largely restored the shattered morale of the American Army' by two principal means. The first was to re-inculcate aggression among the American troops through means such as Operation KILLER at the beginning of March. The sole purpose of the Operation was to kill Chinese and although, as one British officer noted, it was scarcely a lasting objective, it was important in helping to rebuild the Americans' confidence.[40]

The other change he introduced was tactical. Under Walker the Americans had tended to use combat teams or task forces on the principle of isolated troop penetrations, mostly along the roads and with little consideration given to consolidation of ground already gained or of linking up along a wide front. Failure to secure their flanks on the high ground resulted invariably in their being outflanked by the Chinese, who did not share the American aversion to climbing the steep Korean hillsides. The end result was a process of 'barrelling in and bugging out'. The British and Turks had generally consolidated as they worked forward, making smaller gains but over a wider front. It was this form of operation that Ridgway now adopted, gradually but decisively pushing the enemy northwards until, by April, the front again stood north of Seoul in the vicinity of the 38th parallel.[41]

As the situation stabilised the British brigades, so long used in local crises to protect withdrawals or extricate surrounded units, found themselves placed increasingly in reserve. As Bouchier noted, this was welcome, especially among the men of the 27th Brigade, the original members of which 'have had a hard war with no respite and need a rest.'[42] The British brigades had indeed had a hard few months, and plans were already well in hand to withdraw the Argylls and the Middlesex, together with the 27th Brigade headquarters, and replace them with two fresh British battalions and a new headquarters, redesignating the brigade the 28th Commonwealth Brigade. Before the relief could be accomplished, however, and before either force had enjoyed much rest, they were called forward once again into the fire-brigade role to help stem the Chinese Fifth Phase Offensive in late April 1951.

The epic stands of the 27th Brigade at Kapyong and the 29th Brigade on the Imjin have been told numerous times, and need not be recounted here.[43] Rather, these two brigade actions demonstrate both the continuing reliance of Eighth Army upon these two formations, and illustrate further the difference in approach to military problems between the Americans and the Commonwealth.

The 27th Brigade was brought forward from reserve when the 6th ROK Division gave way before the Chinese during 23 April 1951. As the Brigade war diary put it, 'it looked as though another retrograde movement had started as many ROK soldiers were pouring through the gun areas of 16 Fd Regt.'[44] Kapyong is only about sixty miles from Seoul, and the valley of the Kapyong river, a tributary of the Han, provides a natural avenue of approach to the capital. The same is true of the Imjin position occupied by the 29th Brigade. In addition, the Chinese attack there was aimed at the hinge between the brigade and the 1st ROK division, covering the important road junction at Uijongbu, which in turn controlled all the roads in the US I Corps area. They were both important strategic positions, the capture of which would greatly facilitate the Chinese offensive.

In a hard-fought action over the next two days, the 27th Brigade broke the impetus of the Chinese attack along that sector of the front. The main brunt of the assault fell upon 3 RAR and 2 PPCLI, the former suffering thirty-two dead and fifty-nine wounded, the latter ten dead and twenty-three wounded. Between them, and with the aid of the New Zealand gunners and an American tank company, they fought an entire enemy division to a standstill. On the Imjin, the 29th Brigade faced two Chinese divisions, in the 63rd CCF Corps, but here the whole brigade was committed to action, together with the Belgian battalion which had been attached for operational purposes. By stupendous effort, in what has been described as 'the greatest and bloodiest fight of the entire Korean War',[45] the Chinese were stopped there also. But the cost was very much greater than at Kapyong. The brigade suffered over a thousand casualties, with the Gloucesters virtually wiped out, all but five officers and forty-one other ranks being either killed or captured. The commanding officer of the Royal Northumberland Fusiliers was also killed, and the Belgian battalion took about fifty casualties, including its commanding officer. The brigade had lost quite a lot of equipment – including several of the new Centurion tanks – and had been reduced in effective strength by almost twenty-five per cent. The price would appear to have been high.

Ridgway, by now Supreme Commander, did not come under any pressure, from either the British or his own government, to explain the loss of a complete allied battalion.[46] He was clearly concerned, however, to establish the reasons, and pressed the new Eighth Army commander, General James Van Fleet, for an answer. Given the disparity between Commonwealth losses in the two engagements, the question seems worth asking.

The two actions were of similar duration. Although the 29th

Digging a defensive position on the Jamestown Line, 1951

Brigade on the Imjin faced twice the enemy strength that the 27th Brigade met at Kapyong, the former also fielded at least double the strength of the latter. The problem would seem to have revolved less around the size of forces or intensity of combat than around the command decisions made when the forces met the enemy.

In the British edition of his book, *The Korean War*, Ridgway commented that in talks with unspecified senior British officers after the Imjin battle it was pointed out to him that the commanding officer of the Gloucesters, Lieutenant-Colonel J.P. Carne, was noted for 'his exceptional coolness under pressure and his dislike for asking for help until every resource at his disposal had been exhausted.' Ridgway says that he made a point of taking this up with the commanding general of the US I Corps, General O'Daniel, telling him that

it seemed to me that there was a lesson here for all of us. With Carne's well-known characteristics of understating his own problems and not seeking help except as a last resort, it should have been clear to higher commanders that his situation was much worse than his early reports indicated, and that earlier major efforts to break through to him should have been made.[47]

This essentially was Van Fleet's view. In a signal to Ridgway he noted that

it appears that the Gloucester battalion commander did not indicate the seriousness of his position and the need for either additional help or withdrawal. Fortunately it was his decision to hold. I say fortunately because had he not held and inflicted terrific casualties on the [enemy] I believe it would have been a proper decision for higher commanders to order him to hold.

The threat to the withdrawal of troops further north, and to the bulk of the British and the Corps artillery, necessitated that stand. In Van Fleet's view, 'this battalion was not lost in vain . . . this is one of those great occasions in combat which call for a determined stand, and . . . the loss of 622 officers and men saved many times that number.'[48] It was, in other words, a critical situation. The commander therefore very properly utilized the best and most reliable troops he had in meeting the crisis. The American opinion of the British forces in Korea was very high, and had been for some time. They were well-regarded because of their battle-readiness, battle-efficiency, reliability, self-sufficiency, and for the excellent and highly professional use they made of the American supporting arms allotted to them. This was often contrasted with the behaviour of some of the other UN contingents, such as the Filipinos, who were generally regarded as a military liability.[49]

This reputation had been considerably enhanced during the early months of Chinese intervention in the war, when many American units had performed badly. This would appear to be the key to explaining the loss of the Gloucesters. A habit in the American command of relying on the British brigades in a sticky situation, combined with the temperament of the particular battalion commander *and* the fact that the British units had come to believe that they could invariably achieve what their American allies could not, led to the situation where the battalion was cut-off and hopelessly surrounded before it was prepared to acknowledge the seriousness of its situation. One American officer present noted that 'the individual brigades were too proud to call for help at the time of the enemy attack in April 1951. They suffered significant casualties before they would acknowledge that they were even in trouble.'[50]

It is significant that at Kapyong, when 'it became clear that 3 RAR would not be able to hold their position for another night', they were told to withdraw.[51] The brigade commander, by now Brigadier B.A. Burke, was not interested in sacrificing a full battalion simply to hold ground of no intrinsic value in itself, and pulled them out in time.[52] But then Burke was largely allowed to fight his own battle, while Brodie of the 29th Brigade had the corps and divisional commanders involved on the Imjin. As a British officer, Burke was also aware that he was responsible to the Australian government for the safety of its battalion, and that searching questions would be asked if the only Australian ground force in Korea was wiped out. This combination of factors undoubtedly gave him the flexibility in command which eluded Brodie.

The Kapyong-Imjin battles were the last great fight for the brigades before they were grouped to form the Commonwealth division in July that year. In late May the 25th Canadian Infantry Brigade at last arrived at the front, and 2 PPCLI was transferred to it from the 28th Brigade, which once again reverted to a three-battalion establishment. This is not to suggest that the fighting did not continue, or that the brigades took no part, for there were occasional fierce engagements in which the brigades were involved. But with the comprehensive defeat of his Fifth Phase Offensive, the enemy was once more back behind his start-line. After its losses on the Imjin, the 29th Brigade spent a month on the Kimpo peninsula for refitting and reorganisation before again being committed to action.

Writing late in the Korean War, the military historical section of Far East Command wrote of the British brigades that 'there was no problem . . . fitting these units into the fighting team. They took over their jobs like professionals.'[53] The high regard felt by the Americans for the sheer professionalism of these brigades is the most constant theme in all their observations. It cannot be said that the same high opinion was always reciprocated. The early disarray within the United States Army had come as a surprise to the soldiers of the Commonwealth, and in the manner of these things the reasons for this disorder were not always viewed sympathetically. As Barclay noted, the Commonwealth brigades felt that 'with their wealth of military experience in World War II, and equipped with modern weapons, [they] should have been able to stand their ground in face of the Chinese enemy, however great their numbers.'[54]

Ridgway himself has written of the poor state of morale in Eighth Army at the time he took over command. He found it 'a bewildered army, not sure of itself or its leaders, not sure what they were doing here . . . There was obviously much to be done to restore this army to a fighting mood.' He contrasted them unfavourably with the British soldiers he met on his first tours of inspection. And the Chief of Staff of the Army in Washington, General J. Lawton Collins, has also noted that the Eighth Army was 'a dispirited command . . . [lacking] in . . . the drive and elan . . . associated with American troops.' This was one occasion on which the low opinion held by their allies was to an extent matched by the views of the American commanders themselves.[55]

The differences in performance cannot be explained solely by claiming greater experience or length of service for the Commonwealth soldiers. Few of the junior officers had previous combat experience, and the battalions contained a proportion of young soldiers without service in the Second World War. It seems rather that they evinced a more professional attitude to the task in hand. It may also be that the American army still suffered from the policy in the Second World War which saw the better-educated, higher quality recruits combed out into the technical services, with the lowest calibre of recruit being given the most demanding of military specialisations, rifleman in an infantry company. The Marines did not suffer from this problem since they had only four specialisations, all of them combat ones, and the Marines were often judged to be better in Korea than was the Army. Commonwealth commanders were full of praise for certain American units, such as the field engineers or the tanks, and the tank company attached to the 27th Brigade at Kapyong was held in great esteem by the infantrymen there for the risks it took in supporting their positions and evacuating their wounded. The performance of the US Army in Korea was not always bad, but it was certainly inconsistent. It is one of the strengths of the organisation that, with a commander of genius, Ridgway, and the additonal time granted them by the efforts of the best of the UN contingents, they not only rectified the situation, but succeeded in turning it around completely. The strain on inter-allied relations occasioned by poor American combat performance had been serious. With the reversal of the trend, it also proved temporary. Poor initial American efforts at Kasserine and in New Guinea during the Second World War had produced negative, and often scathing, assessments from their British and Australian allies. On both occasions a change of command, with all that implies, soon reversed the situation. The most important distinction to be drawn between these occurrences and US Army performance in Korea in the first year of that war is that only in the latter case did American failure carry with it a strategic liability, and the real possibility of actually losing the war.

Chapter six
The formation of 1 Commonwealth Division, 1950–51

The formation of the Commonwealth Division in July 1951 brought into sharp focus a range of problems in the Commonwealth defence relationship that had already received some attention in the aftermath of the Second World War. Although it numbered among its antecedents the New Zealand and Australian Division (NZ and A) in the Great War and the British and Indian Division (BRINDIV) in the occupation of Japan, the Commonwealth Division went much further than either, both because of the greater number and diversity of national forces involved and because the division was itself part of a different national higher formation. In both the discussions preceding the decision to form the division and in its operations once formed, Britain and the Dominions revealed not only a concern with current issues but a preoccupation with past experiences. If the Canadians displayed both these facets more noticeably than the others, all parties were influenced to some extent by them. In particular, the positions on renewed defence cooperation adopted by the various governments at the post-war Prime Ministers' Conferences were clearly in evidence during the time it took to agree on the final form of the Commonwealth commitment to Korea.

It will be recalled that the Americans had requested that forces contributed to the UNC should be of a minimum strength of a reinforced battalion with organic artillery. They had made no secret of the fact, however, that the minimum useful contribution was a brigade or brigade group, which corresponded to the American Regimental Combat Team, and which was capable of tactical employment as a relatively self-contained formation. When the majority of UN member nations took the United States at its word and contributed individual battalions, the Americans modified their ideas and embarked upon the successful system of unit attachment between a UN battalion and a US parent unit. From Britain and the Commonwealth, however, they expected rather more.

The discussions and arguments over the need to commit forces to the UN police action in Korea and the size of any such force actually sent were examined in chapter 3. What also needs to be understood is that from the beginning, and simultaneously with the other discussions about force size, the various Commonwealth governments were considering the question of associating their forces and, specifically, of doing so by forming a Commonwealth division. Whereas the discussions concerning the initial commitment of forces revolved around manpower problems and the assumptions about the role of the Commonwealth in a general war, the debate concerning the division raised stark questions about the future of dominion cooperation. The two matters have therefore been treated separately here, for they raised different issues.

Before agreement had been reached as to the type of forces to be contributed, the possibility of combining forces was being canvassed. Like Australia, New Zealand's primary theatre of operations in any general or world war was expected to be the Middle East, and this consideration constrained New Zealand thinking on the type of force to be sent. The limits of her resources and the primacy of another theatre would affect her commitment and create a problem in maintaining a balance with the troops of other countries. The New Zealand government suggested that '[o]ne solution would be a composite British force of troops from the United Kingdom, Australia, New Zealand and possibly Canada. Although there is no suggestion that this course will be agreed to it will probably be considered.'[1] The New Zealanders were not the only ones considering it. Two weeks later the Australian Prime Minister, R.G. Menzies, who was visiting Britain and the United States, cabled his colleague and Treasurer, Arthur Fadden, concerning his discussions with the American Secretary of Defense, Louis A. Johnson. Having expressed the wish that Australia and New Zealand between them would provide a brigade of three battalions for service in Korea, Johnson suggested that 'the United Kingdom, Australian and New Zealand contingents might ultimately form a British Commonwealth light division.'[2]

The Australian Defence Committee, with the head of the New Zealand Joint Services Liaison Staff, Colonel D.T. Maxwell, present, considered the matter on 1 August 1950. Having noted the American suggestion that an ANZAC brigade be formed, the committee went on to note and agree to the further suggestion that the contingents should form a British Commonwealth force.[3] This advice was cabled to Menzies who, on the very same day during his address to the United States Congress, stated that he

> would like to see these [Australian] troops and others made available by the United Kingdom and other British Commonwealth countries brought together sooner or later and I would hope sooner into a British Commonwealth Division [for] service alongside your own men.

The text of this speech was cabled to the New Zealand government in fulfilment of the Australian undertaking to keep them fully informed of Australian thinking on the matter.[4]

New Zealand was in some difficulty over its contribution, not only because of the prior commitment to the Middle East but because, as was also the case in Australia, a compulsory military training scheme had been recently introduced. The New Zealand government therefore was quite clear on the need to group its force with those of another Commonwealth country; it was less clear with which country it should be. The American suggestion of an ANZAC brigade had not yet been abandoned, but there was also a suggestion that the New Zealand contingent might join a British brigade. The Australian High Commissioner in Wellington, Roden Cutler, met with the New Zealand Prime Minister, S.G. Holland, and the Chief of the General Staff, Major-General K.L. Stewart, on 2 August. He reported to his government that New Zealand would not approach Australia on the question of an ANZAC brigade until the British had indicated whether a joint British-New Zealand brigade was both possible and desired. Furthermore, Cutler pointed out to Holland and Stewart that, since New Zealand did not intend to provide a self-contained force, their only real alternatives either were to 'join a total British Commonwealth force', presumably a reference to the divisional idea, or to 'join with Australia in an ANZAC brigade, as against a UK brigade.' Stewart agreed, since it seemed likely that the UK brigade would be unable to absorb the offered field artillery regiment in a militarily logical manner.[5] In order to come to early agreement, it was resolved that Stewart should visit Melbourne to confer with his Australian opposite number, Lieutenant-General S.F. Rowell.[6]

Discussions at an army-to-army level between the two Chiefs of Staff and the Chief Liaison Officer, United Kingdom Services Liaison Staff, Major-General A.J.H. Cassels, were held on 8 August. Cassels had been fully briefed by the War Office and was empowered to make policy decisions in his capacity as British representative to the Australian Higher Defence Machinery, the successor to the Joint Chiefs of Staff in Australia (JCOSA).[7] The decisions which came out of this meeting were important, and were to influence the character of the Commonwealth involvement for the rest of the war by laying the ground rules for that involvement.

The meeting began by noting the force commitments for Korea already entered into. The UK had promised a brigade group and an armoured regiment, Australia had offered one infantry battalion and the New Zealanders a field artillery regiment and a small force headquarters component. It was resolved that these forces should be combined into an expanded brigade group under British command but that, if Australia should resolve to increase her infantry contribution to a brigade, then the resulting two brigades would be grouped under one divisional headquarters. This would require an additional commitment of personnel. The meeting also resolved that a base organisation would be provided by the BCOF facilities in Japan and that the non-operational control and administration of the force would be vested in the C-in-C, BCOF. It was also noted that, should other Commonwealth countries choose to join the Commonwealth force, further consideration would need to be given to questions of command and control.[8]

The question of the formation of an ANZAC brigade was not raised. In his thesis dealing with New Zealand government policy towards Korea, Robert Eaddy states that Rowell raised the matter but was rebuffed.[9] There is no mention of this in the minutes of the meeting. Additionally Brigadier Sir Frederick Chilton, a senior Australian defence official at the time, does not recall any serious consideration, at the Defence Committee level, of an ANZAC contribution to the UNC.[10] In any case, events overtook them with the urgent dispatch of the 27th British Infantry Brigade from Hong Kong to Korea later that same month in response to the worsening tactical situation. When the 29th British Infantry Brigade Group arrived in Korea in November, the conditions existed for grouping these brigades under one divisional headquarters, as had been agreed at the August meeting. It was to be some time, however, before the decision was acted upon.

After considerable public debate and not a little pressure from the press, the Canadian government decided on 7 August to recruit the Canadian Army Special Force (CASF) for service in Korea. At the same time the Canadians requested details of force size and command and control arrangements from the other Commonwealth countries which had offered troops. At that stage they were informed by the Australian government merely that discussions were continuing at the official level, and that the question of control would be determined later after consultation with the UNC and 'in accordance with the principles relating to BCOF in Japan.'[11] On 28 August the Canadians communicated their views to the rest of the Commonwealth in the form of an aide memoire to the British government, copies of which were circulated to the other Dominions by the British. This document confirmed just how far Canada had drifted from the Commonwealth connection.

The Canadians began by noting that the idea of forming a Commonwealth division had received attention in the press and had been advocated 'in a number of quarters'. The Canadian government was opposed to this course of action because it wished to stress the UN character of the operations to the maximum extent possible. They were in favour of troops from the Commonwealth serving 'in the same divisional formations' for reasons of efficiency, and indeed hoped that any other UN contingents that were similarly equipped and trained would also serve in this division.

Canadians will be happy to serve alongside their comrades from the United Kingdom and other Commonwealth nations as they have been accustomed to do in the past, and the Canadian Government have [sic] decided that they should do so. But it is felt that this can only be accomplished without sacrificing the political advantage to which the United Kingdom and United States Governments as well as the Canadian Government attach great importance, namely, that to be derived from maximum emphasis on the United Nations character of resistance to aggression in Korea.

The Canadians concluded with an appeal to the effect that, although the term 'Commonwealth Division' would doubtless achieve popular usage, every effort should be made to prevent official usage of the term by participants.[12]

The Canadians themselves did not send a copy of this document to either the Australian or New Zealand governments nor sought their views, despite the fact that their troops would have to be brigaded with the Canadians in any arrangement such as the

Canadians proposed. Other than the Belgian battalion, no other UN unit was patterned or armed along British lines, thus making the formation of a truly representative United Nations division from other, non-Commonwealth, nations even less likely. The government of Canadian Prime Minister Louis St Laurent came under attack from the opposition for a similar expression of views in the Canadian Parliament, being accused of 'trying to ease Canada out of the British Commonwealth by the back door', and the Canadian government indeed was concerned that its attitude was open to misunderstanding.[13] The government was in favour of grouping Commonwealth forces, but opposed to identifying them as Commonwealth. It is hard to see how the one could be attained while the other was avoided. The basic rock upon which the Canadian proposal was to founder was the attitude of the British, who were in favour of the formaiton 'of a balanced and identifiable Commonwealth force.'[14]

The British attitude was made even more explicit in a telegram of 16 September addressed to the British High Commissioners in Canberra, Wellington, Ottawa, Pretoria, Karachi and Delhi, and destined for presentation to the various prime ministers. It confirmed British thinking on the desirability of linking Australian and New Zealand forces with the British brigade, and accepted several of the propositions put up by the Australians with regard to the role of BCOF as a base organisation for the force and the vesting of non-operational control and general administration in the Australian Higher Defence Machinery. Matters of command and control, however, might require reconsideration in the event that any other Commonwealth country decided to link its forces with theirs. The Secretary of State for Commonwealth Relations thought that attention should be paid to the

position of Canada who have told us that they are considering [the] possibility of grouping their Special Force for Korea with [ours]. Until we have reached agreement with [the] Canadian Government upon various points that arise including incidentally [the] important question of nomenclature I think we should regard these arrangements as provisional, ie as subject to confirmation with [the] Canadian Government in due course. This need not prevent study going forward on [an] official level . . . indeed it is essential to press forward on this without delay.[15]

In other words, while details might alter, the general plan to field a specifically Commonwealth force was non-negotiable.

This was made even clearer in a long and considered reply by the

Commonwealth Relations Office to the Canadian aide memoire of 8 August. This United Kingdom response began by noting that agreement in principle had been reached between the British, Australian and New Zealand governments over the grouping together of forces, although the tactical situation in Korea had considerably improved since the Inchon landing in mid-September. The need might still arise for the forces of these nations to be grouped with the force provided by Canada during any continuation of operations. Various problems arose from this supposition, and these would need to be addressed by the parties concerned. The British noted that provisional agreement had been given to the Australian and New Zealand proposals for non-operational control, and that the Indian government had been asked to indicate whether it wished to group its 60th (Parachute) Field Ambulance with the proposed Commonwealth force.

The argument in favour of grouping forces 'for reasons of efficiency and convenience' was endorsed, and the British added that they greatly appreciated 'the statement in the Canadian Government's aide memoire that Canadians will be happy to serve alongside their comrades from the United Kingdom.' The Canadians were also asked to comment upon the acceptability of the provisional arrangement for non-operational control. After these conciliatory and negotiatory passages, the British communication got down to refuting the central positions declared earlier by the Canadian government, namely those concerning nomenclature and the inclusion of 'foreign' troops.

British objections to the use of the title 'United Nations Division' were on two levels. Firstly, it was illogical to call one division taking part in the Korean operation a United Nations division when the others were not so designated. This was not to be taken to mean that the United Kingdom did not attach as much importance as did Canada to the UN aspects of the operations. The second objection was more practical.

It does not seem possible to the United Kingdom authorities to omit the word 'Commonwealth' from the title of a division which would be mainly, or as we would prefer, wholly composed of troops from the Commonwealth. A division so composed would inevitably be called a Commonwealth Division by its own members and by the public and it would be in the view of the United Kingdom Government fruitless to attempt to enforce a title omitting this word.

The British could equally see considerable practical difficulties stemming from the inclusion of 'foreign' troops in such a division, difficulties of language, procedure, training and so on. Accordingly, the British would 'prefer NOT to add foreign troops.'[16]

The official historian of Canada's involvement in the Korean War, Colonel Herbert Fairlie Wood, had noted that Canada

did not wish to fight in Korea with allies in the traditional sense; it wanted to do so as part of an international police force under United Nations command. But ... the antagonism of the Soviet Union and Chinese Communist participation in the war weakened the United Nations international aspect and gave the operations in Korea the appearance of 'a coalition war of the traditional kind.'[17]

It was not, of course, as straightforward as that. Canadian governments in the 1930s had been keen to proclaim their independence of Whitehall while at the same time locking themselves into commitments to support British forces in the event of war. Once the war had been won, however, as English and Hillmer have noted, 'it was downhill most of the way for the British alliance ... North American geography was bound to assert itself with more and more of a vengeance.'[18]

The Commonwealth experience of British operational command in the twentieth century was mixed. Australian soldiers on the Western Front had been highly critical of British senior officers, especially after the Somme. They regarded General Sir Hubert Gough, in particular, as a butcher and many loudly claimed that they would not serve under him again. The commander of the New Zealand division, Lieutenant General Sir Alexander Godley, was detested by men of the New Zealand Expeditionary Force for his supposed indifference to their sufferings. The Canadians fared somewhat better in the Great War, having the good fortune to be commanded for a time by Field Marshal Lord Byng who ensured that his successor would be a Canadian and who worked hard to 'nationalise' the Canadian Corps at all levels. In the Second World War the New Zealanders were comanded by General Lord Freyberg, revered by his soldiers for his solicitous attitude to their welfare, although his tactical dispositions were not always sound. For the Australians, the successes of Operation COMPASS in the Western Desert, under the command of the highly-regarded Lieutenant General O'Connor, did not make up for later frustrations under Wavell and Auchinleck. The fiasco in Greece and Crete, where a predominantly dominion force was placed under the command of the portly General Sir Henry 'Jumbo' Maitland Wilson left a correspondingly sour taste in the mouths of many Australian soldiers.

Canadian experience in the Second World War was not always a happy one, either. The controversy over Dieppe is well known. The legacy of the fall of Hong Kong also left a lasting and bitter memory. The attempt by some British officers to shuffle the blame for Hong Kong's early surrender onto the Canadian battalions involved in its defence was widely resented. So deeply did feelings run that the professional heads of the Canadian and British armies agreed to sanitise their official histories of the campaign in the interests of preserving inter-allied amity.[19] Lieutenant General F.J. Fleury, head of the Canadian Military Mission, Far East, in 1950–51 is in no doubt that 'our Hong Kong experience weighed heavily with the Canadians, both in Ottawa and the Far East.'[20] Additionally, Canada had for some time been undergoing an economic reorientation away from Britain and towards the United States. It is therefore not surprising that the plan for a British Commonwealth division should have been received without enthusiasm by Canada at this time, just as Mackenzie King had rejected centralised defence cooperation in 1944 and 1946. The suggestion that the Commonwealth forces be grouped with other UN units was impractical, however, and a complete negation of the 'efficiency and convenience' which was the impetus for the grouping of forces in the first place.

There was to be little or no problem with the Indian government on this question. When the Indian government had decided to contribute a specialised field ambulance and surgical unit, they approached the British government informally concerning its deployment. Although of the view that any decision was ultimately the prerogative of the UNC, the Indians saw advantage in attaching their unit to the Commonwealth force and asked the British to seek Australia's agreement, which was quickly forthcoming.[21]

The Indian Field Ambulance was one of the outstanding successes of the Commonwealth involvement, earning an extraordinarily high reputation among all the other Commonwealth forces. Initially, however, their arrival was viewed as something of a mixed blessing. The British Army's Director of Medical Services,

Lieutenant-General Sir Neil Cantlie, wrote to Robertson in such a vein in early November. After noting that the Indian unit was already on its way, Cantlie raised the problem of rationing, since he presumed 'that they are all Hindu personnel', and foreshadowed problems in dealing with the rank and file, although 'some of our officers will be found, no doubt, who can speak Urdu'. He also had some advice on their operational deployment.

I have served a good deal in India and I know how well the Indians react if they get a pat on the back and are told what good fellows they are. But if they are not employed in what they would regard as a satisfactory role they might be inclined to be offended . . . Perhaps they could be employed to cover Base troops in some convenient port or area. I am sure that would satisfy their ambitions.[22]

Perhaps because he too was a 'colonial', Robertson did not follow this patronising advice, but was soon able to advise Cantlie that the Indians had arrived and were being supplied by the Americans with full winter kit, and were being 'accepted . . . as part of the Commonwealth forces in every way.' Dealing with the needs of Indian soldiers was not new ground for Robertson. As he pointed out, he had had 12,000 of them under his command in 1946–47 in Japan. As a forerunner of the live export trade, BCOF had even imported live sheep from Australia to meet their rationing needs.[23] There were to be no problems experienced with the Indian unit for the duration of the war. Because the unit was a small, specialised and non-combatant one, the Indian government preferred to deal directly with the Commonwealth commanders in the theatre rather than through the Higher Defence Machinery in Melbourne. To this end they attached a senior liaison office, Lieutenant-Colonel P. Chowdry, to Robertson's headquarters and this officer worked directly between the unit and the C-in-C.[24]

The proposal to join the brigades to form a Commonwealth division was given a considerable fillip by the intervention of the Chinese People's Volunteers in October and November 1950. MacArthur's rosy predictions in September and early October of an imminent end to hostilities crumbled dramatically as UN forces were pushed further and further back from the Yalu. The US X Corps, operating independently of EUSAK in the north-east of the country, was forced to retreat, by way of 'frozen Chosin', to be evacuated by sea from a perimeter around Hungnam. It seemed to be a replay of the desperate days of the Naktong perimeter and, as then, trained soldiers were at a premium.

Most importantly for the formation of a properly balanced division was the War Office decision to leave 27th Brigade at MacArthur's disposal, rather than to withdraw it now that 29th Brigade had arrived in Korea, as had been the original intention. With the worsening situation, the Canadians were expediting the dispatch of their 25th Brigade and, when it arrived, there would thus be three brigades in Korea. On 15 November Robertson raised this possibility in a signal to the Chiefs of Staff in Melbourne and Wellington and the CIGS in London:

General Walker commanding Eighth Army expressed to me the opinion that it would help him greatly ... if we would form a British Commonwealth Division which would take care of all British Commonwealth military units ... I suggest the British Commonwealth might well examine the extent to which it wishes to commit forces and the grouping it desires in the field. The Americans are so used to us managing our own affairs that they cannot understand our present piecemeal organisations and from the top down I get the feeling that they hope we will take over all our own affairs and organise British Commonwealth forces as one body. They already have so many small and odd units from various other United Nations that they are embarrassed in fixing a chain of command in the field but it is obvious that they hope we will not leave any of our problems to them.[25]

The Higher Defence Machinery met on 16 November and agreed that the American suggestion warranted immediate examination, while the next day Robertson was able to report that the Canadians had agreed to the attachment of various advance parties to the Korean Element British Base at Taegu. Robertson further under-lined the desirability of this course of action in a signal to the War Office on 24 November in which he pointed out that MacArthur, Walker and their staffs preferred to deal with one person only on all matters which affected Commonwealth forces.[26]

Just when it might have appeared that the last impediment to the divisional proposal had been overcome, the War Office sought to distance itself from the whole idea. In a signal sent to both the Australian Chiefs of Staff and Robertson in Japan on 27 November, the United Kingdom Chiefs asked that no further action be taken on the proposal to form a Commonwealth division because of the increased comitment of forces such a step implied. The

Defence Committee in Melbourne agreed to comply 'for the present'.

This need for additonal manpower should have been evident to War Office planners from the beginning. Since the Chinese were by now clearly involved in Korea in considerable force it should have been obvious that the previous intention to replace the 27th Brigade with the 29th would be postponed indefinitely, if not cancelled altogether. The problem had been discussed at a meeting of the Army Council on 23 November, at which the VCIGS, General Brownjohn, had restated the desirability of creating as few impediments as possible to the eventual withdrawal of the 27th Brigade and returning it to Hong Kong. This was also made clear to General Cassels in a cable from the Chiefs of Staff on 27th November. The latter stated that they did not wish to further reduce the Hong Kong garrison, by despatching the 40th Division headquarters and supporting units to Korea, or delay the building-up of the 3rd Division in Britain, which was ear-marked for the strategic reserve in accordance with the new NATO commitment. The state of the Hong Kong garrison was in any case their chief concern, and 'if the situation vis-a-vis China deteroriated still further [27th Brigade's] return to Hong Kong might become very urgent.'[27] There was strong irony in the fact that British nervousness over Chinese intentions towards Hong Kong in the aftermath of Chinese intervention in Korea should sharpen the desire to withdraw the 27th Brigade, while the deteriorating military situation as a result of Chinese intervention meant that the brigade could not be withdrawn.

The Defence Committee might concede the point to the British, but in Japan the redoubtable Robertson was prepared to argue. In a cable to the British and Australian Chiefs of Staff he repeated that should the Commonwealth commitment in Korea reach or exceed two brigades then a divisional headquarters should be provided and the division formed. He argued that, should 27th Brigade be withdrawn, the force which would result from joining the Australian, New Zealand, Canadian and Indian contingents to the British 29th Brigade would be 'a complicated force for a Brigadier ... and too big to handle in operations.' Such a force would comprise five infantry battalions, two field artillery regiments, an armoured regiment, two field ambulances and assorted engineering and other support troops. Robertson conceded that he would of course begin planning for such an eventuality, but he was unhappy with this turn of events.[28]

He returned to the attack in his weekly report of 15 December, which was distributed to Wellington, Ottawa, Melbourne, and the Commander-in-Chief, Far East Landforces (C-in-C, FARELF) in Singapore. He noted again that both MacArthur and Walker would be very glad to see a British Commonwealth division formed 'as this would give a self-contained body with its own rear services and ease many problems of Eighth Army'.[29] In the continuing absence of such a formation, Robertson had established an advanced liaison headquarters with General Walker in Korea. The message remained clear. Common sense and the Americans required that sooner or later the decision to group the contingents would have to be made. This report elicited a personal response from the CIGS, who remained 'very much opposed to the formation of a Commonwealth Div[ision]'. He appreciated Robertson's arguments, but stated that British intentions to withdraw the 27th Brigade remained firm.[30]

British insistence on this latter point still centred on Chinese intervention in Korea. The Americans had for some months prior to this been concerned that the recently installed Peking regime might be planning an assault upon Taiwan in an attempt to encompass the final defeat of the Kuomintang. The British, as we have seen, were naturally concerned that the Chinese might have designs upon Hong Kong also. The emergency dispatch of the two battalion brigade to Korea had left a weakened force in the Crown colony, and the British authorities were concerned that this position of weakness should be rectified quickly. But if the 27th Brigade was withdrawn, this action would result in an unbalanced Commonwealth force in Korea, which carried operational penalties of its own. One understrength brigade might make little difference when viewed against the overall numbers of UN troops in Korea, but its absence would result in the remaining Commonwealth brigades continuing to operate separately, and further complicate the operational, administrative and logistical tasks involved.

The eventual formation of the division owed a great deal to this same Chinese intervention. Not only did the worsening tactical situation which resulted convince the Canadians to go ahead with their original intention of committing a brigade, but it also meant that the British could not ignore MacArthur's request that they leave the 27th Brigade in Korea to face an actual threat rather than withdraw it to Hong Kong to face a threat which had not yet materialised. It was to be the Canadians, initially reluctant to join such a force, who now raised again the issue of a Commonwealth division.

The groundwork for this was laid in January 1951. First, on the question of nomenclature, the Canadian desire for due prominence to be given to the United Nations character of Korean operations was accommodated in the proposed title 'First Commonwealth Division, United Nations Forces'. The second matter concerned the lack of Canadian representation on the Australian Higher Defence Machinery, just as there had been no Canadian representation on the JCOSA earlier. The accredited representatives of Britain and New Zealand were located in Australia, and we have already noted that India preferred to work directly through a liaison officer in the theatre, an arrangement made possible by the type of force committed. The Canadians now nominated the military liaison officer of the Canadian Military Mission in Tokyo, Brigadier F.J. Fleury, as their accredited representative. Although Fleury had advised his superiors that the Canadian Army could not live under the shadow of Hong Kong forever, the decision to leave Canada's representative in Tokyo rather than sending him to Melbourne may have been a concession to those who felt that Canada's interests were best looked after on the spot. The Australian Chiefs of Staff indicated that any further decision by Canada to appoint a representative in Melbourne would be 'warmly welcomed', but this was never pursued by either side.[31]

Those on the spot had a clearer understanding of the problems than those observing from a distance. On 9 March Fleury advised Brigadier Rowlandson, Brigadier in charge of Administration in BCOF, that he had recommended to Ottawa the formation of a Commonwealth division, and that Ottawa had no objection although 'the question of manpower rears [its] ugly head in relation to [the] provision of Div[isional] staff and . . . troops'. Although provided to Rowlandson for his information only, it was undoubtedly passed, and probably was intended to be passed, to Robertson, with whom Fleury was also in contact concerning the development of Canadian thinking on this issue.[32] Robertson now weighed in yet again with a signal to the GICS.

Much of this message went over familiar ground. There was one

new observation, and this had serious implications for the continued viability of the forces in Korea. Robertson suspected that

some of our difficulties in the forward areas are NOT unconnected with the
feeling of some of our allies that we should have a division which they could
operate in one place. If operations are to continue for any length of time here
I feel the situation must be faced and a division formed, otherwise we will
get into such difficulties that we will NOT be able to pull our weight.[33]

On the same day he advised Fleury that

GHQ [UNC] have made it quite clear to me that they do NOT regard it as their
responsibility to provide a command and supporting set up for forces which
are large enough to have their own, and I think their view is not unreasonable.

This concern reflected American doctrine and practice evolved in
the Second World War. For US units, the division was the cut-off
point of integration for operational command and control purposes. They did not generally mix brigades in the way the British
sometimes did. Although forced to vary this practice during the
Korean War with regard to smaller UN units, the Americans did
not (and do not) see it as desirable.

Robertson again pointed to the serious implications for the
contingents with the observation that 'if there is not an end very
soon to this campaign the British Commonwealth will get into very
grave difficulties unless it organises itself into a division'. The
Canadian government also was being advised by its chief civilian
official in Japan, the diplomat Arthur Menzies, that 'a division
would make more of a public impression', and that it 'would
demonstrate to other Commonwealth Governments that, when
practical considerations dictate, we are as prepared to put an effort
into cooperation with other Commonwealth Governments as we
are with the United States when different practical considerations
suggest another pattern of military cooperation.'[34]

Faced with renewed pressure, the War Office bowed to the
inevitable, and the British Chiefs of Staff Committee initiated
discussions on the formation of the division. The committee even
noted that there were considerable advantages to be gained by such
a decision, citing in particular the psychological and political effect
of demonstrating 'Commonwealth solidarity and unity of aim.'[35]
Robertson underlined this with another well-timed message to the
CIGS, in which he noted that 'we should do the job thoroughly and

make it a proper division able to stand any test', and also observed that a good division would make a very favourable impression upon American opinion. He went to the heart of the matter when he wrote that

None of us may regard this theatre as of much importance to us . . . but it is the chief one in which the USA has men fighting and dying daily and to them that is much more real than preparations for a major war which many believe may never eventuate.[36]

It was at last no longer a question of whether or not a Commonwealth division should be formed, but of how this should be done. It was not before time.

The final decision to form the division was advised 'off the record' by Major-General Bierwirth, the Australian Defence Representative in London, in a letter to the Secretary of the Australian Defence Department, Sir Frederick Shedden, on 2 April 1951, and was confirmed officially by the Office of the British High Commissioner in Canberra four days later. Although the Army Chiefs of Staff of the Commonwealth were all in favour of the idea, it did not appear to the CIGS that they would be able, or willing, to provide much additional assistance towards completing the division. Since the provision of divisional troops and staff would largely fall upon the British, the first task was to ascertain just what contributions the Dominions would make. New Zealand was asked to provide one transport company, with a headquarters and a light aid detachment. The United Kingdom would provide the remaining divisional troops, although it was hoped that Canada, Australia and New Zealand would contribute towards divisional signals, and that all three together with India would contribute certain officers and other ranks to the integrated divisional headquarters. The United Kingdom hoped also to persuade South Africa to make a contribution to the headquarters, despite the face that South Africa had contributed an air force squadron, but no ground troops, to the UNC.[37]

New Zealand readily agreed to the contribution requested of her. Not only did the formation of the division allow New Zealand's force to operate in a familiar military framework and maintain the national integrity of the unit, but the decision was fortuitous for another reason. As Robert Eaddy has shown in his study of New Zealand policy, the New Zealand government, like the Australian, had been under pressure from the Americans to increase the size of its ground force contribution, specifically to send more gunners. It was much easier to send a support unit than a combat unit, and such a force was unlikely to take casualties. The New Zealand government could claim that, with the reorganisation of Common-wealth forces, the transport company was both needed and welcomed, thus solving its problem and avoiding any embarrass-ment implicit in declining to meet the American request.[38] The Australians decided they were unable to contribute to divisional signals because of the shortage of trained personnel in the Aus-tralian Army, but hastened to point out that the BCOF Signals Regiment already provided services to the Commonwealth forces, and would continue to do so. Australia would contribute five officers and fourteen other ranks to the divisional headquarters.[39] Canada agreed to contribute seven officers and fourteen other ranks to the headquarters, and thirty signalmen.[40] The British were left to provide the artillery staff, field engineers, the bulk of the divisional signals, and the Royal Army Service Corps column, just as they provided the largest proportion of the division itself (see table 6.1).

Table 6.1 *Proportion of national components in 1 Commonwealth Division*

Country	Percentage
United Kingdom	58
Canada	22
Australia	14
New Zealand	5
India	1

Source: CRS A816, 19/323/81

Having decided on the general principle of an integrated headquarters, discussions ensued on the breakdown of specific appointments. A conference was held at the War Office on 9 April to decide this, and was attended by representatives of all the participating Dominions. The position of principal operational staff officer in the division was to be a Canadian appointment, while the commanders of the supporting arms and services, the

artillery, engineers, Service Corps, ordnance, and electrical and
mechanical engineers were all British appointments, as initially was
the assistant director of medical services, which later reverted to the
Canadians.

Australia provided two junior staff officers as well as the Deputy
Assistant Director of Medical Services, the Deputy Assistant
Director of Hygiene and one Chaplain. New Zealand provided two
junior officers for liaison and operational planning. The Canadians
also provided these, and filled several administrative positions as
well as that of the Catholic chaplain. The staffs of the heads of
services were mostly British, with some Canadian representation.
The Forward Air Controller and the Air Liaison Officer on the
artillery staff were both officers of the United States Air Force.
There was eventually some rotation of positions between countries,
and the South African Army later furnished one intelligence and
one supply officer.

Robertson had hoped to extend this principle of integrated staffs
to his own headquarters in Japan. He was only partially successful
in this, because the Canadians declined to participate. Australia's
contribution also came in for some criticism, especially from British
officers who felt, not unreasonably, that the percentage of Australian officers in the divisional headquarters was well below what
might be expected of a nation with their numerical interest in the
division. It was not the only time that the size of Australia's
contribution was criticised.

In keeping with the principle that the nation which provides the
largest part of the force also provides its commander, the position
of General Officer Commanding fell to the British. The first
commander was Major-General A.J.H. Cassels, CB, CBE, DSO.
His appointment was in some ways almost too good to be true. A
Seaforth Highlander, he had served on the North-West Frontier in
the 1930s and had a knowledge of the Indian Army and spoke some
Urdu. As the youngest divisional commander in the British Army,
he had commanded the 51st Highland Division at the Rhine
crossings in 1944–45 and had served alongside the Canadians at
this time. To cap it all off he had just completed two years as head
of the United Kingdom Services Liaison Staff in Australia.

A man better qualified to head the composite Commonwealth
Division and deal with potentially troublesome dominion forces
would have been hard to find, as the British themselves recognised.

In commending the selection of Cassels, the United Kingdom Army Liaison Staff in Ottawa noted that he 'has had an outstanding career especially during the end of the war [and] up to the present time, and is, [we] feel sure, an excellent choice for the appointment . . . He is, incidentally, one of our youngest Major-Generals.'[41] If the success of the division owed a lot to the fact that its constituent national forces all worked on roughly the same pattern, it also owed a lot to the fact that the British appear to have deliberately chosen officers for the division who could 'get on' with their Dominion counterparts. There was to be no repetition of the arrogance and condescension which too often had characterised the relationship in the First and Second World Wars.

It was not merely the potential for friction within the division that needed careful preplanning in order to minimise it. Consideration had also to be given to the possibility of disputes with the American command structure within which the division would operate. Once the decision had been made to form the division and a commander selected, it was decided to issue him with a directive which, it was hoped, would provide him with the authority and standing which would enable him to deal with his American superior officers from a position of strength should any serious disagreement occur.

There were plenty of precedents for this course of action. In the Second World War Generals Blamey and Freyberg, commanding the 2nd AIF and 2nd NZEF respectively, had both been issued with charters by their governments. These charters emphasised the distinctly national character of the forces they commanded, and invested in the commanders the responsibility for maintaining the national integrity of the force and for its administration. In certain circumstances they were also charged with responsibility for the way in which the British high command deployed the force. Although this was a considerable advance on the situation which had existed in the Great War, it did not always function as it was intended, chiefly because Imperial officers like Wavell and Auchinleck did not really accept or act upon the principle that the self-governing Dominions had a right of control over the forces they had put into the field. Within Korea, the commanders of the three brigades fielded by the Commonwealth had each been issued with command instructions which charged them with maintaining the safety of their commands. The commander of the New Zealand

Kay-force, Brigadier R.S. Park, had also been issued with such a document.

The only exception to this appears to have been the Australians, somewhat surprisingly. When Brigadier T.J. Daly took over command on the 28th Brigade in June 1952, he was given a verbal instruction by the Australian CGS to the effect that, if the Australian battalions were placed in a position of extreme risk, he could appeal against his orders. Nothing was committed to paper.[42] The Australian battalion commanders do not appear ever to have been issued, formally or otherwise, with any similar instruction.[43] The explanation may lie in a belief on the part of the Australian Chiefs of Staff that the Commander-in-Chief, British Commonwealth Forces, Korea, being an Australian, would exercise a watching brief over the Australians in Korea, and this was certainly the case during General Robertson's period as C-in-C.

The directive to the divisional commander was drawn up by the War Office and circulated to the participating governments. A copy was also sent to Robertson, who was requested to show it to General Matthew B. Ridgway, who had recently taken command of the UNC following the removal of MacArthur. Ridgway was informally invited to comment upon the directive, but appears to have offered no opinion.[44] The directive was agreed to by the other governments, and was formally issued on 15 October 1951, although Cassels had been in possession of the details since June.

After noting that the division formed an integral part of a United Nations force and detailing the national composition of the division, the directive went on to state that, in the interests of unified direction, the division was placed under the Supreme Command of the UNC and that all orders issued by the Supreme Commander or by American commanders appointed by him were to be carried out. The C-in-C, BCFK, was to act as theatre commander for the purpose of non-operational control, administration and logistic support. To this end he had been issued a directive of his own. There was also a requirement to make periodic reports to the War Office on operations in which the division was engaged, and these would be circulated to all participating governments.

The core of the directive was contained in paragraphs five and six. The first stated that if an order given to the divisional commander by the UNC or an American commander did not, in the former's opinion, conform with the United Nations' objective of restoring international peace and security in the area, then he was at liberty to appeal to the C-in-C, BCFK. Before the order was executed the latter would present the case to the Supreme Commander and would report to the Higher Defence Machinery in Melbourne and the Chiefs of Staff in Ottawa. The divisional commander had also to advise his American superior that he was taking this course of action. Paragraph six also provided for an appeal. In this case, if an order was received that 'appears in your opinion to imperil the safety of the Commonwealth troops under your command to a degree exceptional in war', the American command was to be advised that the order would be carried out but the circumstances and the reason for the appeal would be reported to the appropriate bodies in Melbourne and Ottawa through the C-in-C, BCFK.[45]

It should be noted that the Canadian insistence on being directly consulted on matters affecting Canadian troops was reflected in the directive, even though it was willingly conceded that those troops came under British operational control. As Robertson later noted, cases where operational orders did not conform to UN principles very seldom arose.[46] There was much greater potential for friction in the other case, and this will be examined in chapter 8. It only remains here to note that the 1st Commonwealth Division became operational on 28 July 1951. As the author of the Far East Command history observed, this event 'was the logical conclusion [to] British Commonwealth participation in the Korean campaign'.[47]

The participating governments had arrived at this conclusion somewhat reluctantly. That they did not do so more readily can be put down to an unwillingness to enter into seemingly open-ended commitments coupled with a desire, on the part of Canada at least, not to repeat what were perceived to be old mistakes. That the divisional idea was finally implemented was the result of the hard work of men like Robertson and Fleury, whose cooperation in the task of convincing the Commonwealth governments of the necessity of forming the division provides an illustration of the basic good-will frequently operating between the officers of Commonwealth armies. And underlying all considerations of inter-Commonwealth relations was the powerful stimulant provided by the desire of the Americans to maximise the Commonwealth military contribution in Korea.

Chapter seven

Non-operational control and administration of 1 Commonwealth Division, 1951–53

The British Commonwealth Occupation Force assumed administrative responsibility for all British, Australian and New Zealand troops, including the 27th Brigade, on 24 October 1950. While the struggle to define a role for the base organisation had been fought out BCOF, of course, had been meeting the logistic and administrative requirements of the British Commonwealth forces in Korea as and when called upon to do so. With BCOF's place in Korean operations secured, it now became important to define that place, and to regularise the relationship between the base areas in Japan and Korea and the troops in the front line. This process found expression in the 'Plan for the non-operational control, administration and logistic support of the British Commonwealth Forces, Korea'.

On 9 November 1950 the Australian Defence Committee endorsed the provisional plan covering administration and maintenance of the forces in Korea, and circulated it for comment.[1] It was a bulky document of twenty-one pages with nine appendices. Its several sections dealt with the composition, command and strengths of the forces, policy and procedures for logistic maintenance, personnel administration, and a financial section concerned with the financial powers delegated to the headquarters in Japan together with the procedures covering the Korean Operations Pool Account (KOPA). This latter creation was to be the means through which Commonwealth expenses in Korea were met and administered. It is a large and complex subject, involving not only aspects of financial relations between allies but also separate considerations of Commonwealth relations and the financial constraints facing the relevant governments in the early 1950s, and will be dealt with separately in chapter 9.

Much of the plan dealt with administrative minutiae, and is of little interest to this study. Several of the broader features, however, are worthy of note. The force in Korea was to be known as British Commonwealth Forces, Korea (BCFK), and the Commander-in-Chief, British Commonwealth Occupation Force in Japan was also to fill the position of Commander-in-Chief, British Commonwealth Forces, Korea. Operational control of the force resided with the United Nations Command. The non-operational control rested with the Australian Defence Machinery, augmented by the accredited representatives of the Chiefs of Staff of participating countries and exercised on their behalf by the Commander-in-Chief. On those matters of supply which were the responsibility of an individual service headquarters, BCFK was to deal directly with that service headquarters. The establishments of units were set by their respective services, and in dealing with matters of personnel administration, BCFK was to work through the headquarters of 2 Canadian Administrative Group, the Australian Military Force Component, New Zealand Kay Force, and the Indian Liaison Mission in Tokyo. Only in relation to the United Kingdom component was BCFK itself responsible for these functions. Integrated Commonwealth units were the responsibility of the Australian Chiefs of Staff.[2]

The plan was essentially an administrative document, and was designed to provide the detailed instructions not contained in the directive first issued to the Commander-in-Chief on 27 November 1950. This was a much shorter document, intended to define the Commander-in-Chief's responsibilities rather than his powers as was the case with the plan. The directive set out his relationship to the Australian Chiefs of Staff and the other Commonwealth service headquarters. He was charged with the maintenance of forces in Korea and Japan, and was to interest himself

in the operational tasks allotted to the United Kingdom, Australian, New Zealand and Canadian Forces and for this purpose you are to maintain close contact with the Command . . . in the field. If the Commander . . . in the field in Korea makes representation to you in regard to the operational employment of his force, you are to represent the case to the Commander-in-Chief of the United Nations Forces in Korea, and report to the Australian Chiefs of Staff Committee.[3]

There was also a requirement for him to report regularly on a number of matters, such as the overall progress of operations in Korea, but undoubtedly the most important section of the directive was that charging him with safeguarding the interests of the Commonwealth force.

Both these documents were to undergo amendment during the course of the war and into the post-ceasefire period. Such changes in wording accompanied the introduction or withdrawal of national components, or involved rewording in the interests of clarification. Generally these changes were of a minor administrative nature, and only occasionally did they alter or add to the major thrust of the document. An example of the latter occurred at Canadian insistence in the aftermath of the Koje-do incident which will be examined in detail later.[4]

Canada's entry into the Korean War was a little slower than Britain's or Australia's, but the Canadian government's decision to become involved led to consideration of involvement with other Commonwealth forces and of any necessary amendment to Robertson's directive. On the basis of information supplied by the War Office, the Canadians reviewed their position in relation to the organisation in Japan in November 1950. Provided with a copy of the directive, the Canadian CGS was advised to consider clearing the position of Brigadier F.J. Fleury with the Australians in view of the fact that any Canadian contingent 'will be dealing with Robertson who . . . acts as the agent for the War Office on administrative matters.'[5] Fleury was the founding head of the Canadian Military Mission, Far East (CMMFE), and had been appointed on 23 August as the senior Canadian officer in the Korean theatre. On 16 November he was directed to discuss the support of Canadian troops along the Commonwealth lines of communication with Robertson, while the Canadian Vice-Chief of the General Staff requested the concurrence of the Australian Chiefs of Staff in the arrangements.[6] At this stage Canada was committed to deploying only one battalion to Korea, and a largely independent role for the force was quite impractical. A fortnight later the necessary amendments to Robertson's directive consistent with Canadian participation were proposed and accepted. The most important point was the protection of Canadian interests, and an internal Canadian army memorandum made it clear that there was

no military objection to the Australian Defence Machinery exercising control on policy matters provided Fleury is in a position to protect the

Canadian troops' interests and is available to interpret Canadian adm[inistrative] policy. Both Robertson and CGS Australia seem to be satisfied with the present arrangement whereby Fleury is in touch with Comd [sic] BCOF.[7]

November and December 1950 were months of considerable activity for BCOF/BCFK. Composite Commonwealth units were formed from the various national forces available, particularly in the medical and signals areas.[8] This was because of the increasing pressure upon the base organisation as a result of the heavy fighting concomitant upon Chinese entry into the war. Official agreement concerning the full extent of BCOF's support for all Commonwealth contingents was slow in coming through, despite the activity and general agreement in the various service headquarters, and in mid-December Robertson informed the Australian Chiefs of Staff that for reasons of general Commonwealth cooperation he could not

be in the position of refusing requests from British Commonwealth countries if [we] can meet these requests . . . I have consequently accepted the responsibility for all British Commonwealth countries taking part in the Korea operations to the extent that my resources will permit and at UN Command request.[9]

Such a move did nothing to harm Robertson's sense of self-importance, but undoubtedly it was also a good decision. Only a few weeks previously he had received a telegram from the War Office thanking him for the 'great assistance and cooperation' he was showing to British units, and noting that 'this help . . . has made all the difference in the difficult early stages of getting our force ashore and established in Korea.'[10]

This good work was to ensure BCOF's continued survival. So too was the intervention of the Chinese Peoples Volunteers.[11] When it had looked as though the campaign would end quickly with the advance to the Yalu, Army headquarters in Melbourne revived the idea of reducing the Australian component to the barest minimum.[12] By December 1950, however, it was recognised clearly that BCOF could not be scaled down because of 'irreducible commitments' in support of both the forces in Korea and the continuing occupation of Japan, which also now seemed set to continue for a longer period than earlier envisaged.[13]

As with practically every other aspect of Commonwealth involvement in Korea, American wishes were also important in this regard. It was SCAP policy that 'all allied National contingents will be supplied from National sources as far as practicable. SCAP will supply deficiencies in National supply if they are requested to do so.'[14] There was some confusion still concerning the organisation in Japan, however, and in part this was Robertson's fault.

Principal confusion arose over the relationship between the headquarters for the occupation force and the headquarters for BCFK, both commanded by Robertson and sharing many of the same personnel. Robertson had forwarded a proposal for a head-quarters establishment to the Australian Chiefs of Staff which sought changes, and expansion, in the light of the added responsi-bilities linked to the Korean commitment. Rowell, however, accused Robertson of 'attempting to establish a corps HQ', and asked him to justify, among other things, 'a General Staff element comparable to that provided for a corps HQ ... in a purely non-operational headquarters.'[15] Robertson replied by citing a Chiefs of Staff Committee memorandum of 25 January 1951 which had indicated that 'a small HQ possibly integrated might be considered necessary', and denied that he was establishing a corps headquarters.[16]

The Chiefs of Staff were not impressed, and on 29 March advised Robertson that his proposals had not been approved, and that his intended establishment 'is out of all proportion to the small headquarters envisaged by us in [our] memorandum of 25 January. It is desired that the formation of your proposed headquarters ... should not be proceeded with.'[17] This view was confirmed by a JAPC meeting on 10 April, and Robertson was so informed.[18] The Commander-in-Chief was forced to revise his proposal. The new establishment involved a small headquarters organisation for BCFK, located in Japan and separate from headquarters, BCOF. A sub-area headquarters in Korea would control those rear area and lines of communication units not under the command of the new Commonwealth division. The increase in manpower was minimal. Robertson obtained War Office agreement, and then requested approval from his own Chiefs of Staff.[19] This was the form that HQ, BCFK was to take for the rest of the war.

Robertson may have been indulging in a little self-aggrandise-ment with his proposed establishment. What should not be lost sight of, however, is the merit contained in his proposal for a substantial *integrated* headquarters organisation. In particular, he had wished to involve the Canadians closely in the base establishment, and had sought to have the head of the Canadian Military Mission, Far East, Brigadier F.J. Fleury, appointed as his chief of staff. Fleury himself was in favour, and attempted to convince his superiors in Ottawa of the merit of the proposition. Despite some support in Army circles, the Canadian Chiefs of Staff decided against the idea, largely because they did not wish to make the additional allocation of resources implicit in the suggestion. They may also have feared that the appointment of Fleury to such a position would create a conflict of interest for him and undermine his independence in safeguarding Canadian interests.[20] The negative assessment of the Australian Chiefs of Staff meant that no pressure was placed upon the Canadians to reconsider their position. It was an unfortunate decision. As a result, the headquarters was dominated to all intents by the British and Australians, leading to occasional misunderstandings. There can be little doubt either that had the Canadians been more closely involved in BCFK, the train of events surrounding the Koje-do incident might never have happened, and certainly would not have caught the Canadian government so unprepared.

April 1951 was a month remarkable for other reasons. Chief among these were Truman's decision to relieve MacArthur of all his appointments, and his replacement as Supreme Commander by the then commander of Eighth Army in Korea, General Matthew B. Ridgway. The story of MacArthur's sacking is too well known to require retelling. Its impact upon the Commonwealth organisation is less well known and is of more central concern.[21]

The events leading to MacArthur's removal had built up over a period of time, and the antipathy between the President and the Supreme Commander probably developed initially after MacArthur's thinly disguised bid for the Republican nomination in 1948. Gascoigne had warned of potential trouble in a long telegram to the British Foreign Secretary, Bevin, in September 1950.[22] At the same time that Truman's differences with MacArthur came to a head, problems again arose with both Bouchier and Robertson, and these were not unconnected to the turmoil surrounding SCAP in Tokyo.

The circumstances involving Bouchier illustrated the difficulties of working with MacArthur's headquarters at this time. Officials on the political side of the occupation found it increasingly difficult to see MacArthur once the Korean War broke out. Gascoigne's meeting in September 1950 was the first occasion on which he had seen SCAP since 15 June, that is, ten days before the outbreak of war. On 29 March 1951, Bouchier cabled London with a completely unsubstantiated story that units of the US 7th Fleet, including the Royal Navy cruiser HMS *Belfast* had engaged in a naval operation off the Chinese coast. This of course caused a 'considerable stir' in Whitehall. The report quickly was shown to be false, but it demonstrated the dangers inherent in Bouchier's insistence upon operating quite independently of the United Kingdom Liaison Mission in Tokyo.[23] As a result virtually Bouchier's only source of information was MacArthur's headquarters, and this contained dangers of its own, not least becaue of MacArthur's intense dislike of the British Foreign Office.

Robertson's sin was much more one of commission. On 10 April, as the MacArthur controversy heightened, Robertson called a press conference of all British Commonwealth correspondents to give them the benefit of his opinions on the affair. The conference was 'off the record', and in it Robertson described the criticism that MacArthur had attracted as 'unjustified'. In his opinion 'as a soldier', MacArthur 'was simply trying to draw public attention to his continued lack of a directive'. Throughout, he disclaimed any political implications of what he had to say, but implicit criticism of British policy was clear in his remarks.[24]

Before anything was done about either incident, Truman sacked General of the Army Douglas MacArthur from all his commands. This undoubtedly diverted the attention of Whitehall, fortuitously for Robertson for this time he certainly had gone too far. One might feel more sympathy for British opinion on the matter, however, had they been able to analyse it free from some of their anti-Robertson prejudices. R.H. Scott at the Foreign Office wrote that

We know a great deal about [Robertson] . . . and he was running true to form when he gave that foolish Press Conference. We are taking this up with the Ministry of Defence. Perhaps by this time the fate of MacArthur will have made an impression on him and he may take the moral to heart and amend his ways. But I have no great confidence that anything will change Robertson; the only remedy is to remove him. The time for that has not quite come.[25]

Robertson survived however, partly because the story never broke in the papers, and partly because the removal of the Supreme Commander and the 'Bataan brigade' of senior staff created quite enough turmoil in the occupation forces without further adding to it.

Bouchier, though perpetrator of the lesser offense, found his position under the greater threat. With MacArthur's dismissal, his usefulness as a link between SCAP and the Chiefs of Staff appeared to have ended, and his position was deemed to be 'under review'. It was also suggested, probably correctly, that Bouchier had actually talked to MacArthur on no more than about five occasions, and that most of his information came from MacArthur's staff, the majority of whom had now accompanied their master back to the United States.[26] His appointment was also coming under pressure in some sections of the British press,[27] and he clearly recognised that his condition had changed, for he wrote in his report of 15 June that since MacArthur had left 'it has become more difficult for me to gain access to Ridgway and his top operational staff men for many understandable reasons.'[28] Once again, however, his position was saved, this time by the commencement of peace negotiations at Kaesong in July 1951. As a senior military man he was able to channel to London information gleaned from the UN negotiating team concerning the progress of the talks, and for the rest of his time in Japan his reports consisted almost entirely of commentary on this subject.

The promotion of Ridgway brought many changes. In the last year of his appointment, MacArthur had become increasingly isolated from representatives of the other occupying powers and increasingly controlled by his staff, many of whom enjoyed hostile reputations as a result. Ridgway was much more open, but with the occupation now very obviously coming to an end, this was of less value than it would have been a year earlier.[29] Without doubt, however, the atmosphere in Tokyo improved considerably. Ridgway made a point of reassuring British officials of his belief in Anglo-American cooperation, and they made a point of stressing the change in their reports to London.[30]

The most important issues to confront the Comonwealth for the remainder of 1951 concerned the futures of both BCOF and General Robertson, and the command arrangements to cover the continued existence of BCFK. The Korean War showed no signs of coming to an end, and the hopes placed in the peace-talks, first at Kaesong and then at Panmunjom, produced nothing but frustration and propaganda. The occupation force in Japan now had little to do. Its military function had never been invoked and most of the functions of military government were discharged by the Americans. In July 1951 the Australian Military Board noted that

the retention of these forces in Japan rests on political rather than military grounds. Maintenance of these forces is a constant drain on the limited manpower resources of the three services, and this drain will be sharply accentuated because of the increased personnel required for National Service.[31]

If BCOF was withdrawn, as inevitably it would be, the command of the remaining units of BCFK would have to be resolved. In particular, as a reduced command the role and rank of its commander would have to be defined. This was the next task to face the Australian military authorities, and it again involved considerations of Commonwealth military relations and defence policy.

The initial plan was to replace Robertson in Japan with another Australian in the rank of major-general, and this was discussed between Rowell and the CIGS. The Joint Administrative Planning Committee proposed that Cassels, in the same rank but senior to Robertson's proposed successor, Brigadier (temporary Major-General) King, should assume overall authority with King as his administrative commander.[32] If accepted, this would have required a redesignation of the position of both the commander of the Commonwealth division and of the commander-in-chief. It also implied a complete reversal in the pattern of Commonwealth relations in Japan and Korea to date.

The proposal ran into a number of problems, not the least of which was opposition from surprising quarters. The New Zealanders were the first to express misgivings. To some extent they saw the Australian commander as their representative also, and they were not happy that he should once again revert to a status junior to that of the senior British officer in the theatre.[33] Colonel Maxwell, the New Zealand Joint Services' Representative in Melbourne, made representations to the Department of Defence. His superiors regarded it as

essential for C in C BCFK to have ready access and personal grata [sic] with the Supreme Commander in Tokyo. Proposed change means that there is no

British Commonwealth authority with either long experience of or personal contact with SCAP and a period must elapse during which the latters
confidence which is now freely given as a result of Robertson's excellent
personal relationships might be restricted.

It was then argued that in view of the impending ANZUS treaty it
was unwise to prejudice contacts between Australia and New
Zealand and high level American military authorities. 'The most
valuable direct point of contact is in Tokyo between SCAP and C in
C BCFK and should, we consider, be maintained even though it
may involve some immediate inconvenience.' The final argument
against the change was that Cassels, however able, could not
command his division and represent Commonwealth interests with
SCAP at the same time.[34] The War Office now also expressed itself
as opposed to the new arrangements and for the same reason as the
New Zealanders, namely that Cassels could not do both jobs.

The impetus for the proposed change came largely from the
Australian CGS, Rowell, whose motive appears to have been a
desire to return Robertson to Australia. His relationship with
Robertson was marked by the knowledge that the two had been
contenders for the post of CGS, and Rowell was less than fulsome
in his depiction of Robertson in his memoirs.[35] He now sent an
angrily-worded signal to General Brownjohn, VCIGS, in London.
He began by complaining that the matter had already been resolved
with the CIGS, and added that

the organisation that CIGS and myself agreed on could . . . be made to
work if the will to do so was present. You will appreciate that a lot of
personal considerations have been brought into this matter the chief of
which is Robertson's desire not to come back here. He himself has raised
no objection but has seen that Cassels and Stewart [New Zealand CGS] do
so on his behalf.[36]

If Robertson was brought back, he claimed, it would be impossible
for the Australian Army to provide another officer of lieutenant-
general rank to succeed him.

No reason was given for this latter difficulty, and Rowell
certainly was being unfair to Cassels and Stewart, if not to
Robertson himself. It is difficult to see whence arose the apparently
pressing need to return the latter to Australia. He might not be
viewed with favour in the Foreign Office, but the Americans held

him in high regard and the Commonwealth commanders in Korea and Japan were grateful for the way he safeguarded their interests, even if they did not necessarily see eye to eye with him on every issue.[37]

After consultation with the Army Council, though not with the CIGS who was out of the country, Brownjohn replied that the British stood firm in their objections. He defended Cassels, quite properly, against the suggestion that he was acting for Robertson, and made it clear that in any case they wanted Cassels to continue commanding the division. He also turned Rowell's earlier arguments around on him, pointing out that the new arrangements

would mean that two Commonwealth General Officers would be dealing with US Higher Command. This would be contrary to your views on Commonwealth cooperation as expressed [by you on] 1 Sep[tember 19]50 in which CIGS concurred and would [be] likely to lead to the sort of muddle which you then feared. We support strongly Stewart's arguments which seem to us difficult to refute.[38]

Check, but not mate! The matter was left in abeyance while Australian defence authorities sought a solution to the impasse which would be acceptable to New Zealand and the War Office. The Foreign Office, on the other hand, was furious.

We assume that this decision was taken on military grounds, and naturally do not wish to question it . . . we hope [however] that the period of his retention in Japan will be no longer than is absolutely necessary for military reasons.[39]

The compromise achieved was generally satisfactory, one supposes, to all parties other than Robertson himself. On 6 October he was informed officially that he was to return to Australia to fill the post of Director-General of Recruiting. The Australian Chiefs of Staff decided that there were benefits to be gained after all in keeping the senior position in Australian hands and, although no officer of lieutenant-general's rank was available, 'some special effort should be made . . . to appoint an officer who is senior to . . . Cassels, even if the promotion of some officer to the (acting) rank of Lt General would be inconsistent with the normal scale of promotions and establish-ments.'[40] This led to the appointment of the Quartermaster-General of the Australian Military Forces, Lieutenant-General William Bridgeford, to the position. Bridgeford, like Robertson and Rowell, was an early graduate of Duntroon, had seen service in both world wars, and had extensive staff experience as well as a period

General Matthew B. Ridgway, C-in-C, UNC and Lt-Gen Sir Horace Robertson, C-in-C, BCOF/BCFK on the occasion of Gen Robertson's departure from Tokyo, October 1951

commanding the 3rd Australian Division in the South-West Pacific Area. In Bouchier's opinion, 'Australia could not have made a better choice'.[41]

The Secretary of State for Commonwealth Relations cabled his government's appreciation of Robertson's services, and Brigadier Fleury ensured that the Canadian government did the same.[42] In Tokyo, Clutton wrote to his superiors that 'it is a very welcome relief to know that Robertson is really going', but expressed reservations about the appointment of another senior Australian officer to Japan. 'Bridgeford may not be so touchy or pretentious as Robertson, but there are occasions when difficulties are bound to arise.'[43]

In just over five years commanding in Japan Robertson had made a distinguished contribution to his nation's, and the Commonwealth's, affairs. In particular, his period of command in Japan had strengthened Australia's claim to a principal part in Pacific affairs as the leading Commonwealth nation in the region. No matter how much the Foreign Office might carp about him, they could not change that fact. Indeed, the volume of criticism directed at him would seem to be closely related to it. The difficulties experienced within the Commonwealth over the matter of non-operational command of the forces in Korea was one of the most serious obstacles to smooth relations between them. From an inter-allied viewpoint, it was fortunate that Robertson's detractors could be answered with Robertson's achievements. Like all really successful generals he was also lucky, in that no serious inter-Commonwealth dispute arose within his jurisdiction during his period of command. His successor was not so fortunate.

The winding-up of BCOF proceeded apace, with careful consideration given to which units would need to be transferred to BCFK to provide continued back-up. The whole of BCOF simply could not be withdrawn, for BCFK had been erected around it, and in areas such as signals and medical facilities had come to rely upon the BCOF units extensively in order to avoid expensive and unnecessary duplication. Thus, for example, the BCOF Signals Regiment and Cipher Troop handled all British Commonwealth military signals traffic in and out of Japan. It would have to stay, as would certain ordnance, engineering, and medical services, which would be transferred to the command of BCFK and joined with other units to form integrated Commonwealth units.[44]

The occupation of Japan was to end with the ratification of the Treaty of San Francisco, which had been signed in September 1951. The United States-Japan Security Treaty had been signed at the same time. This raised questions about the future basis on which BCFK would continue to use facilities in Japan, since neither the Commonwealth nor the Americans could continue to do so by right of conquest and occupation. The peace treaty had been a long time coming, but even after it was signed it still had to be ratified, and there was a clause in the treaty which specified a further time period after ratification before it would come into effect.

The continued use of facilities in Japan was the first important issue to face Bridgeford after he assumed command. There were two problems. The first, as the United Kingdom pointed out, was that the Japanese 'are likely to be sensitive to any suggestion that British Commonwealth Occupation Force facilities will be retained after the occupation ends, on any other basis but for the specific purpose of the Korea Campaign.'[45] There was some doubt as to under whose auspices these post-treaty forces would operate, although the British thought that it would be best for these matters to be conducted by the United Nations Command. The other problem was that the Commonwealth could not simply follow the Americans in finding a workable solution. Under the terms of the United States-Japan Security Treaty the Americans were to maintain forces in Japan. This was a strictly bilateral treaty, however, and did not apply to any third parties.[46] The problem, therefore, was to balance the requirement to maintain support for the forces in Korea with the necessity of withdrawing the occupation force under the terms of the peace treaty.

Detailed planning went ahead quickly. The Australian Minister for Defence, P.A. McBride, and the Australian Defence Committee nominated 15 December 1951 as the date on which all those functions which related to Korea but which were carried out by BCOF were to be transferred to BCFK. This in fact meant the transfer of the bulk of the units and personnel of the former to the control of the latter. This date did not signify the date by which BCOF itself was to cease to exist, merely the date by which the reorganisation was to be completed in anticipation of that withdrawal. The demise of the occupation force, in other words, was to be conducted in two stages.[47] (See table 7.1.)

The securing of Japanese agreement to continued use by the

Table 7.1 Proposed ceiling for National Forces in BCFK after the disbanding of BCOF

Nation	Officers	Rank and file	Total
United Kingdom	291	2,880	3,171
Canada	95	732	829
Australia	177	952	1,129
New Zealand	23	146	169
India	–	–	–

Commonwealth of facilities in Japan dragged on into 1952 and was dependent, as the Australian Department of External Affairs noted, upon the Americans. This was not because of American dominance of the United Nations Command, but because the basis for any such use would stem from the basis on which American forces operated in Japan and, although the presence of US forces had been agreed in the treaty, the administrative agreement which would actually give force to the provision in the treaty had yet to be negotiated. Rather than take independent action, the Australian government accepted the intercession of the Assistant Secretary of State for Far Eastern Affairs, Dean Rusk. The latter indicated that the negotiations would be on a government to government basis, and would not involve SCAP. As the Australians noted, they 'could not usefully try to make arrangements independently of the Americans' in such circumstances.[48]

In 1952 the great issue for the Commonwealth was the question of adequate consultation concerning planning operations in Korea. As O'Neill has shown, the problem was that little information on future policy found its way from Korea to the governments with forces in Korea, and at the heart of this was the fact that the Commander-in-Chief, United Nations Forces, took his orders from, and reported back to, the Joint Chiefs of Staff in Washington.[49] The government most aggrieved by this state of affairs was the British, and this had implications for other Commonwealth governments also.

Most governments with forces in Korea saw their involvement in terms of a UN police action, but made little effort to interfere in its conduct or demand a voice in American deliberations.[50] The British, however, still regarded themselves as a great power and as the principal partner of the United States in world affairs, and this tendency to trade upon the supposed 'special relationship' became even more pronounced after Churchill returned to the prime ministership in 1952. There had been earlier incidents where the British had requested increased consultation, such as in December 1950 when Attlee had flown hurriedly to Washington to prevail upon Truman not to use atomic weapons in Korea, but 1952 was to see a succession of such incidents which brought the question to a head.

The British attempt to forge the special relationship was doomed to failure because the Americans, while in favour of its development, were only prepared to countenance it on their terms. The problem for the British lay in the fact that American policy assumptions 'were more hegemonic than pluralistic . . . [T]here was not much room for independent manoeuvres by [America's] allies, particularly on the issues on which they [the Americans] felt sensitive.'[51] This attempt to assert an independent and exclusive role as an indispensable ally of the United States lay at the heart of the moves to gain effective senior British, but not Commonwealth, representation on the headquarters of the United Nations Command.[52]

On 12 May 1952 the adroit and widely-experienced General Ridgway left Japan to take up the appointment of Supreme Allied Commander in Europe. He was replaced by General Mark W. Clark, an officer with considerable experience in the European theatre, especially Italy, in the Second World War, but with little knowledge of local conditions in Korea. Clark had been criticized for some aspects of his command of Fifth Army in Italy, especially his decisions concerning the liberation of Rome. In his recent and definitive biography of Eisenhower, Stephen Ambrose has pointed out that the Supreme Commander gradually lost faith in his old friend Clark, and at no time considered taking Clark to England and a command in OVERLORD, although he took from Italy every other senior officer he wanted. In both cases, the criticism and doubts concerned Clark's judgement.[53]

Clark's judgement was thrown into question again in Korea, at least for some of the allies, by two events soon after his appointment, the Koje-do incident and the bombing of the hydro-electric power stations on the Yalu river. To be fair to Clark, neither situation was of his making, since the administration of prisoners-of-war was still governed by decisions made in MacArthur's time, while the Yalu bombings had been carried out with Truman's approval as a means of increasing the pressure on the Communists in the hope that they would become more tractable at Panmunjom. As O'Neill notes, these incidents 'may have led the British Government to doubt his judgement, or at least to desire more direct information on his plans'.[54] Equally, they may simply have provided the opportunity the British had been seeking to increase their role within the United Nations Command. Much was made of the fact that the British Minister for Defence, Lord Alexander, a friend and former commander-in-chief in Italy, had been visiting Korea at the time that the Yalu bombings were planned, and had not been briefed on them.[55]

The suggestion that the bombings were the cause of the request for greater participation in the conduct of the war is not borne out by the evidence. As early as 29 May the Foreign Office had prepared a brief concerning the command arrangements in Korea, and it was intended that Alexander should discuss the matter with Clark during his visit. The brief noted that there were political arguments favouring the alteration of the command structure, and that these followed on from 'a serious lack of confidence in the United Kingdom and other countries concerned'. While the principle of American leadership, set out in the Security Council resolution of 7 July 1950,was not being questioned, it was felt that the present situation, if allowed to continue, would have harmful effects upon future attempts at cooperation. The Foreign Office felt that Commonwealth and non-Commonwealth staff officers could be placed with advantage at Eighth Army headquarters in the operations, intelligence, and prisoner of war administration branches. The headquarters of the UNC in Tokyo was also still responsible for US forces in Japan, and clearly therefore was less susceptible to arguments favouring an integrated headquarters. In Tokyo, it was recommended that the British Chiefs of Staff appoint an officer of higher rank than Bouchier to the position of personal representative.[56]

Two aspects of the brief were queried by the Commonwealth Relations Office. The first concerned the Foreign Office idea that the approach to the Americans should be a strictly British exercise, and that the other Commonwealth governments should not be consulted until after the decisions had been reached. On balance, the CRO accepted this idea, although perhaps someone should have pointed out that the British did not have the power to pledge the other Commonwealth forces to any manpower commitment. Of more interest was the suggestion that as a solution to the perceived problem, the proposal was not wholly satisfactory, since as staff officers on a headquarters the individuals appointed, of necessity, would have no right of reporting back to their parent organisations and the influence they could have upon the conduct of the war therefore would be indirect at best.[57]

The air attacks began on 23 June, and prompted Eden to call for better political guidance for Clark, possibly in the form of a 'political advisor'.[58] But before the air attacks had commenced, the suggestion of appointing a British Deputy Chief of Staff to Clark's headquarters was already under active, and favourable, consideration. The Commonwealth dimensions of the appointment were also discussed. In the view of the Commonwealth Relations Office, Canada, Australia and New Zealand

will be very greatly interested in any proposals for finding a place for [a] non-American in the higher command. It is therefore *most* important that we should consult with these other Commonwealth Governments *before* any sort of *definite* arrangements are discussed with the US.

But the mainstream of Foreign Office opinion was less concerned with Commonwealth susceptibilities. The Secretary of State was advised that

it will be important to secure the agreement of the other Commonwealth countries concerned to this appointment, and to this "Commonwealth" appointment being held by a United Kingdom officer. The Australians, in particular, may be sensitive over this question, and we shall need to handle the matter carefully . . . [59]

The form of appointment probably was suggested by Clark himself, largely as a compromise to head off proposals by Lord Alexander that a British officer should be added to the negotiating team at Panmunjom. According to Clark's later recollection, he also proposed the individual who was to occupy the position, Major-General Steven Shoosmith.[60] Both these claims are perfectly plausible, since Clark had been under Alexander's command in Italy, and knew him well, and because Clark had had British units under command in Fifth Army, and Shoosmith had served on his staff there at one time. Despite any other failing, Clark was one American officer who understood that 'national interest[s] infringe one upon the other'. He was therefore less likely to resist the idea.

The problem now was for the British to gain Commonwealth approval. Sir Oliver Franks, British ambassador to Washington, lunched with the Australian ambassador, Spender, and his prime minister, Menzies, and gained the latter's concurrence with little apparent effort and without consultation with the Australian Chiefs of Staff. The Canadians indicated that they would 'greatly welcome' the arrangement, but revived the rather curious argument they had used in 1950 in opposing the formation of the Common-wealth division by stating that any Deputy Chief of Staff to Clark should be a United Nations, not a Commonwealth, appointment.[61] It is safe to assume that the British simply ignored this latter point.

One of the things that the proposal highlighted was the complete inadequacy of Bouchier. Clark confided to Sir Esler Dening, British ambassador in Tokyo, that Bouchier never came near him. Bou-chier's relationship with Dening was also bad, and active consider-ation was given once more to supplanting him. The Foreign Office favoured replacing him with an army officer of brigadier rank, so as not to cause any problems with Lieutenant General Bridgeford, the more so since it had by now abandoned any hope of establishing some sort of political advisory mechanism at Clark's headquar-ters.[62] Clark certainly seems to have appreciated the desirability of the appointment, writing in the wake of the Yalu bombings to his old wartime friend Lord Ismay that 'I am looking forward to having him, and I am sure things will be better from your point of view.'[63]

The problem for the British now was to reconcile the desires for the Commonwealth governments with the actual conditions of the Americans had imposed when agreeing to the appointment of Shoosmith. This particularly concerned the flow of information and the representation of views other than British to Clark and his senior staff. The Australian government recognised that, while the strengthening of consultative machinery was to be desired, 'we would not wish to press for formal machinery which necessitated the participation of other countries less likely to be entrusted with information.'[64] This being so, it is difficult to see how the other Commonwealth governments could make 'similar arrangements for themselves' to the ones the British were setting up. That it was to be a British appointment was also clear from Whitehall's disinclination to have Shoosmith either visit the Commonwealth capitals for consultation or be briefed by the High Commissioners in London. This of course

would not mean that we should refrain from briefing the officer ourselves . . . There is a further consideration. The Canadian's general view is that the Deputy Chief of Staff should be regarded as *wholly* responsible to the United Nations Command. They might, if the question were put directly to them, argue tiresomely that neither we nor they should attempt to indoctrinate him.[65]

This still left the matter of liaison with Clark's headquarters, and here the British Chiefs of Staff were inclined to abolish the position still held by Bouchier and replace it with a separate service liaison group. To date, general liaison for the Commonwealth had been the responsibility of the Australian liaison group acting under Bridgeford's control on behalf of the whole.[66] But in addition to this Canada had maintained a separate and additional liaison group, and Bouchier had filled a similar function. The British now wished 'in the interests of efficiency to regularise this' since it was claimed that Bridgeford himself had devoted little time to liaison, and they expressed the hope 'that Australian *amour propre* will not be hurt by [the] present suggestion'.[67]

In the end Bouchier was replaced, and the position continued to be one answerable to the British Chiefs of Staff. Bridgeford had argued that the functions of the office ought to be broadened to include the other Commonwealth Chiefs of Staff, since he conceded that his other work left him little time for close liaison duties, a recommendation that Dening felt sure would 'doubtless find an echo in Australia'. Bouchier's view, and one confirmed by the British Joint Service Mission in Washington, was that the flow of information would cease quickly if there was any suggestion that such information would be passed to other members of the Commonwealth such as Ceylon, which was not a member of the United Nations, or India, whose ambassador in Peking was too close to the Chinese Government for Washington's comfort.[68]

It was inevitable that the previous arrangements would come to an end, and that Australia and the other dominions would be largely excluded from any privileged relationships the British managed to establish with the Americans.This was the product of Britain's striving after the special relationship, but it also reflected the fact that, over and above the day to day tasks of administration and non-operational control, the Australian organisation headed by Bridgeford was no longer indispensable as a channel of inform-ation, intelligence, and influence with the Americans. From the British point of view at least, it had outlived its usefulness in that regard. One positive consequence of all this was that Bouchier, also, was perceived finally to be an impediment and, despite a late intervention by Churchill to have him kept on, was replaced by Air Vice Marshal Barnett in October 1952. Of this appointment the Foreign Office wrote to Dening that their impression of him 'was of a very sensible and agreeable fellow who should be a great improvement on his predecessor.'[69] The Canadian service liaison staff in Tokyo did not much favour the new arrangements but they, likewise, were ignored.[70]

The negative perception of Bridgeford did him less than justice. Although he had taken over a relatively settled organisation and had not had to fight for his position in the way that Robertson had been forced to, his job was by no means easy. The peace talks did not mean any lessening of the fighting, and 1952 was an eventful year with the finalising of the Japanese peace treaty, the shifting relationships within the Commonwealth described above, and the increasing frustration of the Americans in their inability to force a decision in Korea. On top of this Bridgeford's command supported the forces in Korea fully and well. It was a considerable achievement.

Apart from difficulties with the British, Bridgeford was also the target of intermittent sniping by the Canadians. In February 1952 they were speculating on his replacement by a British officer and the handing over of responsibility for administrative and non-operational control to the British Chiefs of Staff. Such an arrange-ment was to be accompanied by the appointment of a Canadian brigadier as chief of staff, precisely the situation that Robertson had tried to bring about in late 1950, and which the Canadians then had rejected.[71] The major questioning of Bridgeford's position arose as a result of his part in the mis-handled Koje-do incident. In the end, and despite considerable criticism of his actions within the

Canadian government, the latter contented themselves with an amendment to the directive requiring that 'political' matters should be referred to the political representatives of the countries concerned, in effect the civilian liaison missions based in Tokyo. Bridgeford was advised that these amendments originated with the Canadian government, and was 'requested therefore to pay particular attention to Canadian aspects in this respect'.[72]

Bridgeford in fact did a much better job than he was given credit for at the time, and this was belatedly recognised in December 1952 when it was announced that he was to be relieved the following February. The British Quartermaster General, on a visit of inspection to Japan, cabled London that 'Bridgeford has been great success here, is popular on all sides and has done an excellent job . . . Ambassador and American HQ both support this view.'[73] Dening also cabled his support for Bridgeford's retention, stating that Shoosmith agreed with this view and that the Americans 'both respect and trust' Bridgeford 'to a degree which . . . is unusual between Americans and Australians'.[74] But the appointment of his successor, Lieutenant General Wells, was already under way, and was not interfered with. In February 1953 the American commander of I Corps, operationally responsible for the Commonwealth division, noted that he 'was sorry to see General Bridgeford leave as he and I got along very well'.[75] The fairest summary came from the head of the Canadian Military Mission, Far East, by then Brigadier Morton, whose comments also made some shrewd judgements on the nature of the Commonwealth enterprise in Japan.

During his fifteen months here, 'General Bill' has attained considerable respect and great popularity, both of which it was his aim to establish after he succeeded his able but 'difficult' predecessor Lt-Gen Robertson. He has filled an important and hard position here and carried it out firmly, tactfully, wisely, and with commendable forebearance. BCFK, with its complicated organisation and chain of responsibility and national interests, is like the British Commonwealth itself. While there is excellent cooperation and a lot of integration, there is no hard and fast compulsion. This comparatively loose organisation has worked well under General Bridgeford's genial leadership . . . The general [also] got on well with the Americans who like and respected him.[76]

Bridgeford's successor, Wells, appears to have asserted his authority in a rather heavy-handed manner, and to have attempted to usurp certain functions in regard to the Canadian forces which the Canadian government was not prepared to concede.[77] He was firmly restrained, and the war ended in July 1953 before he could damage further an already rather tense relationship. With the end of hostilities came the rapid run-down of the Commonwealth presence in Korea and Japan, although some forces and base organisation remained until final withdrawal in 1957.

The administrative and non-operational aspects of the Commonwealth involvement in Korea demonstrated the strains in the relationship and the clash of interests more sharply than did the interaction of the forces in the field, both with each other and with the Americans. Personalities were as important as policies, with differences in the former often being used to justify disagreements in the latter. This was particularly true during Robertson's period of command, and the occasional difficulties experienced in dealing with him were allowed to obscure the considerable accomplishment of his time as commander-in-chief. Britain's pursuit of the special relationship with the Americans led to the dominions being gradually excluded, with the 'Commonwealth' nature of various arrangements being no more than convenient fiction.This is particularly true of the appointment of Shoosmith to Clark's headquarters. Australia's attempts to assert for itself a clearly independent position in Pacific affairs, while broadly successful, led to increasing clashes with the British in this area, though not to a fundamental deterioration in relations overall. The Canadians also were in conflict with British aims, but they were so concerned to preserve a distinctly Canadian position that they did not coordinate their actions with the Australians, to their mutual cost on occasions. The New Zealanders appear largely to have been taken for granted by everyone concerned.

Conflict within the Commonwealth in Japan was not matched by disputes with the Americans, and this is owed in very large part to the excellent personal and professional relations enjoyed by Robertson and Bridgeford with successive American supreme commanders and the commanders of Eighth Army. Whether a commander-in-chief of British provenance would have fared any worse is impossible to say, but MacArthur's well-known dislike of the Foreign Office might have precluded the level of cooperation that was gained, and that was so necessary, to the effective establishment of the base and maintenance organisations in the first chaotic months of the Korean War.

Relations down the chain of command were cordial also. The British commanders of the Commonwealth division, Generals

Cassels and West, may not always have been in complete agreement with Robertson and Bridgeford on every issue, but both divisional commanders were well aware that they would receive the necessary support and that Robertson, in particular, was prepared to fight hard with both his own superiors and with the Americans, if necessary, to ensure that the forces were adequately supplied and maintained.

The success of BCOF was sufficiently unusual in itself, given the conflicting national interests involved, but the successful transformation of the occupation force into an effective base organisation, undertaken after the war in question had begun and with the same conflict of interests again to the fore, is little short of remarkable. It is highly unlikely that any other group of forces outside the British Commonwealth could have done it.

Chapter eight

The integrated division in the multi-national command – the Commonwealth division in battle, July 1951 – July 1953

The activation of the 1st Commonwealth Division, United Nations Forces, on 28 July 1951 brought to an end the long series of disagreements over the combining of Commonwealth forces in Korea which had characterised intra-Commonwealth relations during the preceding twelve months. The ensuing two years, until the signing of the armistice on 27 July 1953, were also marked by disagreements and friction both between the different Commonwealth forces themselves, and between the Commonwealth and the United Nations Command. It should not be lost sight of that, overall, no disagreement ever proved sufficiently serious to jeopardise either the viability of the division or its relationship to its US parent formation, and that there were positive features to both. These two considerations, however, should not lead us to downplay the fact of friction or its potentially serious consequences, nor should we smugly present the two year combat experience of the Commonwealth Division as being incident-free as has tended to be the case.

The Commonwealth Division was part of the American I Corps. The Eighth Army at this time comprised three US Corps – I, IX, and X – and I ROK Corps, later joined in the spring of 1952 by the reconstituted II ROK Corps. I ROK Corps occupied positions on the east coast, with the line from east to west being occupied by X, IX and I Corps (see map 3). The Corps had performed occupation duties in Japan, before finally being deactivated in March 1950. It was quickly reactivated in the United States on 2 August that year, and was involved in operations on the Pusan perimeter by the end of that same month. In July 1951 I Corps comprised five divisions, 1st ROK, 1st Commonwealth, US 1st Cavalry, and US 3rd and

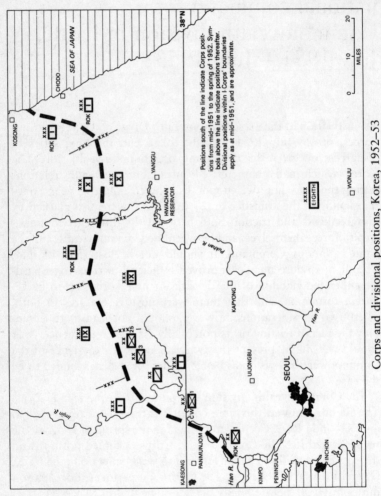

Positions south of the line indicate Corps positions from mid-1951 to the spring of 1952. Sym-
bols above the line indicate positions thereafter.
Divisional positions within I Corps' boundaries
apply as at mid-1951, and are approximate.

SEA OF JAPAN

38°N

CHODO

KOSONG

ROK

ROK

YANGU

HWACHAN
RESERVOIR

ROK

Pukhan R.

WONJU

EIGHTH

KAPYONG

Han R.

UIJONGBU

SEOUL

Imjin R.

Han R.

KAESONG

PANMUNJOM

ROK

KIMPO

PENINSULA

INCHON

0   10   20

MILES

Corps and divisional positions, Korea, 1952–53

25th Infantry Divisions, and held a sector of front from the Kimpo peninsula on the Yellow Sea coast to a point east of Kumhwa. The whole corps position was some thirty miles north of the capital, Seoul, thus giving the corps the sobriquet 'the shield of Seoul'. Within this, the Commonwealth division held a line about 11,000 yards long to the right of 1 ROK Division. I Corps had already had two commanding generals, and at the time of the formation of the Commonwealth Division was commanded by Lieutenant-General John W. O'Daniel.[1]

The Commonwealth Division and the Americans

Before considering the disagreements and problems between the national formations which made up the division, this chapter will examine the relationship between the division on the one hand, and the Americans at several levels on the other. If one leaves aside those areas more properly handled by higher commands, such as logistic support or the higher direction of the war at the level of the supreme commander, there were three basic areas where differences were most noticeable and the potential for conflict greatest : relations between units and commanders, the organisation of staffs and prevailing staff concepts, and the conduct of operations, or approach to tactical situations. To an extent, these are merely different aspects of the same problem basic to any coalition, namely, how to combine different national forces into an effective combat force. There are distinctive national styles of warfare. There is an American way of war, to use Russell F. Weigley's phrase.[2] Equally, there is a British way of war, and the two are not the same. Reconciling them was the challenge in Korea, just as it had been in the later stages of the war in Europe.

Contact with the Americans in a direct command relationship was confined almost entirely to the divisional commander and to the divisional headquarters staffs. Although there was a constant stream of visitors to the brigades and battalions these, when not of a social or VIP nature, were normally in the nature of liaison visits. An example of such visits is provided by Lieutenant-General Sir Thomas Daly who, when in command of the 28th Brigade in 1952–53, 'visited and was visited by the Commander US Marine Division on the Comwel [sic] Division's left, especially when arranging lie-up patrols'.[3] Such a visit was made because 28th

Officers of the Commonwealth Division and the UNC reviewing
Commonwealth troops, 1952. Rear group, left to right, Lt-Gen Bridgeford,
General O'Daniel, Maj-Gen Cassels

Brigade at that stage was occupying the left hand position in the divisional line; the commander of a brigade in the centre of the line or in reserve would obviously receive no such calls. Very properly, battalion commanders had even less contact with the US command structure except, again, in the form of social or VIP visits. One British battalion commander noted that he received 'no visit by [the] American Corps etc Commanders ... until we had been in Korea several months',[4] while several Australian battalion commanders recalled little contact at all with the American command.[5]

In discussing relations between US and Commonwealth commanders during the last two years of the Korean War, therefore, we are concerned with relations between the two wartime commanders of the Commonwealth division, Major-Generals A.J.H. Cassels and M.M. A-R-West, and three commanders of the US I Corps, Lieutenant-Generals John W. O'Daniel, Paul W. Kendall and Bruce C. Clarke. This was in contrast to the situation pertaining in the period before the division's formation, when the individual brigade commanders were a direct part of the UNC chain of command, and in which individual battalion commanders might from time to time find themselves in the same position.

The most serious disagreements were between Generals Cassels and O'Daniel. In part this was to be expected, since the period immediately after the formation of the division involved adjustments on both sides to each army's differing methods. But O'Daniel did not relinquish command of the Corps until June 1952, and the two commanders appear to have been in dispute from time to time during the entire period of O'Daniel's appointment. These disputes highlight the difference in approach to the two armies; equally clearly, however, it was 'Iron Mike' O'Daniel's personal approach that caused Cassels, and others, serious misgivings and led to disagreements between them. Lest the impression be given that this problem was confined to these individuals, it is worth noting that the judgement of the officers of the Japan and Korea desk in the Foreign Office at about this time was that although 'this is the first UN war, ... the US Army find it pretty difficult to act in any capacity save their own, and the other members of the UN concerned are in a very small minority.'[6]

The impression has been given since the war that relations were largely trouble free, or that disagreements were minor and temporary. Thus Brigadier C.N. Barclay, writing immediately after the war, makes no mention of them. The Canadian official historian, Colonel Herbert Fairlie Wood, describes them as 'problems of adjustment', while a later Canadian historian, Denis Stairs, concedes the initial difficulties but, since he based his account on Wood, examined the matter no further.[7] In fact they were more serious and longer-lasting than these accounts imply.

Cassels now plays down the seriousness of his disagreements,[8] but there is no doubting the extent of his unease at the time. Thus in his periodic report to the War Office covering the period from 2 May to 15 October 1951, he noted:

My main trouble during this period was to convince I Corps that, though we were more than ready to do anything that was required, we did like to know the reason behind it. On many occsions I was ordered without any warning, to do things which I considered militarily unsound and for which there was no apparent reason. Eventually I asked the Corps commander for an interview where I put all the cards on the table. I pointed out that we worked quite differently to them, and it was impossible to expect that we would suddenly change our ways to conform to American procedure . . . The Corps commander could not have been more helpful and, since then, things have been much better and both sides are happier. *Nevertheless I regret that I can not state that everything is now completely right.* There is no doubt that they look at military problems in a very different light to us and I never know for certain what the future plan is likely to be.[9]

Earlier he had endured 'three days of argument and discussion' before convincing I Corps headquarters that the 25th Canadian Infantry Brigade should be physically located with the other two brigades in time for the activation of the division.[10] Corps headquarters had assigned the brigade to the 25th US Infantry Division to protect their left flank, and at issue was the actual physical control of his own troops.

Cassels has stated that at times the American plan of action was, in his view, nonsensical 'and the reason for the operation obscure or non-existent'[11] and this continued to be the case despite his interview with O'Daniel noted above. There was the Corps policy on taking prisoners, for example, supposedly for intelligence purposes. Cassels eventually felt the need to raise this also in his reports. After noting that he was being required to produce at least one prisoner every three days, and to use up to a battalion to achieve this, he went on to comment that

I am being harassed and ordered by Corps to produce a prisoner every third day, apparently regardless of cost. As we know quite well what enemy divisions are in front of us I cannot see the point in this and I have said so . . . Personally I believe the reason behind the order was to keep the US Army divisions "sharp" regardless of casualties, and at least one of their divisions has taken very considerable casualties – between 2,000 and 3,000.[12]

The commander of the 1st US Marine Division on the Commonwealth division's left expressed agreement with this view. Neither division needed to be kept 'sharp' by this method; they were generally considered the two best divisions in the Eighth Army. Additionally, neither division could afford continuous heavy casualties, the Marines because they drew on a smaller replacement pool than the US Army, the Commonwealth for both political and manpower reasons. The desire to avoid pointless casualties motivated Cassels in many of his dealings with Corps. In the same report quoted above he noted yet another disagreement over 'certain operations which I considered either unsound or pointless.' On this occasion he specifically mentioned a proposed raid to Kunwha-ri involving two infantry battalions and an armoured regiment in an operation 18,000 yards behind the enemy's forward defended localities and against considerable enemy opposition. The only object given for the operation was to show the enemy that the UN could still be offensive. 'In my view it would have led to heavy casualties . . . and the corresponding gains would have been small.'[13]

It should not be thought that Cassels was merely being difficult or uncooperative; a little of the flavour of O'Daniel's style of command can be gained through some of his orders and comments. In a letter of instruction to all formations in the corps after the commencement of peace talks at Kaesong, he ordered that commanders and staffs should

use aggressive phrases in all communciations. Use Medal of Honour winner's names or the names of outstanding commanders, for phase lines on operational overlays. Use every means conceivable to maintain morale and esprit-de-corps. The signal for combat will be "sharpen your bayonets". Use this phrase at every available opportunity.[14]

This message was not the product of some over-zealous junior staff officer, for at a conference of divisional commanders and staff officers on 4 September 1951 O'Daniel addressed his audience in similar terms. Everyone, he stated,

must continue to be alert, sharp. Men must be made to eat, sleep, live "killing" so as to be able to destroy this barbaric, cunning enemy whose wish is to "distribute poverty". This enemy will bring us down to his level if he can.[15]

And in his Christmas order of the day to all officers and men in the corps he observed that 'with God's help and a sharp bayonet we will all fight toward that goal [peace], and will not let up until we have gained it.'[16]

There were two consequences to this 'cold steel' rhetoric. The first, as Cassels had stated, was that it got people killed for no good reason. There is some evidence that the troops also perceived this, and were unhappy about it. Private William Speakman, a regular soldier in the Black Watch who won a VC in the heavy fighting in November 1951 while serving with the KOSB, was quoted by the head of the United Kingdom mission in Japan, Sir Esler Dening, as stating that 'his mates got killed in Korea to no purpose at all.' This was felt to be in contrast to service in Malaya. In the same despatch Cassels, an old friend of Dening, was quoted as describing his corps commander as being 'of the "Two-Gun Patton" type ... always wanting to undertake foolhardy stunts which had no serious military purpose.'[17]

If Cassels, an upright soldier of great personal integrity, was 'telling tales out of school' then he must have been seriously concerned about his situation. It certainly deserved more consideration than the laconic Foreign Office observation that the Commonwealth Division 'seem to be unfortunate in their Corps Commander.'[18] Concern was expressed at the same time from another quarter, moreover, in the form of a personal and very secret letter to the Supreme Commander, Ridgway, from the Canadian Chief of the General Staff, Lieutenant-General Guy Simonds.

After a recent visit to Korea, Simonds had come away 'with real misgivings as to the competence of ... O'Daniel as a corps commander ... I was left with the most serious doubts as to his ideas and abilities.' It was the tone of the briefings and instructions issued, together with the ordering of operations to 'maintain the offensive spirit' which had caused this concern.[19] In likening these operations to 'that period in World War I when imaginative military leadership descended to its nadir', Simonds was concerned about casualties. But he was also worried by the fact that Cassels or one of his subordinate commanders might feel the need to invoke their right of appeal against their orders, and of the effect this might have on inter-allied relations. 'I regard it as most undesirable that any of our formation commanders should feel they have to exercise their right of appeal to a higher commander and I know none of them would resort to such an appeal except in an extreme case.'[20]

Cassels had been sorely tempted. In his first three months of command there had been at least five occasions when he considered invoking the directive, and he had also come close to doing so over the proposed raid to Kunhwa-ri, mentioned earlier. That he did not to do so in the end was owed to his preparedness to argue with the corps commander, which shocked the American divisional commanders present, and the existence of the right of appeal itself. Cassels is sure that the latter had a deterrent affect.[21] Equally, the requirement that he carry out the operation over which an appeal might be pending was, as the Foreign Office noted, 'cold comfort'.[22] Ridgway did follow up Simonds' expression of concern. At a meeting of corps and divisional officers on 11 March 1952 he asked Cassels privately whether any operational demands made upon him were, in his view, unsound. Whether out of loyalty to his commander or a desire not to muddy further the inter-allied pond is not clear, but Cassels answered in the negative.[23] In a sense, of course, this was correct, since he had managed to talk O'Daniel out of most of his wilder flights of fancy. But his answer could not be said to convey the whole unvarnished truth, either.

O'Daniel was reassigned in June 1952, eventually leading the Military Assistance Group to the French in Indochina. Cassels returned to Britain, a knighthood, and promotion in September the same year. Their successors, Lieutenant-General Paul W. Kendall and Major-General M.M. A-R-West, seem to have enjoyed a quieter, if not smoother, relationship. Kendall however had an argument with Cassels within a week of taking over the corps command, stating, in what must have been a frosty 45 minute meeting, that he would not give the Commonwealth Division what he saw as preferential treatment over Cassel's request to shorten the Divisional line and rationalise his defences.[24] Many of the same causes for disagreement reasserted themselves, with West complaining at one stage about the renewed pressure to produce prisoners, and of high-level interference in such low-level matters as the number of patrols to be sent out by the forward battalions.[25] Although Kendall was widely recognised as being a very different personality type from his predecessor, even being described by the then Supreme Commander General Mark Clark 'as one of the better officers in the US Army',[26] this did not necessarily equip him to deal successfully with his allies. He was replaced on 10 April 1953 by Lieutenant-General Bruce C. Clarke after he had publicly rebuked West in a divisional commanders' meeting and had made a number of disparaging remarks about the British.[27] The experience of dealing with his principal commonwealth subordinate was not a particularly happy one for either O'Daniel or Kendall.

After the Chinese Fifth Phase Offensive of April and early May 1951 had expended itself against the UN forces, Ridgway and Van Fleet went over to a limited offensive all along the line. By 1 June the Eighth Army had regained all the territory lost to the enemy in his previous offensive, and set about establishing a strong defensive line slightly to the north of the 38th parallel. This was to become known as the Kansas-Wyoming line.

From here, Van Fleet launched a number of more limited offensives to improve particular portions of the line and to push the enemy further back from important features such as the Hwachon reservoir, which eventually lay to the rear of the central part of the front. From 2 to 15 October I Corps conducted a major offensive operation on the western front, codenamed COMMANDO, in which the Commonwealth Division played a major part. The Commonwealth Division was assigned an advance of between 6000 and 8000 yards to a new position, dubbed the Jamestown Line, taking and fortifying a number of key features. After intense fighting, particularly for the feature known as 317 or Maryang San, the advance was successfully completed, and the task of establishing the new line commenced.

The US and Commonwealth conceptions of defence had obvious points in common. Both acknowledged the importance of depth, and both agreed on the need to protect important points of observation, which was why so much blood and effort was expended taking and then holding positions such as 355 and 317 in the Commonwealth sector. Both made extensive use of wire and minefields, and both dug, though neither ever matched the Chinese in the depth or rapidity of their digging. One Commonwealth officer noted that

The Americans like digging, if possible, rather less than we do, but all along the front the emphasis ... has been on the improvement of existing defences and the construction of new ones and everyone has been digging hard ... The Chinaman is doing the same both in his forward and rear areas and ... as a peasant digging seems to come rather more easily to him than to us.[28]

Commonwealth doctrine decreed that the infantry be disposed in Forward Defence Localities in depth, capable of all-round defence, and placed on the crest and side slopes of the hills. Where necessary, by day and/or night, observation posts would be pushed forward of the line. The Commonwealth forces also engaged in extensive patrolling. The Americans, on the other hand, placed their Main Line of Resistance at the forward base of the hills and tended to rely on a linear defence, attempting to avoid gaps between localities. In front, they placed the Outpost Line of Resistance. This was designed to discover, resist, and possibly yield to an enemy assault, a concept designated as 'fight and roll' or 'roll from the punch'. In these circumstances the enemy then would be halted by the main line. I Corps orders noted that outposts were expected 'to give timely warning of enemy attack and to delay and harass his advance but are not expected to hold outpost positions at all costs ... outpost commanders may withdraw on their own initiative if their unit is in grave danger of being overrun or annihilated.'[29] The American doctrine also called for forward patrolling.

This was fine in theory, but in practice revealed a number of shortcomings. The Main Line of Resistance was too shallow and, if penetrated by the enemy, required major counter-attacks to retake the position. A Chinese penetration of the line was also potentially more dangerous, as illustrated by an observation of the Commonwealth division's chief engineer officer in November 1952. When the battalion of the Black Watch moved to take over the Hook position from the US Marine Division it found that 'the shattered remnants of their defences were almost completely useless to our troops.' In order to give the Black Watch 'something fit to hold', a squadron of engineers and an entire company of the Korean Service

Corps had to be employed, often under shell fire and on one occasion through a night attack by the Chinese. The reason for this state of affairs was bluntly stated as being 'because the American tactical doctrine in defence is so radically different from our own.'[30] Even more serious was the teaching regarding the outpost line. Despite the requirement to withdraw if in danger of being overrun, there was a strong tendency to 'feel that the retention of an outpost is a matter of honour and [to] insist that it shall be defended to the last man and the last round, regardless of its tactical significance.'[31] This caused excessive casualties and further weakened the main line of resistance by drawing troops away to retake the outposts.

A Canadian report in September 1952 illustrated the problem. A company of the 3rd US Infantry Division, placed in an outpost position nearly a mile in front of the main line, had been heavily attacked by the Chinese and overrun. Several strong counter-attacks were mounted, but were unsuccessful, with the result that several battalions sustained heavy casualties. The Chinese then abandoned a feature of no real value to either side, and one entire American company was killed or captured. The Canadian officer went on to note that a check of all UN divisions had revealed that those divisions with the most ouposts also suffered the heaviest casualties. While conceding that the nature of the ground and the varying quality of the divisions might account for this, he nonetheless reported that US commanders had a tendency to fight for the retention of outpost positions at any cost. He had expressed a similar view in an earlier report, noting that 'despite their theory, we claim that the Americans reinforce and counter-attack to assist their OPLR if overrun . . . thus putting their MLR off-balance.'[32]

Not all American higher commanders were guilty of such tactical excesses. The battle for Pork Chop hill in July 1953 was brought to an end when the corps commander brought in heavy concentrations of tactical air and artillery fire, over the objections of the US divisional commander concerned who wished to continue with the costly assaults.[33] The majority, however, seem to have been perfectly willing to take the level of casualties imposed by these operations, leading one analyst to note that 'some of the bloodiest battles were fought over these seemingly inconsequential outposts.'[34]

The differences in doctrinal assumptions are explained by past experience, especially in the two world wars. The men who led

Britain's armies in the Second World War had been subalterns in the trenches of the First, and there is no doubt that the experience caused them to value the lives of their soldiers and to husband them accordingly. The Americans did not share in the blood-letting on the Western Front to anything like the same extent. In any case, as Weigley has shown, American doctrine was the product of two conflicting legacies, mobility and power, born out of 19th century experience in the Civil War and fighting the Indians. 'The Civil War', he contends, 'molded the American army's conceptions of the nature of full-scale war in ways that would profoundly affect its conduct of the Second World War.'[35] This holds true for Korea also. And the criticisms of unnecessary casualties incurred in unnecessary actions resurfaced in Vietnam as well.

Given this tendency, it is not surprising that the commanders of the Commonwealth Division should have resisted stoutly attempts to impose American operational assumptions on them. It should not be construed from this, however, that the Commonwealth did not at times fight fairly bloody engagements for the possession of ground. The fierce fight to gain Maryang San has already been referred to, and various battalions fought bloody engagements on the position known as the Hook. A Canadian battalion repulsed a strong Chinese assault on the Hook in March 1952, a battalion of the Black Watch withstood a similar attempt in November the same year, the Duke of Wellington's Regiment fought the heaviest action of all in May 1953, and 2 RAR were fiercely engaged on the position just hours before the cease-fire came into effect in July. But the essential difference was that the Hook was a key feature; it dominated the Sami-chon valley below at the point where the river turned south, towards Seoul, hence the frequent Chinese attempts to take it. The position was summed up in a Foreign Office minute at the beginning of 1953.

American discipline is poor, and to keep up the morale of the troops they must be given action and employment whether there is any military purpose to be solved, or objective to be taken, or not. I discussed this matter with several British officers in Korea, and as they put it: "we do not need casualties for training purposes. Some of the American units do."[36]

A further feature of American conduct of operations, and which again emphasised the level of interference by higher commanders, also surprised Commonwealth officers. In the words of one

American company grade officer, this was 'the penchant for senior commanders to play squad leader.'[37] General West complained in one periodic report that there were signs of increasing centralisation of command manifesting themselves in, among other things, searching inquiries into minor incidents.[38] One Foreign Office official in Tokyo even reported an occasion on which a US corps commander allegedly had directed a platoon assault against an enemy strongpoint.[39] Where this behaviour did not impinge upon Commonwealth units it was little more than a source of amusement. Where it did, it caused aggravation and bemusement. One commanding officer of 16th New Zealand Field Regiment one night found himself the only responsible officer left in an American regimental headquarters because the assistant divisional commander, regimental commander, and two of the battalion commanders had all descended on the command post of a single company in action with the Chinese.[40] It was a bad command practice that the US Army was to repeat in Vietnam.[41]

This seeming reluctance to trust NCOs and junior officers in the execution of their duties also affected such vital matters as the provision of artillery fire support. The fighting in Korea was very much an infantryman's and gunner's war, and the prompt and accurate provision of supporting fire by the artillery was vital in breaking up Chinese attacks, aiding surrounded patrols to regain their lines, and generally assisting in the vital task of maintaining domination of no-man's land.

In the Commonwealth system, the officer commanding the field regiment lived side-by-side with the commander of the brigade of which the regiment was in direct support. Each battery commander was attached to the battalion his unit supported. The Forward Observation Officer (FOO), usually a lieutenant or a captain, was located in the forward areas with the rifle companies. The FOO could call for fire support and the request would immediately be complied with because firstly, the system gave that officer the authority to do so and secondly, because the commanders were well forward and in a position therefore to assess the situation on the ground. The American system placed an enlisted man or perhaps a sergeant in the forward area whose request for fire had to be passed back through various command levels until it reached the divisional headquarters, where the decision was made. There was therefore a considerable time-lag in the provision of fire-support by US gunners. The Commonwealth artillery was also able to respond rapidly because all batteries in the divisional artillery were inter-linked with both radio and line communications. If the guns in direct support of a unit were already engaged, guns from another battery, or indeed from another regiment, could be brought to bear almost immediately.

The superiority of the Commonwealth system was marked, and remarked upon. I Corps artillery units sent officers to study the Commonwealth's communications discipline; the commander of the artillery school at Fort Sill asked for a demonstration of the division's methods when he visited Korea in October 1952; specific favourable mention was made of the support given the US 2nd Infantry Division when it relieved the Commonwealth Division in the line in February 1953.[42] In an exercise conducted with two American field artillery regiments in January 1952, the Common-wealth batteries reported 'ready' in 69 seconds while the American units came up in three minutes. This latter performance was considered good for an American unit. On another occasion, the Commonwealth guns engaged targets on the front of the Marine Division to their left well before the US units responsible for answering the call for fire. This led to an enquiry by US authorities, including General Van Fleet, in an attempt to ascertain how this could be possible.[43] Despite being impressed by the system, the US Army made no effort to modify their own procedures accordingly.

There were no significant changes made to staff practices and organisation, but attempts were made to smooth the path of both sides, since British and US staffs had (and have) little in common except function. Commonwealth headquarters issued a detailed memorandum for the benefit of US formations dealing with the division which explained the differences between the staffs, listed the Americans' 'opposite numbers', and explained such mysteries as the use of the term 'regimental' which, for the Americans, has a precise organisational definition that it does not enjoy in Common-wealth armies. When the 2nd Division relieved the Commonwealth Division in February 1953, the headquarters of the Commonwealth artillery issued a staff list of the American division and its constituent regiments to all the field regiments which would be in support of them.[44] Aside from any less formal steps, the Americans for their part published articles on the Commonwealth staffs in major service journals both during and after the Korean War.[45]

Orders and instructions emanating from I Corps were generally 'translated' by divisional headquarters into Commonwealth terminology before being transmitted to the brigades. On the one hand this prevented confusion over standard but ambiguous American terminology such as 'initiate offensive action'. On the other, it enabled the divisional commander to modify the emphasis consistent with Commonwealth procedures when this was necessary. The brigades and battalions were able to operate happily in a thoroughly familiar environment and without some of the problems that had assailed the brigade commanders before the division's formation.

One very bad practice that amazed the Commonwealth staffs was the constant American requirement for estimates of casualties and damage inflicted.The American system worked on the premise that the expenditure of a certain amount of ammunition for a certain period of time should result in a certain number of enemy casualties. In part this was necessary so that American staff officers had something to say at the daily briefings, held every morning regardless of the level of activity in the previous 24 hours. As in a later American war, the enemy made it difficult to gauge the effectiveness of American actions through his habit of carrying away his dead and wounded with him when he broke contact. Hence the constant pressure for estimates. Generally the Commonwealth refrained from this sometimes meaningless exercise, much to the irritation of higher headquarters. The first commander of the Canadian brigade, Brigadier J.M. Rockingham, recalled an incident which well demonstrated the sorts of excesses which such a system generated. A three-man enemy patrol had been detected near Canadian positions, with one being killed, one captured, and one making his escape.

Later US Army HQ said that the report did not match their statistical methods . . . the figures should be three killed, ten captured or wounded, and any number got away. I said that I was sorry, but only three had come in and what I had reported had indeed happened to them. The next day in Tokyo I visited the C in C's HQ and found that the board had the US figure for the patrol against us. I again explained that only three had come in and what had happened to them. A rather tolerant shrug greeted my announcement as much as to say these crazy Canadians don't know the rules.[46]

A system that could turn a three man patrol into a platoon size action to satisfy statistical requirements was well capable of the body count excesses of the Vietnam War.

As the Australian official historian has noted, the US Army exposed its characteristic strengths and weaknesses in Korea.[47] Because of its very different methods and procedures, the Commonwealth Division probably considered the weakness more marked than the strengths. If the differences between the two did not at any time develop into serious political problems, they always had the potential to do so. Dealing with the Commonwealth Division cannot have been an altogether happy task for either O'Daniel or Kendall, while Cassels and West resolutely refused to follow methods or embark upon operations whose only outcome would be heavy casualties. They were right to do this, but it cannot have done anything for inter-allied relations. Overall, and despite the sometimes heavy-handed attempts to make them conform to US practice, the Americans learned to leave the Commonwealth Division to conduct operations in its own fashion. In doing so, they granted it in practice a far greater level of practical autonomy than ever would have been allowed a ROK or US division. Not to have done so, however, would have caused more problems that it solved.

The Commonwealth experience

The internal difficulties of the Commonwealth Division in some ways mirrored the problems faced by the United Nations Command as a whole. Manpower problems, rotation policy, the provision of arms and services suited to the Korean climate and terrain, disagreements between allies, and command relations all had to be faced within the Commonwealth organisation just as they were faced by the Supreme Command.

Units drawn from the Empire of course had served together in the past on numerous occasions and in all parts of the world. Although generally successful from a military point of view, these had not always been happy experiences for all concerned, with the Canadians and Australians in particular at times feeling that they were asked to do the work and take the casualties without corresponding recognition or reward. Commonwealth land units had only rarely before worked in a formal, integrated formation such as the Commonwealth brigade or division.[48] Because the size of the forces in Korea was not large, much of the decision-making was made in the theatre without consulting national governments. Provision for this had been made in the directive issued to Cassels upon his appointment as operational commander. In practice he and his successor kept in close touch with Robertson and his successors, who had responsibility for non-operational matters, and with the heads of the New Zealand and Canadian military missions in Korea and Japan. Equally this was 1951, not 1914, and there were matters, seemingly trivial in themselves, which had to involve the home governments. Failure to do so could produce major repercussions.

Relations between units and individuals, on the whole, were of a high order. Many officers had seen service in the Second World War, and were therefore generally familiar with the various national idiosyncracies they could expect to encounter, and often with individuals as well. In 1950 the various Dominion forces were still very closely patterned on the British model, and although Canada had begun to realign more closely towards the United States in such matters as procurement of equipment, this had not yet-seriously affected the ability of the Canadian army to operate virtually interchangeably with other Commonwealth forces. All shared the same tactical organisations and establishments, the same staff procedures, and to a greater or lesser extent the same doctrine, although as will be seen the latter was often practiced inconsistently from unit to unit. Many of the causes of friction with the Americans were therefore absent from the start.

Relations within 28th Brigade were usually harmonious, although there was some ill-feeling generated with the replacement of Brigadier George Taylor in October 1951. This was not necessarily the case outside the brigade. In particular, relations between the Australians and New Zealanders on the one hand, and the Canadians on the other, were much less close and at times quite strained. The Australian official historian has noted that the Australians objected to Canadian sanitary habits, and relieving a Canadian battalion in the line has been compared to occupying a fresh midden.[49] While unpleasant, this was trivial when compared to the Canadian attitude to camouflage and concealment. Canadian units tended to dispose of rubbish by the simple expedient of throwing it out in front of the wire. Since much of this consisted of empty ration tins and the like, it meant that the positions were clearly outlined in bright, reflective material easily visible to the Chinese and giving a good indication of the strength in which the position was held. British and Australian battalions relieving the

Canadians had then to send out working parties beyond the wire for the dangerous and totally unnecessary task of cleaning up the position. The Canadian brigade also tended to keep to itself, and officers of other nationalities on the divisional headquarters soon came to leave liaison with the brigade to the Canadians among them.[50]

Of equal seriousness were some of the Canadian attitudes to operations. Their defensive positions were generally inadequate, and prompted complaints from battalions of other brigades. The war diary of 28th Brigade recorded a number of these. Comments such as 'Bns say wire in positions . . . was not very thick', '1KOSB say they are going to need a lot of def[ensive] stores in new positions', 'Brigade Major said that the [search light] position we were taking over from 25 Cdn Inf Bde had NO defences', appeared frequently during and after the relief.[51] Their objection was again based on the fact that working parties from the new battalions would have to go forward of the wire for the dangerous task of improving the positions under enemy observation. The criticisms eventually produced some action on the part of the Canadian command; in a personal memorandum of 1 May 1953 the brigade commander, Brigadier Jean Victor Allard, issued *Notes on Defence* to all units as a guide for conduct, on the surprising grounds that 'deliberate defence is in many respects foreign to the average Canadian officer.'[52] Since the brigade had by then spent two years in Korea, it should not have been.

The other cause of serious criticism of the Canadians related to their apparent unwillingness to patrol vigorously. Aggressive patrolling was necessary not merely to gather intelligence and maintain contact with the enemy, but to achieve dominance of no-man's land by keeping the Chinese patrols well away from the Commonwealth positions and to frustrate his activities. Failure to do this meant that the enemy could form up and launch attacks with considerable advantage. Once the enemy was 'sitting on the wire', the process of pushing him back down into the valley had to begin all over again, and this meant taking anew casualties that had already been incurred when the units had performed this task the first time. This failing could prove costly for the Canadians also. On the night of 23–24 October 1952 the positions occupied by B Company, 1 Royal Canadian Regiment, on Hill 355 were overrun by strong Chinese attacks and had to be retaken by counter-attack.

A night patrol moving up to the front line, 1952–53

The Chinese had formed up under cover in six large bunkers constructed for the purpose just beyond the defensive wire.[53] A similar attack against C Company, 3 RCR, on the night of 2–3 May 1953 also enjoyed the advantage of enemy domination of no-man's land. On this occasion, the enemy had profited from the prior occupation of the position by the US 2nd Division, whose patrolling also left a great deal to be desired, but weaknesses in the Canadian arrangements contributed.[54]

It is only fair to add that the Australians erred in the other direction, patrolling too aggressively on occasions and finding themselves well beyond the agreed patrol lines. This could lead to fierce small-unit actions inside the Chinese positions, and Australian patrols sometimes required heavy artillery covering fire in order to extricate themselves from areas in which they were not supposed to be in the first place. By straying into free-fire areas, they also risked casualties from their own guns.

Dissatisfaction with the consequences of Canadian practices led, in part, to West's decision in late November 1952 to vary the deployment of the division in the line.[55] Previously the division had deployed two brigades up front and one in reserve, with relief in the line being carried out on a brigade basis. The change, completed on 1 December, placed all three brigades in the line, with each brigade having two battalions up and the remainder in reserve, and reliefs being conducted on a battalion basis. Each brigade now had its own sector, which did not vary. This removed the cause of the complaints from 28th Brigade, but it also meant that contact between contingents was even further reduced. Generally speaking, however, the nationalities got on well together, which is to say that there were few ugly incidents between them. In some ways, the fact of national diversity aided this, since it led to competitiveness within the division which Cassels at least was not slow to exploit in overcoming day-to-day problems.[56] Most remaining difficulties arose out of the interaction of personalities.

Somewhat ironically, the most serious difference of opinion involving the use of Commonwealth forces had little to do with operational matters, although these were invoked as justification. The Koje-do incident in 1952, alluded to earlier, in which a company of Canadian troops was detached, on American orders, and sent to help deal with rioting prisoners of war without reference to higher Canadian authority, has been dealt with briefly by both Wood and O'Neill, and the general account of events provided by them is not disputed.[57]

However, the Canadian attitude was not only a product of the dispute over the sending of troops to Koje, as the official historians imply. In a minute to the Canadian Department of External Affairs, dated 6 July 1951, the Chairman, Chiefs of Staff, Lieutenant-General Charles Foulkes, stated that in the view of the service chiefs

the channel for dealing with operational disputes should be the Chiefs of Staff of the participating countries . . . there may be certain decisions in regard to occupation which may be highly political, therefore, it is essential that any decisions affecting Canadian troops should come through this channel.[58]

The Canadian attitude was also consistent. It applied equally to decisions concerning Canada's force contribution to NATO, and stemmed from a recognition of 'the obvious growth in stature of the individual Commonwealth countries, and particularly Canada's natural evolution into political and constitutional independence.'[59]

In assessing the events surrounding the Koje affair, the Canadian CGS absolved both Cassels and the Canadian brigade commander, Brigadier Bogert, from any blame. He took considerable exception to the role of General Bridgeford, the Australian C-in-C, BCFK, whose directive, he argued, required reference to and consultation with Commonwealth governments on matters with political implications. He additionally raised the possibility of reassesment of the effectiveness of the Commonwealth command organisation in the Far East.[60] He also blamed Brigadier A.B. Connelly, the head of the Canadian Military Mission, Far East, for the incident by not keeping him informed of events.

This much is generally known. What is not appreciated is that Canadian feeling was so strong that the Minister for External Affairs, Lester Pearson, raised with the Department of National Defence the possibility of action being taken against Bridgeford for his part in the affair.

If he acted improperly, the Canadian Government should consider what action, if any, should be taken with the Australian Government. In the alternative, or in addition, his Directive should be revised to clarify his duty to consult the Canadian Chiefs of Staff.[61]

The Canadian chiefs *did* feel that he had acted improperly, but there were problems in having their view accepted. The British were concerned by the prospect of any action which might 'impair the effectiveness of the Commonwealth command organisation which has been working so smoothly up to date' and declined to take any action themselves.[62] The Australian Defence Committee, in resolving to permit Australian troops to be sent to Koje if required, also declined to take any action or find any fault with Bridgeford's behaviour.[63]

The Canadians thus found themselves isolated in their stand, and in some ways had only themselves to blame, for they handled the public statement of their objection badly. They based their objection, as the External Affairs Minister Lester Pearson made clear in the Canadian House of Representatives on 26 May, on the principle of the national integrity of their brigade, and opposition to its being broken up. There was also the consideration, not publicly aired, that a mess of American creation was for the Americans to clean up. The latter was clearly untenable, all the more so when it is noted that in addition to sizeable ROK and US forces, detachments from the Netherlands and Greek battalions were also being employed on Koje.[64] The former objection was undoubtedly designed to appeal to the other Commonwealth governments, and one suspects particularly to the Australians for whom this had been a serious issue in the Second World War. The issue that should have been emphasised, however, was that concerning lack of consultation. The Americans recognised this implicitly by quickly dismissing the question of separation of forces, observing that the entire brigade could be sent to Koje, thus keeping it intact. They then answered the latter point with the quite erroneous suggestion that what the Canadians proposed was to inject 'into combined operations in the field the concept of Governmental consultation and consent.'[65]

Pearson did not make public the American reply of 17 June. Had he done so, the other Commonwealth countries might have been given cause to reconsider their positions, since the movement of troops for guard duty on Koje scarcely constituted a 'combined operation in the field'. The lack of support, however, obliged the Canadians to take the matter no further.

It must have been one more cause for Canadian disaffection with the conduct of Commonwealth affairs in Korea, and had clear implications in both the NATO and the wider Commonwealth context.[66] Two further outcomes were that Connelly was relieved of his post and forcibly retired soon after, and Bridgeford's directive was amended to require explicit consultation with national governments in regard to the employment of their forces.[67]

Manpower problems afflicted the Commonwealth forces as they did the Americans, although not always for the same reasons. The American system had two fundamental characteristics; relief of individuals as opposed to relief by units, and rotation of officers through a number of positions, sometimes known derogatorily as 'ticket-punching'. The American practice of relief and reinforcement by individual dated back to the Second World War. It had not been an altogether satisfactory system in that war because the open-ended nature of enlistment meant that units were often made up of large numbers of newly-trained and inexperienced soldiers, especially after a heavy engagement. In addition, the front-line soldier was faced increasingly with incapacity or death as the only means of release from combat duties because the policy of sending home men who had served a set period of time in a combat zone proved impossible to implement due to the overall shortage of replacements and shipping space. In Korea, the exacting nature of climate and terrain ensured that soldiers only had to face a tour of twelve months, and only one winter, in the country, and priority for relief was worked out under a fairly complex points system. The personnel changed, but the units and formations remained, in name at least. There was some limited relief of units: the 24th Infantry and 1st Cavalry divisions were relieved by two National Guard divisions at the beginning of 1952, but these were exceptions made to return units to the Japanese occupation force which had been reduced at the outbreak of the war. Rotation was the means by which regular officers filled a number of positions, both staff and field assignments, during their tour of duty. While the abuses of the practice, which were so evident in Vietnam, do not seem to have emerged in Korea, there was appreciation of its weaknesses, in particular the additional responsibility placed on NCOs by the replacement of company grade officers just when they had learned their jobs properly and were in a position to provide effective combat leadership.[68]

Because war had not been declared, and the country therefore had not been mobilized on a war footing, the Americans experienced some difficulty in establishing and maintaining the necessary manpower commitment in Korea. The I Corps diarist complained in September 1952 that

the flow of replacements was not adequate to replace personnel who departed on expiration of term of service and rotation. Personnel requisitions for officers and enlisted men were not filled by proper MOS [military occupation specialty] or in numbers requested. The critical shortage of enlisted specialists, qualified senior noncommissioned officers, company grade infantry, artillery and engineer officers has jeopardised the efficiency of combat units.[69]

Commonwealth practice differed from contingent to contingent, and generally reflected the nature of the force committed and the means by which it had been raised. New Zealand had raised the 16th Field regiment by special enlistment specifically for service in Korea. Although staffed by a handful of regulars, the men served eighteen month tours before relief, while the unit itself remained in Korea throughout the war and into the early years of the shaky cease-fire. Because service with the guns was less dangerous and (a little) less arduous than in the infantry, these volunteers served a longer tour than those in the battalions. Canada began with one system and ended with another. As noted in chapter 3, the Canadian Army Special Force had also been raised by special enlistment specifically for Korean service. This was done because the Canadian government did not wish to interfere with its commitment to NATO, and the small post-war Canadian army lacked the resources to meet both simultaneously. The Canadians raised second battalions for each of the three regular infantry regiments from this pool of special enlistees. This naturally disappointed the personnel of the regular first battalions, who felt that as regular soldiers it was they who should be fighting in Korea.

They need not have worried, however, for in April 1952 they relieved the original battalions in Korea on a unit basis. Third battalions were also raised, initially out of the reinforcement companies of the special force battalions, and were held back for training at Fort Lewis in the United States, where the entire Canadian force trained. These latter had originally been intended to relieve the second battalions, thus preserving the non-regular character of 25th Brigade, but they were not up to establishment or trained when the decision was made regarding unit relief in August 1951, and did not proceed to Korea until March-April 1953.

The Australians, by historical accident, relieved on both a unit and an individual basis. Under the Defence Act, in 1950 members of the Army, but not of the Navy or Air Force, had to volunteer individually for specified overseas service. The members of BCOF had volunteered for service in Japan; they had to come forward again for service in Korea. Australia's military capacity had run down to such an extent in the five years since the end of the Second World War that the provision of a single battalion on active service was the most the army was able to provide, and 3 RAR was supported initially from the resources of its two sister battalions in order to meet even that small commitment. When Australia agreed to American requests to increase the size of its forces in Korea, 1 RAR was prepared for active service. 1 RAR served in Korea from March 1952 to March 1953, and was then replaced by 2 RAR. 3 RAR served continuously in Korea from September 1950 until the cease-fire, and its members were relieved in groups. In this way a force of two battalions was maintained from a pool of only three.

The British always relieved on a unit basis, but the composition of their forces was the most diverse of all, being made up of regulars, National Servicemen, and recalled reservists. The British were the largest single contingent in Korea after the Americans and the Koreans themselves, and they were also the most hard-pressed for manpower because of the range of their overseas commitments. At the outbreak of the Korean War these included Germany, Malaya, Egypt, and Hong Kong, to which was added the Mau Mau rebellion in Kenya in 1952.

This manpower problem had faced the British from the beginning, and generally speaking it got worse, not better, the longer the war went on. Cassels brought it to the attention of the War Office even before the division was activated. Both the British battalions in the 28th Brigade, he advised, were

at terrible disadvantage owing to low strength which naturally hits rifle companies hardest. This is very much [an] Infantrymans battle and companies of reasonable strength are essential. Again I realise general shortage but urge most strongly that we be allowed to increase each Bn by 100 men or more if possible. This will make whole difference to their fighting value.[70]

He did not get them, and approximately eighteen months later his successor, West, wrote to the Adjutant-General in similar terms. British manpower deficiencies were now manifesting themselves not only among the infantry, but in the artillery and signals as well. Not only did this pose the sorts of difficulties for the British battalions that Cassels had noted earlier, but West was also placed

in the invidious position of having always to put either Canadian or Australian battalions into certain key localities (which are inevitably the more dangerous ones) simply because the British battalions are not strong enough. Another difficulty is that when a British battalion relieves an Australian or Canadian one it has too few men to fill the holes, and we have to alter the whole layout.[71]

West was supported in this by Bridgeford, who also wrote to the War Office on the subject. Cautioning the British authorities not to be misled by the static nature of operations, he went on to point out that the division had suffered 262 killed, wounded, and missing in the month of November alone and that, should this rate of casualties continue, 'you will agree [that] . . . the UK reinforcement situation will become extremely worrying.'[72]

On 1 November 1952 the two British artillery regiments in the division were 170 other ranks under strength and likely to remain so for several months, while the divisional signals regiment had been fifty men short ever since it had been formed. But the real problem still lay in the infantry battalions. The authorised strength for infantry units destined for Korea was set at War Establishment less ten percent, or 942 less ninety-two, giving a posted strength of 850. Of these, approximately sixty were always on leave, courses, hospitalised, and so on, leaving a frontline strength of around 790 men. This was often insufficient to man properly the localities allotted to them. In addition, by mid-1952 battalions were arriving in Korea anything up to 150 men under strength, and these deficiencies had to be made good out of the basic reinforcements held by BCFK in Japan. This meant in turn that the numbers available to replace normal wastage in units were much reduced, and created extra administrative problems with a considerable amount of 'rebadging'.[73] Crocker's reply to Bridgeford, however, was not hopeful. Stating himself appreciative of the points raised by both officers, he went on to advise that although the War Office was considering the possibility 'of raising establishment of Bns above the minus ten percent . . . I am very doubtful whether we will be able to do so.'[74]

There was clearly potential for strife in this situation. In December 1951 the Canadian brigade commander, Brigadier Rock-ingham, complained to the Canadian mission in Tokyo that his brigade was holding half the divisional front and providing far more than their share of engineering and transport services because their units were up to strength while the British were not.[75] Several months later the head of the British mission, Sir Esler Dening, reported to the Foreign Office that the Canadian Defence Minister, Brooke Claxton, had also complained about the employment of the brigade, and the attendant casualties.[76] Yet at the very time that these objections were being voiced, the British were engaged in attempts to further reduce their strength in Korea by withdrawing one battalion.

The opportunity appeared to present itself when Australia announced that it would despatch a second battalion to Korea. Bridgeford established that the American command, incredibly, had no objection to the proposed British action and in short order the Minister for Defence in London approved the proposal to withdraw the battalion.[77] It is easy to sympathise with the British in their predicament, for as Field Marshal Slim noted, 'we have not nearly enough infantry battalions and have had to accept gaps in Germany and the loss of a strategic reserve in this country' to meet the commitment in Korea.[78] But it seems remarkably short-sighted of the War Office to have imagined that they could avoid the political repercussions which would accompany such a move. And these were precisely the grounds on which the Foreign Office successfully opposed the decision. They pointed out that not only had the Minister for Defence, Lord Alexander, himself recently called for greater reserves in Korea, but that the British were about to support a UN resolution calling for additional forces for the UN Command. In such circumstances, 'we can hardly hope that the withdrawal of this battalion, without replacement, would escape notice.'[79]

And so the problem remained. Cassels had wanted to use the second Australian battalion as a floating reserve, since technically it was surplus in a nine battalion division. The Australian government insisted, however, that it be attached to the 28th Brigade, and the War Office had no choice but to agree.[80] But an excellent example of the desperate situation facing the War Office is provided by the preparation of the 1st Battalion, the Duke of Wellington's Regiment, for Korean service. This chronically understrength battalion had been ear-marked for service in Germany when it was directed to prepare for Korea instead. In order to make it up to something approximating the approved establishment it was necessary to cull drafts of regulars and national servicemen from the 1st York and Lancs and the 1st East Yorkshire regiments, thus further weakening units in Germany. In addition, the Army Council reduced the existing residual service rule from twelve months to nine, and altered the lower age limit for Korea from nineteen at the time of embarkation, to nineteen at the time of disembarkation, in an effort to spread thin resources even further. The ill-effects of these moves were recognised and regretfully accepted.[81]

It should not be thought from the foregoing that the British were the only Commonwealth member with problems in this area. The Canadians had difficulty maintaining the flow of men to the French-Canadian battalion of the R22eR, but this affected only one unit. The Australians had problems keeping up the supply of infantry subalterns to the battalions, and ended up posting officers from the artillery, engineers and signals corps to the battalion's anti-tank, pioneer and signals platoons respectively. They also recruited a large number of Englishmen, who saw service with 1 RAR, when they failed to attract enough recruits from domestic sources.[82] The New Zealand field regiment, being a specially raised force, had too few members with sufficient technical training in some of the more arcane arts of the gunner, and this deficiency was made up by posting a small number of Australian artillery officers to the regiment. (Offsetting this, however, was the number of New Zealander regulars from corps other than artillery who were attached to Australian units for experience.) But it was certainly the British who faced the most serious problems, and a fairly radical solution was finally adopted to alleviate the situation – KATCOM, or Korean Augmentation Troops Commonwealth.

This scheme was in fact based upon an American programme which had enjoyed mixed success, the Korean Augmentation to the US Army, or KATUSA. It was initially a response to the desperate manpower shortage confronting MacArthur in the early months of the war. Some of the US divisions received several hundred Koreans, while the 7th Division was 'augmented' by over 8600 Koreans only a few weeks before the division was to take part in Operation CHROMITE, the Inchon landings. On this occasion it was observed that some of these Koreans 'participated heroically and some of them disappeared at the first sign of danger. The great majority behaved just as any other troops with less than three weeks training would have – they just didn't know what was going on.'[83]

By mid-October 1950 over 26,000 Koreans had been incorporated into the US Army. To say that they had been integrated would be misleading, and the gradually easing manpower situation, coupled with general dissatisfaction at the Koreans' performance, led to widespread demands that no more be sent to US divisions. By March 1952 the number involved had dropped to a little over 9000. Two factors, however, conspired to revive the programme and increase confidence in it at the same time that the Commonwealth was looking to it as a solution for its own problems. Firstly, the Koreans came to recognise that their continued presence in American units, with their better rations, weaponry and equipment, depended upon their level of performance, and they began to improve. It should be recalled that the alternative was service in the ROK army, where private soldiers were not infrequently executed for minor disciplinary offences. The second factor was American unwillingness to continue taking heavy casualties. Increased numbers of Koreans in the front line meant that more Americans could be rotated out of combat. By May 1953 the number of Koreans in US units had increased to nearly 24,000.

The proposal to emulate the American scheme originated with Cassels, and was received somewhat hesitantly by the various governments.[84] There was some questioning of the practicability of the proposal within the Foreign Office, with the suggestion that a composite Korean company or battalion to serve within the division might be better suited to its needs.[85] On being advised by the Commonwealth Relations Office that it was a question of military requirements, although with some political implications, the Foreign Office merely requested the opportunity to comment 'at the appropriate stage'.[86]

The scheme envisaged the attachment of 100 Koreans to each infantry battalion, giving a total of 1000 for the division as a whole. As New Zealand had contributed a field artillery regiment, the NewZealand government not unreasonably wished to know on what basis the programme would be financed, as a charge against the Korean Operations Pool Account, or against the individual countries whose forces employed Koreans. The British, with bal-

General Mark W. Clark, Maj-Gen Cassels, and General J. Lawton Collins reviewing Commonwealth positions on the Jamestown Line, 1952

ance of payments difficulties, were also concerned to limit expenditure on the attachment scheme. The Australian Defence Committee resolved that expenditure by the British Commonwealth was to be limited to feeding, clothing and equipping the Koreans, with the costs to be charged to KOPA, on the basis that the force as a whole would benefit from the scheme. The British and New Zealanders agreed, although both expressed the hope that the ROK government would make a contribution to overall costs.[87]

Table 8.1 Estimated initial cost of the integration of KATCOMs

Item	£ per month
Rations	10,375
Clothing	9,079
Arms	213
Accommodation	905
Transport	281
Total	20,853

Source: Defence Committee Agenda 80/1953. CRS A5799.

Although the Canadian government and the Chief of the General Staff were in favour of the scheme, objections were voiced by Brigadier M.P. Bogert, by then in command of the 25th Brigade. He stressed the difficulties of language and 'national characteristics', and expressed concern over the 'grave danger of misunderstanding and a lack of homogeneity which would almost cerainly reduce the battle-worthiness and ultimately perhaps the reputation of Canadian units . . . I am not very strongly in favour of this scheme.'[88] It is worth noting that this lack of enthusiasm on the part of the Canadian soldiers in the field did not change. In a confidential briefing paper prepared after the cease-fire, the problems of language, discipline, administration, pay scales and so on were analysed, and the recommendation made that 'preferably . . . the attachment of KATCOMS to Canadian units [should] be ceased.'[89]

The Koreans were given sixteen weeks' basic training in American methods at the ROKA Replacement Training Centre before being posted to the Commonwealth Division. They were then given further training in British weapons before being distributed to the companies, two per section. Each British battalion received ninety-four Koreans, the Australians and Canadians 100 each, with thirty being attached to the divisional signals regiment, where they proved very adept as linesmen.[90] Following experience in American units, the New Zealanders requested that consideration be given to extending the use of Koreans to the artillery and other technical areas, but the war ended before anything could be done, although approval in principle had been given.[91]

Opinions about the value of the scheme differed. One commander of the 28th Brigade later recalled that the KATCOMS ensured that sections were always up to strength, while an Australian battalion commander noted that they 'undoubtedly became a useful addition to the under strength UK battalions but the RAR need for augmentation was nowhere near as great.'[92] The unfavourable Canadian assessment should not be overlooked. Overall, the scheme seems to have worked quite well, but since the Koreans did not begin to see service with the Commonwealth until March 1953, the system was only tested under active service conditions for a few months.

If the Commonwealth experienced difficulties in putting enough men in the field, there could be problems also in the provision of combat arms and supporting services, and this reflected the undesirability of being forced to rely upon the Americans for such things. This is particularly well illustrated by the growing need, by late 1952, for the provision of medium artillery within the division. Although superbly well served by the divisional field regiments, the growing sophistication of the Chinese artillery emphasised the need for an additional counter-battery capability that the 25 pounder field guns, because of range limiations, could not supply. The normal British practice was to group medium guns under corps or army command, whereas the American practice was to place an integral medium regiment within each division. In addition, in the last winter of the war there was a critical shortage of the necessary 155 mm artillery shell used by the American corps medium artillery. The results of these two shortages were operationally unacceptable.

Both West and Bridgeford made representations on the matter.[93] To rectify the situation meant an additional force commitment, and the various governments were unwilling of course to countenance this. Australia at this time had no regular medium artillery units. New Zealand was unable or unwilling to assist, and pointed out that on a population basis they were doing enough already. The

Canadian government, while fully appreciating the desirability of the proposal, was also unable to assist, citing the commitment in Germany as a factor in the decision. Eventually it was the British who provided a single battery of medium artillery from Hong Kong for service until the cease-fire in July.[94]

This episode consolidates the impression, if such were needed, of the appallingly run-down state of Commonwealth defences. Australia, which in 1945 had maintained six divisions in the field, had some trouble fielding two battalions in Korea. Canada, which had supplied most of the First Canadian Army to Montgomery's 21st Army Group, was now under strain with just two brigades overseas, only one of which was actually engaged with the enemy. It was the British, with the greater resources but far greater commitments, who had to make good the deficiencies, thus placing those resources under even greater stress. And it made the point, yet again, that if a government is not prepared to provide its forces with the necessary services and equipment, those forces must rely upon what their allies can spare and are prepared to give them.

Shortage of equipment was serious, but could be made up more often than not at the expense of other priorities. As was noted after the cease-fire, the Commonwealth division had often 'had more than their proportional share of any item or commodity in short supply'[95] through the generosity of Eighth Army. The most valuable element of all, trained manpower, was much more difficult to improvise. Guns could be taken from the Hong Kong garrison for Korean service and, although undesirable, without fatal consequences. The garrison itself could not be reduced below a given level without its ceasing to function, and this also held true for the forces on the Rhine or in the Middle East. The post-1945 run-down of the armies' stocks of equipment was short-sighted; the reduction of the armies' manpower to levels below which they were incapable of swift reaction in an emergency was the height of folly. It was a folly widely shared in the late 1940s.

Chapter nine
Finance and logistics

The Korean War was not a great conflict of national economies in the way that the two world wars had been. Indeed, a product of the insistence upon regarding the war as a United Nations 'police action' was the absence of any attempt to mobilize the economies of participating UN member states and place them on a war footing. This was not a total war for anybody except the Koreans themselves. In terms of international law it was not a war at all. This did not mean that economic questions were absent, however, merely that they took a somewhat different form from that of the Second World War.

During the Second World War the United States had operated the Lend-Lease scheme to help finance the war effort of the British Empire generally, and the United Kingdom specifically, following the British dollar crisis in 1940. There had been some mutual aid between the Dominions, but a comprehensive scheme of Empire mutual aid never eventuated largely because of the different economic and military situations which confronted each Dominion, and which proved irreconcilable.[1] A good example of the failure of mutual aid between the Dominions is provided by the attempts of the Australian government to establish bilateral military cooperation with Canada in early 1942. This took the form of an appeal both for Canadian troops to be sent to help in the defence of the Malay barrier and for equipment, since the traditional sources of supply in Britain of course had dried up.

The Canadian Prime Minister, Mackenzie King, rejected the troop request out of hand, and the Canadian government was not prepared to meet Australian orders for equipment, especially munitions, because this would have meant diverting production from British and American requirements in these areas, and the latter might then have placed their contracts elsewhere.[2] It was a convincing demonstration not only of the realities of alliance warfare but of the frailty of Imperial defence and Dominion solidarity.

The Lend-Lease scheme itself was terminated suddenly and without warning just two days after the Japanese surrender, on 17 August 1945. It was replaced by a cash reimbursable Lend-Lease scheme, in which material would continue to be supplied through the same channels, but on a strict cash basis. The scheme was to be financed by a thirty year loan at near commerical rates of interest, or by credits arranged through the American Export-Import Bank. This caused a considerable shock in some allied circles, for there had been an optimistic belief that the United States would agree to wipe clean the financial slate at the end of hostilites. Such a view took no account of the domestic pressures which faced President Truman in the Congress. Equally, however, the proposed thirty year loans were unrealistic and Britain, Australia and most other Lend-Lease recipients agreed to reject the offer.

Eventually, separate agreements were reached between the US and the contracting parties such as Britain and Australia. The latter did very well out of the agreement, because in terms of mutual aid Australia had furnished reverse Lend Lease to the value of approximately 70 per cent of the material provided to them by the United States.[3] Britain was granted a generous settlement of Lend Lease also, but the British economic situation was much more parlous. Britain was bankrupt, spending over £2000 million overseas in 1945 and earning only about £350 million, and with a war debt of US $20 billion. The British economy was to be rebuilt with American and Canadian loans, but the economic strategy upon which hopes of recovery rested soon collapsed as the result of a number of factors, not the least being inflationary government policies in the United States and the insistence by the Americans that sterling be made convertible. This latter move was proceeded with in July 1947 with disastrous results.[4]

Britain's only solution was to embark upon a further round of borrowing while attempting to shed or transfer as many overseas obligations as possible. Thus British support for the anti-communist struggle in Greece and Turkey was transferred to the Americans in 1947. A further round of financial sustenance, not merely for Britain but for western Europe as a whole, came with the

Marshall Plan. Much of this took the form of an outright gift, but some was on loan, and in the period 1948–51 Britain received some £681 million.[5] Thus even before the Korean War prompted a new, and expensive, round of rearmament the British economy was in crisis. Its dollar reserves were depleted, not least because of the rush on the currency following convertibility, and the balance of payments was critical.

Another post-war cost that the British dispensed with as quickly as decently possible was the participation in the occupation force in Japan. The British had hoped to derive some economic benefit from a role in the occupation, but American insistence on placing BCOF in isolated and largely rural prefectures in the south of Japan, and their blocking of British attempts to re-establish themselves in Osaka and Kobe, soon diminished whatever enthusiasm for the occupation there had been in Whitehall.[6] There were also disputes from time to time over the provisioning of the occupation force, with both Australia and New Zealand wishing to export agricultural surplus in this manner. In the end, most foodstuffs were supplied from Australia, and the Australians were also responsible for the shipment of supplies and equipment to BCOF.[7]

Costs for the occupation were pooled, and paid by the participating governments on a pro-rata basis. In keeping with the dominant role played by the Australians this pool account, as it was called, was set up and administerd by the Australian Treasury in Melbourne. The entire edifice was a highly complicated piece of acounting, but a little needs to be said of it because it became the model for the Korean Operations Pool Account (KOPA) which followed it, and which was the instrument through which the costs of Commonwealth involvement in the Korean War were eventually met.

The Australian Treasury rendered quarterly statements of expenses upon the participating governments. Such expenses did not include pay and allowances for the national forces concerned, and items of expenditure incurred exclusively by one force might not be adjustable through the pool account, but could be met in full by the government concerned. Just as there were debits against a country for expenses incurred, so adjustments were made to credit the account for equipment or services supplied by that government. When BCOF was eventually wound up, in 1952, the disposal of stores and equipment also led to adjustments in the accounts, with

Australia paying-out over £4½ million to the other three governments.

The expenses incurred, expressed as a percentage of the total BCOF establishment, are shown in table 9.1. The overall expenditure charged to the pool account during the life of BCOF was in excess of £21 million, broken down in the manner shown in table 9.2. The most notable features of the two tables are the predominance of Australian expenses, and the decline of the forces contributed by Britain and India after 1947.[8] Between the outbreak of the Korean War and the disbanding of BCOF, occupation costs were kept separate from costs incurred in Korea just as a distinction was drawn between the tasks of BCOF and BCFK.

Table 9.1 BCOF expenditure as a percentage of total establishment

Country	To 28.2.47	From 1.3.47	From 15.6.47	From 1.9.47	Subsequent to 20.3.48
Australia	31	37	39	59	75
Britain	32	26	27	26	6
India	24	23	24	–	–
New Zealand	13	14	10	15	19

Table 9.2 BCOF: Expenditure by member nations (£)

Country	Expenditure
Australia	14,416,348
Britain	2,829,027
India	3,031,541
New Zealand	892,197
Total	21,169,113

Although President Truman was the executive agent of the Security Council in carrying out United Nations' action in Korea, it was clear from the outset that the United States was not prepared to bear the cost of defeating Communist aggression alone, just as the Americans were not prepared to be the only UN member nation to commit troops. There was domestic political pressure for America's allies to support her in Korea, especially in view of American commitments to the defence of Western Europe through NATO and the generous provisions of the Marshall Plan. It was the sort of pressure that no president could withstand for long. Section seven of the 'Policy for Integration' dealt with accountability for logistic support rendered by American forces and outlined the procedures for reimbursement. It stated that reimbursement for logistic support

furnished to [the] Republic of Korea and other nations participating in the Korean operation will be effected at inter-governmental level except that British Commonwealth Occupation Force's accounts will be settled under present procedures. United States Army, Navy and Air Force will each maintain separate accounting for support furnished and will render reports through normal channels.[9]

The question of reimbursement and of military expenditure is closely related to the problems of supply and logistics, and a little should be said therefore about the overall logistic picture in Korea and about the situation specifically pertaining to Commonwealth forces before Commonwealth policies and decisions are examined. The financial aspects of the alliance may appear to affect operational considerations only indirectly, but some of those charged with their administration were also closely involved in operational questions. The issues raised here reflect the general pattern of relations within the Commonwealth, and between the Commonwealth and the Americans, at this time and clearly underscore many of the points already raised concerning other facets of the relationship.

The supply system which sustained the United Nations Command in Korea was slightly unusual. The 2nd Logistical Command had been established when American troops were committed to action in Korea. As the forces advanced and the supply lines lengthened, an army service area and forward supply points were organised. Since Korea was a theatre of operations, the next step would normally have been the establishment of a communications zone headquarters which would have assumed responsibility for rear area logistics. However General Matthew B. Ridgway, on assuming command of Eighth Army, had insisted that his responsibility should begin at the shoreline. His motivation presumably was to forestall interference by the Supreme Commander, MacArthur, but his decision meant that Eighth Army headquarters exercised control over the Korean railroad system, rear area security, civil affairs, prisoners of war, and the training of the ROK army. 2nd Logistical Command was responsible only for direct logistic support and was the primary requisition agency.[10]

This situation remained unchanged until the middle of 1952 when the chain of events surrounding the riots in the prison camps on Koje-do demonstrated clearly that Eighth Army could not conduct the war and run the rear areas at the same time. 2nd Logistical Command was replaced by a Communications Zone, with three new subordinate commands responsible for prisoners of war, civil assistance, and rear area administration. Although aimed primarily at resolving difficulties in prisoner of war administration, it also reformed and regularised practices at all levels of base area responsiblities.[11] Throughout the war there were three main supply lines in Korea, all of which entered the country through the southern port city of Pusan. The largest line serviced US forces and the bulk of the UN units attached to them. The other two were for the forces of the British Commonwealth and Republic of Korea. These latter two ran parallel to the main line, while Pusan was chosen as the main resupply point because it was the only deep-water port available, Inchon being subject to large tidal variations.

British Commonwealth forces generally used a mixture of British and American equipment and services. Most of the basic equipment was British, but the infantry units drew such items as flame-throwers and 3.5 inch rocket launchers (bazookas) from the American Army. All drew varying levels of support from American engineer, signal and medical services, and some rations were also supplied from US Army sources. Specialised equipment such as winter clothing was entirely drawn from the Americans, as were supplies of petrol, oil and lubricants. The contingent most heavily reliant upon the American supply system was the Canadian. As well as drawing the above items, the Canadians also required parts and services for their signals equipment, all of which was American, and ammunition and spare parts for their tanks, which were American Shermans rather than British Centurions. This greater reliance reflected their closer proximity to the United States, but it was to be a source of great difficulty in arriving at a common financial policy with the other Commonwealth governments, especially since Canada was not a member of the sterling area.

Canadian orientation towards the Americans was one consistent theme of fiscal arrangements during the Korean War. The other was the critical state of the British economy, and this was raised even before the first British troops had set foot in Korea. As early as the beginning of August 1950 the British government told the Australians that they did not wish 'to be committed to any system which might result in [the] accumulation of further sterling balances' in the area, and that therefore they were 'opposed to the setting up of a general fund which presumably would involve [the] Commonwealth in liability to contribute.'[12] If such a liability could not be avoided completely, however, it was considered desirable for British forces to rely upon the resources of BCOF since these at least remained within the sterling area and did not, therefore, involve a dollar commitment which would otherwise be the case if British forces relied upon the American supply line.

Events in the first six months of the war were confused, with a wider war brought about by the entry of the Chinese and a more extensive commitment than originally envisaged on the part of all Commonwealth governments concerned. With forces arriving in a piece-meal fashion, and with one 'expending bandages while . . . another is expending Centurion tanks and quantities of expensive ammunition', Robertson advised his government that 'the financial interests of each country [should] be assessed on a man/day basis at the end of the campaign and not each time a major change in strength is deemed to have taken place.'[13] An added bonus was that such a scheme would release combat units and 'heavily pressed depots' from the extensive paperwork necessary in any pool account arrangement.

Robertson was arguing for a capitation system of the kind which had worked well during the Second World War. Its great virtue was its simplicity. Presumably because of the integrated nature of the Commonwealth effort in Korea, it was decided to follow the example of the BCOF Pool Account and set up a Korean Operations Pool Account which, according to the report of the Australian Joint Administrative Planning Committee which recommended it, was 'a very simple account' requiring merely 'proper documentation of transactions.'[14] The Chief Finance Officer in the Australian Department of Defence drew attention to the fact that the integration of units would cause problems for a pool accounting system, and suggested that 'the practicability of a simple method of financial adjustment should be examined', but the Australian Chiefs of Staff decided otherwise.[15]

The implementation and administration of the Korean Operations Pool Account was carried out almost entirely at the service and departmental level, with little or no political direction from government. Thus the United Kingdom Army Council advised the Australians of their agreement to the financial plan,[16] while the Indian government's suggestion that the costs of its small, non-combatant medical unit should be settled directly was passed to the Defence Committee for consideration and agreement.[17] Only when there were serious difficulties did discussion even intermittently move to the governmental level, and it was this situation which occurred with the Canadians.

Initially there had appeared to be few problems. The draft financial plans had been circulated, to the agreement of the British and New Zealand authorities, while the Indians had reached an amicable and practical alternative. In July 1951 the War Office declared that it had no knowledge of the state of negotiations with Canada over the pool acount, but in August the Australian Department of External Affairs told the Commonwealth Relations Office in London that agreement had been reached with Canada 'on the official level', without indicating who or what this comprised.[18] At virtually the same time, however, headquarters in Japan was receiving complaints from the 1st Commonwealth Division in Korea that the Canadians' continuing refusal to join the pool account was making logistic administration difficult,[19] while the Canadians were also issuing separate terms of reference to their own lines of communication headquarters.

Clearly, Canadian agreement had simply been presumed and it was not until the end of 1951 that any Australian official thought it worthwhile to try and establish exactly what Canada's position was. On 3 December the Canadians replied that the financial plan was under consideration and that a reply would be forthcoming. At the same time the Director of the Canadian Army Budget, Colonel Purvis, made a visit to Commonwealth headquarters in Japan to discuss financial arrangements, although he left the clear impression that he was opposed to Canada joining the pool account because it did not provide a prompt means of settling Canada's liabilities.[20]

The Canadian reply, when it came, caused some consternation. Canadian military authorities had given the proposals careful consideration, but regretted 'that they [were] unable to participate in pooling arrangements by your government.' They requested a simple capitation rate for settling costs within the Commonwealth, and reserved to themselves the right to deal directly with the Americans on the issue of reimbursement.[21]

This was the crux of the disagreement. On the one hand, Canada's objection was founded on the question of budgetary convenience, as Australian Treasury officials rightly assumed. On the other, it had a great deal to do with the Canadian desire to manage their own affairs free of the impositions of a joint Commonwealth position. They had not been enthusiastic about the formation of a Commonwealth force in the first place, and they accurately foresaw the delays in settlement that a pool accounting system would occasion, not least in the area of reimbursement of the Americans. They may have guessed also, although there is no direct evidence for it, that British economic difficulties might further delay settlement with the Americans. Given the process of Canadian readjustment away from Britain and towards the United States which had been going on since the 1920s, they undoubtedly viewed such an eventuality with dismay.

A compromise was eventually reached which enabled the Australian Treasury to incorporate the Canadians into the Pool Account while preserving for the Canadians their freedom of action in relation to the Americans.[22] On 28 May 1952 the Canadian High Commissioner in Canberra advised the Australian Treasury 'that the Canadian authorities are prepared to participate in the Commonwealth Korean Operations Pool Account'.[23] The terms of Canadian participation were not altogether welcome, for Canada was to have no restriction placed upon her with regard to dollar purchase from American sources, and it was felt that this would worsen the overall dollar position of the Commonwealth in the long term. It was equally, and wisely, recognised that Canada was unlikely to participate under any other terms.[24] As the Canadians themselves put it, 'if Canada wishes to incur expenditure and pay for it without debit to the Pool Account, it is their own concern.'[25] The break-down of costs expressed as percentages of the total is shown in table 9.3

During the course of the Korean War the United Nations Organisation made no attempt to distribute the costs between the participants. As a result, it was necessary for the United Nations

Table 9.3 KOPA: breakdown of charges

Country	Percentage
Britain	54.3
Canada	27.9
New Zealand	5.3
Australia	12.5

Note: Figures as at 31 December 1952.
Source: CRS A571, 53/652 Part 1.

Command, which in practice meant the Americans, to devise a basis for reimbursement by separate agreement between the country providing the logistic support and the country receiving it. Since most countries which contributed forces did not then maintain and resupply their units, the US Army had to make up these deficiencies. The Americans also supplied much logistic and administrative back-up, even to the otherwise relatively well-supplied Commonwealth forces. All of this was an expensive process.

It was also an administratively complex one, because most of the smaller UN contingents were intermingled with American units by virtue of the unit attachment system. Logistic support flowed into a common supply line, and this made it very difficult to determine exactly the amount of support received by any indidivual unit. For a variety of reasons a solution was not forthcoming quickly, although the Department of the Army in Washington had first issued directions on the subject on 29 June 1950, just four days after the war broke out.[26] In fact it was not until the (northern) summer of 1951 that a system of control and accounting was actually fully working. The delay was occasioned largely by conflict between the Department of the Army, Eighth Army in Korea, Far East Command headquarters in Tokyo, and the Department of Defense in Washington over what sort of information collection was required and whether the units in the field were actually able to provide it. On at least two occasions Eighth Army recommended a simple capitation system, but was over-ruled.

The adoption of a pool accounting system by the Commonwealth also complicated financial arrangements with the Americans, and not only because of Canadian disinclination to join. American authorities favoured bilateral agreements covering reimbursement with each participating government. But as the New Zealand government pointed out to its Australian counterpart when presented with the draft of such an agreement in early 1951,

these drafts, providing as they do for separate agreements between the United States of America and New Zealand . . . appear to be inconsistent with the principle of accounting embodied in an operations pool account. There would thus appear NO reason for separate and private arrangements between individual governments and the United States.

The Australian Defence Committee had already recorded similar reservations.[27]

In order to accommodate the United States over the question of reimbursement, the Defence Committee sought and obtained agreement for Australia to settle the cost of supplies and services on an actual basis on behalf of the pool account members. The costs would then be recovered by apportionment through KOPA.[28] Thus by adopting a pool account to cover the operations in Korea, the Commonwealth had not only created difficulties with the Canadians but had also ensured that the system of financial relations with the United States would be more complicated than was necessary, or perhaps desirable.

The greatest difficulties faced by the Commonwealth in this respect were caused not by the Canadians, however, who simply refused to be co-opted, but by the weakness of the British economic position. Britain had entered the Korean War in difficult economic circumstances, and the dollar cost to the sterling area of US maintenance and support now became the central question facing them and, by extension, the Australians charged with administering the pool account. Although seemingly of little interest, the issue in fact raised important questions about the Anglo-Dominion relationship and illustrated the drift in that relationship since the end of the Second World War, particularly with regard to Australia.

In a cable on 15 December 1951 addressed to all Commonwealth governments the British, citing a precarious dollar position, requested their agreement to indefinite postponement of the settlement of accounts with the United States. The occurred while the Secretary of the Australian Treasury, Dr Roland Wilson, was in London attending the Commonwealth Finance Ministers meeting, and it prompted a flurry of signal traffic between London and Canberra.

The Australian position was cabled to Wilson by a First Assistant Secretary, F.H. (later Sir Frederick) Wheeler. The latter noted what should have been evident from the beginning, that Commonwealth forces would have to make some use of US supply lines, that dollar liabilities would occur, and that efforts should be made to minimize them. He also stated that no thought had been given to evading such dollar liabilities, either by means of a US grant or through outright evasion. This was not high-mindedness on Wheeler's part, but reflected the relatively low level of expense incurred by Australia to that time, approximately three million dollars per year, and the fact that the sterling area dollar position had been stronger in the first half of 1951.

This had now altered, and Wheeler detected 'an element of panic' in the British Treasury. They had estimated a sterling area liability of fifty million dollars a year, which he dismissed as fanciful. Even if it were not, Wheeler wrote that he remained 'very hostile to the UK proposal for handling it. Up to the present Australia has a good record in meeting its overseas financial commitments punctually and we have always been careful to preserve that record in the United States and elsewhere.' At a time when Australia was seeking new loans in the United States, any suggestion of default was to be avoided, and the British suggestion that the US Department of Defense would not publicise such a failure to settle was naive in the extreme. Wilson was further cautioned to remember that the United Kingdom 'has in the past made a similar request to us with some embarrassing results'. This was a reminder of the negotiations over the winding-up of Lend-Lease, when the British had made an agreement with the United States over the disposal of machine tools behind Australia's back and in breach of prior agreement, leaving the Australian government to salvage what it could. In short, it was suggested that Wilson should take 'a fairly strong line'.[29]

Wilson did just this. British Treasury officials reiterated that they could not pay in dollars, and did not wish to pay in sterling since this might then be used by the Americans to meet their own expenses in the United Kingdom, thus occasioning an indirect dollar loss. Invoking sterling area solidarity, they requested cooperation in seeking such an indefinite deferment of negotiations. The Australians responded that the British should take the lead in seeking such postponement and that Australia was not necessarily averse to this, but that they were anxious not to jeopardise their own negotiations with the World Bank or put their own good financial record at risk.[30]

Had Wheeler and Wilson been aware that Whitehall was giving serious consideration to defaulting, the outcome probably would have been very different. At a meeting on 2 October 1951 the Mutual Aid Committee had resolved that if the Americans pursued the matter 'we should seek to avoid payment on the grounds of our general balance of payments difficulties.' This was followed by the extraordinary suggestion that 'we should also point out to the Americans the dangers of their discouraging joint United Nations operations of this kind in future if they insist on involving participants in severe dollar liabilities'.[31] Other voices in the Foreign Office pointed out that this was 'politically an impossible thing to say', but in May 1952 the Mutual Aid Committee was still arguing that Britain should 'admit liability but . . . argue on balance of payments grounds against settlement.'[32] The same minute went on to note that it was important 'that the Sterling Commonwealth should speak with one voice on this. The Australians are wobbly as they fear repercussions on their attempts to obtain a dollar loan. The C.R.O. will do their best to keep the Australians in line.'

Once again the British invoked 'Commonwealth unity' in an attempt to solve purely British problems, apparently regardless of any adverse affect this might have upon one or other Dominion. When the Americans again raised the issue of reimbursement in May and June 1952, the British representative stalled negotiations with the assistance of his Australian counterpart who had been so instructed by his government. Nothing in fact was resolved during the course of the war, although the Americans signed agreements with a number of other participating governments, such as the Dutch and South Africans, during 1952. It must be considered most unlikely that the Australians would have agreed to the British request had they known of the deliberations of the Mutual Aid Committee. Nor did the views of the latter change once the war was over. In early 1954 it was still being argued that '[t]he longer we leave this question in oblivion, the better for our balance of payments position now . . . I see no advantage (other than rather expensive tidiness) in awakening this sleeping dog . . . I would recommend that we leave well alone.'[33] The matter was not resolved until long after the cease-fire in Korea, not finally until

February 1964, in fact, after seven years of intermittent negotiations which had begun in 1957 following the final withdrawal of Commonwealth forces. The final settlement was well below the nervous projections of the British Treasury, and is shown in table 9.4.

Table 9.4 KOPA: Final settlement ($)

Country	Share of pool costs	Direct charge	Total
Britain	24,164,317	1,214,965	25,379,282
Canada	10,320,596	–	10,320,596
New Zealand	2,379,535	–	2,379,535
Australia	5,501,663	1,819,661	7,321,324
Total	42,366,111	3,034,626	45,400,737

Note: Direct charges were those costs for items drawn from US sources and directly applicable only to the country drawing them.
Source: 'Some notes on the Korean Operations Pool Account', DAK 1/10/1, NZA.

The financial administration of Commonwealth involvement in Korea is a large and complex subject, worthy of further study, and only a number of the more important aspects have been dealt with here. The war ended up costing the Commonwealth over £207 million.[34] Over and above the financial cost, the administration of the Korean Operations Pool Account and the conduct of negotiations with the United States raises several interesting points. The first of these is that a capitation system, such as had been widely used during the Second World War, would have saved everybody a great deal of trouble. For reasons that are not entirely clear neither the Commonwealth nor, generally, the Americans adopted this approach, although both were urged to do so from various quarters. The Canadians, on the other hand, insisted upon capitation in their dealings with the Americans and experienced no difficulties in so doing. There is undoubtedly a lesson here.

The delay in settling outstanding accounts with the Americans does not appear to have affected American-Commonwealth relations in any way. Indeed the figure finally arrived at in 1964 was rather less than half the original total of $102.34 million presented to Commonwealth officials in 1957. The United States would seem to have been quite prepared to accommodate its allies in this matter. This flexibility may have owed something to American desires at the time to convince Australia, New Zealand and Britain to fully support US intervention in Vietnam, but this cannot be proven at present.

Australia's management of the pool account arose almost by default, as a result of Australia's principal role in the occupation force in Japan. Like the appointment of an Australian to command that force, however, the Australian part in KOPA marked a departure from previous practice and further emphasised the drift in Anglo-Dominion relations. Canada had been charting a more independent financial course since, at least, the signing of the Halibut Fisheries Treaty with the United States in 1923.[35] The willingness of Australian officials like Wheeler and Wilson to put Australian interests ahead of Britain's, together with the seeking of large investment capital in the US, was a further sign of the realignment of Australia away from Britain. Such a development would have been unthinkable before the Second World War. In invoking 'Commonwealth unity' in a moment of purely British difficulty Whitehall demonstrated not only that nothing much had changed in its thinking, but that it still did not appreciate the extent of the changes in the Commonwealth relationship which had been wrought by its own failures in the Second World War and after. An area of Commonwealth participation in the Korean War that might appear to amount to little more than balance sheets and accounting ledgers can in fact be seen almost as a paradigm of Commonwealth relations at this time.

Chapter ten
Conclusion

The peace-talks at Panmunjom finally led to a cease-fire, although not to a peace treaty, on 27 July 1953. From an operational point of view there were three immediate tasks to be performed. These were the withdrawal of forces from both sides of the newly-declared demilitarised zone within 72 hours of the cease-fire, the construction and occupation of new post-armistice positions to the south of the Jamestown line, and supervision of the exchange of prisoners of war including the potential difficulties implicit in the decision not to repatriate forcibly POWs who did not wish to return to their own side.[1]

The immediate withdrawal southwards was hectic but uneventful. The defensive positions, erected with such skill over the almost two year period that the Commonwealth Division had held its section of the UN line, were demolished, while stores and equipment were removed in order to leave nothing of potential value to an enemy by no means trusted to keep the cease-fire agreement which he had just signed. Uncertainty concerning the Communist intentions led the Americans to insist that all governments with forces in the UNC should maintain those forces until it was clear that the terms negotiated at Panmunjom would be adhered to. The South Africans withdrew their fighter squadron during October 1953, but the other Commonwealth governments maintained their forces in Korea although all had reasons for wishing to terminate the involvement as quickly as possible. The governments concerned also agreed to maintain the Commonwealth nature of the forces in Korea, thus precluding any other unilateral withdrawals.[2]

India had withdrawn its medical unit from Korea, but this was because India was to provide the Custodial Force supervising the exchange of POWs as well as chairing the Neutral Nations

Repatriation Commission.[3] The requirement for field medical units
had largely disappeared with the cessation of hostilities, but the
Indians also felt that they could not provide the custodial force and
continue to contribute a unit to the forces of one of the belligerents,
even a non-combatant one.[4] The Indians in any case had held a
rather equivocal attitude towards their Korean involvement, going
so far as to state in mid-1952 that, although they had a unit in
Korea, they did not consider themselves associated with the operations there.[5]

The return of POWs to the UNC was conducted in two stages. The
return of some sick and injured prisoners, LITTLE SWITCH, had
been conducted between 20 April and 3 May, before the cease-fire in
fact. BIG SWITCH, the repatriation of the remaining prisoners, was
conducted between 5 August and 6 September. Over 22,000 Chinese
and North Koreans refused repatriation, compared with 359 soldiers
from the UNC. The latter comprised 325 South Koreans, twenty-
three Americans, and one Royal Marine. The break-down of
Commonwealth POWs may be followed in table 10.1.

Table 10.1 Commonwealth POWs – repatriates

Country	Little switch	Big switch	Total
United Kingdom	32	945	977
Canada	2	30	32
Australia	5	21	26
New Zealand	–	1	1
South Africa	1	8	9

Source: Hermes, *Truce Tent and Fighting Front*, 514.

The United States' government would not agree to any reduction
in forces until August 1954.[6] In September of that year the JCS
agreed to a plan for the gradual reduction of Commonwealth forces
in line with the American announcement that their own commitment to Korea was to be reduced from six divisions to two. The
Commonwealth Division was reduced to a Commonwealth Brigade
Group, and from May 1956 until final withdrawal in August 1957
to a Commonwealth Contingent which was little more than an
expanded battalion. This latter unit was largely supplied by the

British with small admixtures of troops from the other three governments.[7]

Commonwealth experience in the Korean War confirmed the alterations in Commonwealth relations suggested by developments during the Second World War and in the immediate post-war period. Britain emerged from that war victorious but exhausted, lacking the means to maintain a world empire and thus retain great power status, but as yet unaware of the fact. The old Dominions emerged with their status and capabilities enhanced. The circumstances and needs of each Dominion continued to differ as they had done before the war. And just as during the war no common Dominion position developed on anything, least of all the question of defence cooperation, so the situation remained unchanged in the early post-war years.

Proposals for the strengthening of defence cooperation in the period 1945–50 foundered on the same sorts of objections that had greeted such proposals in the lead-up to the Second World War. At the last Imperial Conference, in 1937, British attempts to impose a common front were defeated by

the incompatibility of British preponderance, dominion autonomy, and Commonwealth unity in international affairs. The discussions in 1937 once more demonstrated that the diversity of external interests and of internal problems (and particularly those of nation-building in the young dominion societies) continued to defy any working definition of mutual responsibilities or a lasting disentanglement of policies.[8]

Commonwealth unity at the 1937 Conference was a myth, albeit one carefully fostered by the British Prime Minister, Neville Chamberlain. He recognised that the partnership with the Dominions raised Britain 'from the status of a fourth-rate power to the heart of an Empire which stands in the front of all the powers of the world.'[9] To maintain this position he withheld essential information from Dominion delegates while assuming responsibility for the direction of policy, and thus relegated the Dominions to a role of passive acceptance of that policy. This generally set the tone for the conduct of Commonwealth affairs during the Second World War.

This state of affairs was not to last forever, and even as the Second World War was entering its final phases the facade of Commonwealth unity was beginning to crack. Mackenzie King's

opposition to the centralising of Commonwealth defence cooperation had been mirrored earlier in 1944 by the signing of the Anzac
Pact, or Canberra Treaty, in which Australia and New Zealand had
stated their position on the defence of the South-West and South
Pacific areas. Domestic critics of the agreement charged that the pact
weakened the Imperial connection, the Americans that it indicated an
isolationist tendency, the British that it was presumptuous.[10] What
particularly disconcerted the British and Americans, however, was
the statement that decisions regarding the settlement of territory in
the Pacific should not be made without Australian and New Zealand
agreement. This indicated that Australia, in particular, was
determined to be accorded the status of a principal belligerent of the
Japanese, with all that flowed from that.

This development led naturally to the events surrounding the
creation of the Commonwealth occupation force for Japan. If the
Australian Labor government had expected generous consideration
of its Pacific aspirations from its British Labour counterpart,
however, it was quickly disabused of the notion. Britain had not
abdicated an Imperial role in the Far East, and the projection of a
military presence east of Suez was an obsession common to British
administrations, Conservative and Labour alike, until the mid
1960s. The message was clear, and vindicated Mackenzie King's
stance; defence cooperation was to be on British terms and under
British direction. The centralising tendency of Whitehall which
discounted the interests of the Dominions continued to assert itself.

The experience in the Korean War demonstrated again this
conflict between Dominion aspirations and increasing independence in policy formulation, and the British desire to maintain their
status as a great power by drawing on the resources of the
Dominions in 'friendly cooperation' while at the same time arro-
gating to themselves the benefits which accrued from such association. The importance of Commonwealth cooperation was stressed,
but the primacy of British interests was served. 'The declining
British Empire had to cope with increasingly difficult Commonwealth affairs, while maintaining cordial relations with the US
without injuring British prestige. The former dominions . . . became
annoyingly assertive of their "independence" as "mature" sovereign states.'[11] It may be that the Korean War was the last occasion
on which this familiar pattern of Anglo-Dominion defence relations
was able to assert itself.

In the area of strategic policy British actions were dictated by a preoccupation with strengthening the special relationship with the United States. Thus, at the military level, the British government sought to influence the planning and conduct of operations through successful agitation for the appointment of Shoosmith as deputy chief of staff to Mark Clark's headquarters. Although reluctant to form the Commonwealth division because of the additional manpower commitment concomitant upon such a move, the decisions arrived at in Melbourne on 8 August 1950 were acted upon not, in the final analysis, because of the military logic of the proposition but because it was widely recognised that the formation of a balanced and identifiable Commonwealth division would both enhance the combat contribution already made and, as a result, find favour with the American supreme command and government circles in Washington. This merely reinforced the fact that, in any case, the initial commitment of combat forces in August 1950 was primarily a means of acquiring a status with the Americans in the process of supporting the United Nations to resist aggression in Korea. British annoyance at being beaten by the Australians in publicly announcing the commitment, and their subsequent insistence upon being the first physically to commit the troops, were both reflections of this aspect of the relationship.

The appointment of Air Vice Marshal Bouchier to MacArthur's staff can also be seen as part of this process. It fulfilled an additional function, however, in that it was designed to minimise the role of the Australian commander-in-chief in Japan, General Robertson. This deliberate confusing of the command system once again sprang from a belief, widespread in some British government circles, that command of British forces was not to be vested in Dominion officers. The prestige accruing from occupancy of the senior Commonwealth position went to the Australians, and the capable manner in which they exercised the non-operational control and administration of the forces in Korea and Japan strengthened Australia's claim to a principal role in Commonwealth affairs in the Asia-Pacific region. This did not match British desires or intentions, but the time was long past when they could simply ride roughshod over Dominion interests. It did not prevent them trying, especially during Robertson's period of command in 1950–51. His eventual replacement by the genial Bridgeford did nothing, however, to stop British efforts to enhance their own relationship with the Americans at the expense of any Commonwealth position.

Disharmony in command relations at this level was of an intra-Commonwealth nature, and generally did not extend to the Americans. At the operational level the opposite applied. With one or two exceptions which were quickly, and sometimes ruthlessly, dealt with in the interests of good relations, British and Dominion officers worked smoothly together. This process was assisted by the fact that successive British divisional commanders, Cassels and West, exercised command in a manner devoid of the condescension and superiority which too often had been a feature of Anglo-Dominion military relations in the past. Clearly, different considerations governed official attitudes at different levels. It was one thing to treat Robertson in a disdainful and even hostile manner in order to enhance British interests; at an operational level such attitudes might endanger men's lives, and the senior British officers sent to Korea, especially in the Commonwealth division, were selected for their ability to get on with their Dominion counterparts. Relations with American higher formations were much more strained, and in large part resulted from operating within a different national command structure. Satisfactory, if not always amicable, resolution came through the expedient of allowing the Commonwealth division much greater operational flexibility than would have been tolerated in its American counterparts. Whether this arrangement would have worked successfully under the stresses of, for example, a further major Chinese offensive like the ones of November 1950 or April 1951 is open to serious question, and the difficulties experienced by Coad and the 27th Brigade in late 1950-early 1951 further add to the doubt.

The combat performance of the ground forces was generally of a high order, but demonstrated that even with a common military system there was still potential for disagreement and friction. The poverty of post-war defence planning, both a symptom and a cause of the inability to construct a realistic common defence scheme after 1945, led to serious deficiencies in manpower and equipment. The provision of under-establishment British battalions forced West, unwillingly it must be said, to revert to the old habit of using Dominion units in 'fire-brigade' roles because the British units lacked the means to carry out important, and often additionally dangerous, tasks. Inability or unwillingness to meet equipment shortages highlighted the risks inherent in reliance or semi-dependence upon the major force in the theatre, in this case the

Americans. The difficulty experienced in the provision of medium artillery to the division in the last winter of the war courted operational penalties which should not have arisen in the first place. It illustrated once again, however, the disinclination of the parties concerned to incur additional commitments and expenditure in support of a Commonwealth position to which none were fully committed.

The supply of the forces caused much less difficulty than their financing. All the dominions had enjoyed closer dealings with the United States in the course of the Second World War, and the Canadians in particular continued along this path after 1945. Their insistence upon dealing bilaterally with Washington in the matter of reimbursement for logistic support illustrated this, as did their much greater reliance upon American equipment and supplies. British officials misled Dominion, and especially Australian, representatives as to their thinking and intentions in this area, and a problem which faced Britain only was once again shared by the Commonwealth as a whole. Britain's economic and dollar position was clearly serious, but the withholding of vital information concerning the deliberations of the Mutual Aid Committee was an abuse of Dominion cooperation which, had it gone further, might have jeopardised Australian loan negotiations with the Americans.

As Mackenzie King and others had stated, the principle behind the Commonwealth was, of necessity, one of non-coercive cooperation in the furtherance of mutual interests. Increasingly, however, the pattern of inter-allied affairs illustrated the conflict of interests, not their mutuality. Commonwealth participation in the Korean War might demonstrate the continuing ability of the Anglo-Dominion armies to operate successfully together, but at a level above that of combat operations it has to be doubted that such joint action represented the Dominions' best interests. And even in the operational sphere, frictions were revealed more sharply than before. It is for these reasons that the Korean War can be said to mark the beginning of the end of successful and realistic defence cooperation of a specifically and recognisably Commonwealth nature. And the breakdown of the Commonwealth ideal in defence would be mirrored gradually by the erosion of a Commonwealth emphasis in other areas, such as trade preference or the placing of investment capital.

Contemporaries were generally agreed upon the didactic value of the inter-allied experience in Korea. The American combat analyst and historian S.L.A. Marshall thought that the US Army 'would have been well-advised had this area . . . been subjected to intensive study throughout [the] Korean operations', since the problems of dealing with such a range of allies 'would arise in another Alliance operation in Europe'.[12] Another American officer observed that Korea

furnishes a great testing ground for inter-allied relationships, a problem we will continuously meet at all levels in any future war. These experiences and lessons gained and formed should be passed on as soon as possible . . . We certainly have many favourable instances of inter-allied cooperation in Korea. We have to depend on our allies – let us learn how now before it is too late.[13]

The Korean example has been studied occasionally, although not always in the positive manner that Marshall and others intended. Representatives of the ABCA armies have used the fact of their Korean involvement to underscore the alliance features of that agreement favourably on several occasions.[14] Warning the President and National Security Council against over-reliance upon the good intentions of allies in Vietnam in 1964, however, the Joint Chiefs of Staff stated that the Americans 'had NO significant support in Korea, other than verbal. Except for the South Koreans themselves, the US did essentially all the fighting, took all the casualties and paid all the bills.'[15]

Clearly there is some disagreement concerning the on-going value of the coalition experience in Korea. The recent pronouncements of the parties to the ABCA agreement would seem to indicate that the importance of the alliance in Korea lies in its demonstrating that the American and Commonwealth forces concerned have cooperated successfully in operations since 1945. This is a lesson with less than universal significance. Alternatively, the Korean War may be said to illustrate that the armies of the Commonwealth still possessed that higher degree of interchangeability and common understanding that made the Commonwealth Division a success and which has been demonstrated, in considerably more limited form, in subsequent engagements in Malaya and Borneo in the late 1950s and mid 1960s, and in the Rhodesian Monitoring Force in 1980. This too is of limited significance, since neither Canada, India nor South Africa were involved, and the fielding of a specifically Commonwealth force for combat operations in the future must be considered highly improbable.

Commonwealth involvement in Korea does demonstrate three things. Disagreements or lack of common purpose in matters of common defence will be reflected in the performance of the forces concerned. Lack of preparedness to meet an emergency will make the forces of the smaller partners in a coalition even more reliant upon the major force in a theatre, increasing the difficulties between the partners on the ground and with the potential for the dependent force to find itself operating on inadequate resources. If protracted, this may prove disastrous. Finally, even allied forces operating with the benefit of common doctrinal and organisational assumptions and a high level of standardisation will experience friction and disunity. In Korea the Commonwealth forces overcame or minimised these, not without difficulty.

The observation of the JCS in 1964, quoted above, was well wide of the mark. The forces contributed by the Commonwealth had made an important contribution over and above their diplomatic significance, and as demonstrated in chapter 9 considerable efforts were made in ensuring that, in their case at least, the Americans were not left to 'pay all the bills' resulting from their participation in the Korean War. Fighting in coalition makes the conduct of war infinitely more complex for the nations concerned, but fighting without allies is a luxury few can afford. However dismissive the JCS may have been, there is no doubt that the Americans were resentful and disappointed at the failure of the British to make even a token force contribution in support of American action in Indochina,[16] while the American pressure brought to bear upon Australia and New Zealand emphasised the political benefits which may accrue to the nation acting in concert in the field with its allies, however small those allies' contributions.[17]

Taken as a whole, Commonwealth military involvement in Korea was a success, if not a uniform one. Two recent analysts have noted that 'the closer national forces integrated into an allied force resemble each other in organisation, doctrine, and equipment, the less likely they are to experience major problems in interoperability. This should be a prime consideration . . .'[18] The units of the Commonwealth Division resembled each other to a greater degree than any other force in the United Nations Command. This did not prevent difficulties arising, although it may have been important in limiting those difficulties. As Commonwealth experience in Korea demonstrated, however, this is not of itself sufficient to ensure smooth operations however important a step it may be towards that goal.

Despite the wealth of historical experience concerning the perils and pitfalls of inter-allied operations, little systematic attention has been given to planning ahead for the exigencies of coalition warfare.[19] Even with a heavy and deliberate emphasis upon the fostering of mutual understanding between allied armies, as in NATO since 1975, experience suggests that the problems inherent in coalition warfare will never be eliminated. Given this, it must be wondered whether the forces in such an alliance will be capable of emulating the success of the Commonwealth when faced with operations instead of exercises. They are unlikely to better them.

Appendix 1
Composition of Commonwealth forces in Korea, 1950–1953

(Open ended date indicates that the unit concerned was still on active service in Korea at the end of 1953)

Infantry brigades

27th Commonwealth Infantry Brigade (27th Infantry Brigade to 30 September 1950)
HQ 27th Commonwealth Infantry Brigade, August 1950–April 1951
1st Battalion The Middlesex Regiment, August 1950–May 1951
1st Battalion The Argyll and Sutherland Highlanders, August 1950–April 1951
3rd Battalion The Royal Australian Regiment, September 1950–April 1951
2nd Battalion Princess Patricia's Canadian Light Infantry, December 1950–April 1951

28th Commonwealth Infantry Brigade

HQ 28th Commonwealth Infantry Brigade, April 1951–
3rd Battalion The Royal Australian Regiment, April 1951–
1st Battalion The King's Shropshire Light Infantry, May 1951–September 1952
1st Battalion The King's Own Scottish Borderers, April 1951–August 1952
2nd Battalion Princess Patricia's Canadian Light Infantry, April 1951–May 1951
1st Battalion The Royal Australian Regiment, March 1952–March 1953
1st Battalion The Royal Fusiliers, August 1952–August 1953

1st Battalion The Durham Light Infantry, September 1952–
September 1953
2nd Battalion The Royal Australian Regiment, March 1953–
1st Battalion The Essex Regiment, August 1953–
1st Battalion The Royal Warwickshire Regiment, September
1953–

29th British Infantry Brigade

HQ 29th British Infantry Brigade, November 1950–
1st Battalion The Royal Northumberland Fusiliers, November
1950–October 1951
1st Battalion The Gloucestershire Regiment, November 1950–
November 1951
1st Battalion The Royal Ulster Rifles, November 1950–October
1951
1st Battalion The Royal Norfolk Regiment, October 1951–
September 1952
1st Battalion The Leicestershire Regiment, October 1951–June
1952
1st Battalion The Welch Regiment, November 1951–November
1952
1st Battalion The Black Watch, June 1952–July 1953
1st Battalion The King's Regiment, September 1952–October 1953
1st Battalion The Duke of Wellington's Regiment, September
1952–October 1953
1st Battalion The Royal Scots, July 1953–
1st Battalion The King's Own Regiment, October 1953–
1st Battalion The North Staffordshire Regiment, November 1953–

25th Canadian Infantry Brigade

2nd Battalion Princess Patricia's Canadian Light Infantry, May
1951–November 1952
2nd Battalion The Royal Canadian Regiment, May 1951–April
1952
2nd Battalion Royal 22e Régiment, May 1951–April 1952
1st Battalion Princess Patricia's Canadian Light Infantry, October
1951–November 1952
1st Battalion The Royal Canadian Regiment, April 1952–March
1953

1st Battalion Royal 22e Régiment, April 1952–April 1953
3rd Battalion Princess Patricia's Canadian Light Infantry, October 1952–October 1953
3rd Battalion The Royal Canadian Regiment, March 1953–
3rd Battalion Royal 22e Régiment, Arpul 1953–
1st Battalion The Black Watch (Royal Highland Regiment) of Canada, October 1953–

Armoured units

8th King's Royal Irish Hussars, November 1950–December 1951
'C' Squadron, 7th Royal Tank Regiment, November 1950–October 1951
5th Royal Inniskilling Dragoon Guards, December 1951–December 1952
1st Royal Tank Regiment, December 1952–December 1953
5th Royal Tank Regiment, December 1953–
'C' Squadron, Lord Strathcona's Horse (Royal Canadians), May 1951–June 1952
'B' Squadron, Lord Strathcona's Horse (Royal Canadians), June 1952–May 1953
'A' Squadron, Lord Strathcona's Horse (Royal Canadians), December 1953–

Artillery units

45th Field Regiment, Royal Artillery, November 1950–November 1951
11th (Sphinx) Independent Light AA Battery, November 1950–October 1951
170th Independent Mortar Battery, Royal Artillery, November 1950–October 1951
14th Field Regiment, Royal Artillery, November 1951–December 1952
120th Light AA Battery, Royal Artillery, October 1951–December 1952
42nd Light AA Battery, Royal Artillery, November 1951–February 1952
(The above two units joined 61st Light Field Regiment)
61st Light Field Regiment, Royal Artillery, January 1952–

20th Field Regiment, Royal Artillery, December 1952–December 1953
42nd Field Regiment, Royal Artillery, December 1953–
16th Field Regiment, Royal New Zealand Artillery, December 1950–
2nd Regiment, Royal Canadian Horse Artillery, May 1951–May 1952
1st Regiment, Royal Canadian Horse Artillery, May 1952–April 1953
81st Field Regiment, Royal Canadian Artillery, April 1953–

Engineer units

55th Field Squadron, Royal Engineers, November 1950–July 1951
57th Canadian Independent Field Squadron, Royal Canadian Engineers, November 1950–July 1951
(the above units joined 28th Field Engineer Regiment in July 1951 upon the formation of 1 Commonwealth Division)
28th Field Engineer Regiment (integrated unit), July 1951–
64th Field Park Squadron (integrated unit), July 1951–

Medical units

60th (Para) Indian Field Ambulance, November 1950–August 1953
26th Field Ambulance, RAMC, December 1950–
No 25 Field Ambulance, RCAMC, May 1951–April 1952
No 25 Canadian Field Dressing Station, July 1951–
No 37 Field Ambulance, RCAMC, April 1952–May 1953
No 38 Field Ambulance, RCAMC, May 1953–

Notes

Records with the prefixes FO, WO, DO, CAB, and PREM are located in the Public Records Office, Kew. Records with the prefix CRS are located in the Australian Archives. The bibliography contains a full listing of the location of all material cited.

Introduction

1 The literature in this area, admittedly, is scanty. Material on the South African Air Force Squadron in Korea includes Colonel P.M.J. McGregor, 'The History of No 2 Squadron, SAAF, in the Korean War', *Military History Journal*, (Johannesburg), 4,3, June 1978, and material at AWM 114, 665/7/4. RAAF involvement is treated by Robert O'Neill, *Australia in the Korean War 1950–53*, volume II, *Combat Operations* Australian War Memorial, Canberra, 1985. Robert F. Futrell, *The United States Air Force in Korea 1950–1953*. Revised Edition, Office of Air Force History, Washington DC, 1983, has little to say on the role and problems of attached UN air units. RAN activity may be followed in O'Neill, who sees the most significant problem as being the challenge of naval operations, especially blockade, in peninsular waters. See also 'The Royal New Zealand Navy in the Korean War', Navy Office, Wellington (no author, no date), Thor Thorgrimsson and E.C. Russell, *Canadian Naval Operations in Korean Waters 1950–1955*. Department of National Defence, Ottawa, 1965, and Ministry of Defence, *British Commonwealth Naval Operations, Korea, 1950–53*. Historical Branch (Naval), London, 1967. The last-named concedes that the system of command was the most important question facing the Commonwealth navies (279), but then glosses over any inter-allied problems and concerns itself entirely with technical and organisational aspects (280–3).

2 Field Marshal Lord Wavell, *Soldiers and Soldiering or Epithets of War*, Jonathan Cape, London, 1953, 22. The text of this lecture was delivered originally in 1936 to Trinity College, Cambridge.

3 Christopher Duffy, *Russia's Military Way to the West. Origins and Nature of Russian Military Power 1700–1800*, Routledge and Kegan Paul, London, 1985, xii.

4 David Fraser, *And We Shall Shock Them. The British Army in the*

Second World War, Hodder and Stoughton, London, 1983, ix–x.
5 *ibid.*

Chapter 1

1 Cecil Woodham-Smith, *The Reason Why.* Penguin, Harmondsworth, 1973, 162.
2 Clausewitz, *On War,* Princeton University Press, Princeton, 1976, 596.
3 For example, the disagreememt over the deployment of the British 2nd Army in October 1918. John Terraine, *To Win a War, 1918. The Year of Victory,* Sidgwick and Jackson, London, 1978, 225–6.
4 B. Franklin Cooling and John A. Hixson, *Combined Operations in Peace and War,* United States Army Military History Institute, Carlisle, 1982, 96–123, 180–87.
5 Bill Gammage, *The Broken Years. Australian Soldiers in the Great War,* Penguin, Ringwood, 1975, 85–7, 208–9.
6 D. Cameron Watt, *Succeeding John Bull. America in Britain's Place 1900–1975,* Cambridge University Press, Cambridge, 1984, 52–3.
7 Fraser, *And We Shall Shock Them,* 26–7.
8 Paul Kennedy, 'Military Coalitions and Coalition Warfare over the past century', in Keith Neilson and Roy A. Prete (eds), *Coalition Warfare. An Uneasy Accord,* Wilfred Laurier University Press, Waterloo, 1983, 11.
9 Cooling and Hixson, *Combined Operations in Peace and War,* 68.
10 Montgomery of Alamein, *The Memoirs of Field Marshal Montgomery,* Collins, London, 1960, 56–7. '[F]rom the point of view of command and control of the forces available in France in May 1940, the battle was really almost lost before it began.'
11 Of the evacuation, however, Major-General Sir Edward Spears could write that 'if we were in such dire jeopardy, it was due to colossal French incompetence and, steeped as I was in French atmosphere, I knew that in French eyes we only came into the picture in so far as we could help France . . . [we] ought not to sacrifice our chance of survival to the French, who certainly would not do so for us.' Major-General Sir Edward Spears, *Assignment to Catastrophe,* Reprint Society, London, 1956, 301.
12 Basil Karslake, *1940. The Last Act. The Story of the British Forces in France after Dunkirk,* Leo Cooper, London, 1979, 142.
13 David Dilks, 'The Unnecessary War? Military Advice and Foreign Policy in Great Britain, 1931–1939', in Adrian Preston (ed), *General Staffs and Diplomacy before the Second World War,* Croom Helm, London, 1978, 107–8; Donald Cameron Watt, *Too Serious a Business. European armed forces and the approach of the Second World War,* Temple Smith, London, 1975, 81, 103–30 passim.
14 Fraser, *And We Shall Shock Them,* 26–7.
15 Kennedy, 'Military Coalitions', 13.
16 The so-called 'Color' Plans. Louis Morton. 'Germany First: The Basic Concept of Allied Strategy in World War II', in Kent Roberts

Greenfield (ed), *Command Decisions,* Office of the Chief of Military History, Washington DC, 1960, 12–18.

17 *ibid.,* 19–20.

18 Maurice Matloff and Edwin M. Snell, *Strategic Planning for Coalition Warfare 1941–1942. United States Army in World War II.* Office of the Chief of Military History, Washington DC, 1953, 4–8.

19 *ibid.,* 12–13.

20 Morton, 'Germany First', 31.

21 *ibid.,* 35

22 Richard M. Leighton, 'OVERLORD versus the Mediterranean at the Cairo-Tehran Conferences', in Greenfield, *Command Decisions,* 255–6.

23 Richard M. Leighton, 'OVERLORD Revisited: An Interpretation of American Strategy in the European War, 1942–1944', *American Historical Review,* LXVIII, 4, July 1963, 923. Matloff, however, holds to this view. Maurice Matloff, *Strategic Planning for Coalition Warfare 1943–1944,* Office of the Chief of Military History, Washington DC, 1959, 262. 'The British position merely confirmed the suspicion that the British goal was increased emphasis on the Mediterranean and that the OVERLORD pattern would be upset.'

24 Leighton, 'OVERLORD Revisited', 936–7.

25 Christopher Thorne, *Allies of a Kind. the United States, Britain, and the War Against Japan. 1941–1945,* Oxford University Press, New York, 1978, 520–1.

26 The most lurid and extreme treatment of this is David Irving, *The War Between the Generals. Inside the Allied High Command,* Allen Lane, London, 1981. For a more scholarly work see Russell Weigley, *Eisenhower's Lieutenants. The Campaigns of France and Germany 1944–45.* Sidgwick and Jackson, London, 1981.

27 Peter Calvocoressi, *The British Experience 1945–75,* Penguin, Harmondsworth, 1979, 209–10.

28 Richard A. Preston, *Canada and 'Imperial Defense'. A study of the origins of the British Commonwealth's defense organisation, 1867–1919,* Duke University Press, Durham, 1967, vii.

29 Lieutenant-Colonel H.D.G. Crerar, 'The Development of Closer Relations Between the Military Forces of the Empire', *Journal of the Royal United Service Institution,* LXXI, August 1926, 443. Crerar's three factors closely resemble the modern US Army doctrine of RSI – Rationalisation, Standardisation, Interoperability – which currently dictate the American approach to inter-allied relations in NATO and elsewhere.

30 Ian McNeill, 'General Sir John Wilton: A Commander for his Time', in D.M. Horner (ed), *The Commanders, Australian Military Leadership in the Twentieth Century,* George Allen and Unwin, Sydney, 1984, 318–9.

31 A system begun in 1885. Preston, *Canada and 'Imperial Defense',* 165.

32 Colonel J.E. Lee, *Duntroon, The Royal Military College of Australia 1911–1946,* Australian War Memorial, Canberra, 1952, 181–4.

33 Crerar, 446.

34 Richard A. Preston, 'The Military Structure of the Old Commonwealth', *International Journal,* XVII, 2 Spring 1962, 107, 114. A third college was

set up at Haifa during the war to cater for the needs of Middle East Command.

35 John McCarthy, *Australia and Imperial Defence, 1918–39. A Study in Air and Sea Power,* University of Queensland Press, St Lucia, 1976, 66. 'It had a doubtful application to Australian defence.'

36 Robin Higham, *The Military Intellectuals in Britain: 1918–1939,* Rutgers University Press, New Brunswick, 1966, 25. On the same page, however, he concedes that 'relatively little is known about what took place in the staff colleges.' This remains the case.

37 *ibid.,* 29–31.

38 D.M. Horner, *High Command, Australia and Allied Strategy 1939–1945,* George Allen and Unwin, Sydney, 1982, 6.

39 S.F. Rowell, *Full Circle,* Melbourne University Press, Melbourne, 1974, 27; Horner, *ibid.,* 5.

40 Preston, 'The Military Structure', 114.

41 Northcott Papers, MSS 1431/26, 1431/28, Mitchell Library.

42 McCarthy, 133.

43 Horner, *High Command,* 5–6.

44 Preston, 'The Military Structure', 117.

45 Kenneth Taylor, 'The Challenge of the Eighties: World War II from a New Perspective – The Hong Kong Case', Timothy Travers and Christon Archer, *Men at War,* Precedent, Chicago, 1982, 197–212.

46 Horner, *High Command,* 322–6.

47 Nicholas Mansergh, *The Commonwealth Experience,* Weidenfeld and Nicolson, London, 1969, 384–5.

48 Visit of Churchill to Washington and Ottawa 1952–3. RG25, B3. vol 2124, file U-1/2–20–1, Public Archives of Canada (PAC). Churchill 'picked up a remark by Mr Wooton in introducing him to the effect that a union between the might of the United States and the prestige of Great Britain was unconquerable, and went on to demonstrate that Britain still had a share of might to throw into the common pool. In doing so, he added, as he has done so often before, the white population of other members of the Commonwealth to that of the United Kingdom in order to arrive at a total of over 70 millions. He will certainly continue to talk and think of the older Commonwealth members as sure to be united in action against danger in any circumstances.'

49 Robert O'Neill, *Australian in the Korean War 1950–53,* volume 1. *Strategy and Diplomacy,* Australian War Memorial, Canberra, 1981, 39.

50 *ibid.,* 205–8.

52 *ibid.,* 209 n.

53 *ibid.,* 218–23.

54 T.B. Millar, *Australia in Peace and War,* Australian National University Press, Canberra, 1978, 176.

55 Preston, 'The Military Structure of the Old Commonwealth', 104–6; Lieutenant General Sir Sydney Rowell has an account of the first meeting of the revived Imperial General Staff under Montgomery in 1946. Rowell, *Full Circle,* 164.

56 This was the precursor of the ABCA (America, Britain, Canada,
    Australia) programme. Australia was admitted in 1964, and New
    Zealand was granted associate status in 1965. This programme
    remains the basic standardisation agreement between the armies
    involved.

Chapter 2

1 Peter Lowe, *The Origins of the Korean War*, Longman, London,
   1986, 5.
2 *ibid.*, 8–9.
3 Gavan McCormack, *Cold War Hot War. An Australian Perspective
   on the Korean War*, Hale and Iremonger, Sydney, 1983; Karunakar
   Gupta, 'How did the Korean War Begin?', *China Quarterly*, 52, 1972,
   and replies 54, 1973; critique of McCormack by Colonel F.S.B.
   Peach, *Defence Force Journal*, 82, January–February 1986, and
   McCormack's reply, *DFJ*, 86, July–August 1986. British left-wing
   writer Jon Halliday also favours a variation on this argument, Bruce
   Cumings (ed), *Child of Conflict. The Korean-American Relationship,
   1943–1953*, University of Washington Press, Seattle, 1983, 163–8.
4 Cumings, *Child of Conflict*, 40–1.
5 James F. Schnabel, *Policy and Direction: The First Year*, US Army in
   the Korean War, Office of the Chief of Military History, Washington
   DC, 1972, 77–9.
6 Robert O'Neill, 'The Chongchon River', Noble Frankland and
   Christopher Dowling (eds), *Decisive Battles of the Twentieth
   Century*, Sidgwick and Jackson, London, 1976, 295.
7 *ibid.*, 290.
8 Schnabel, *Policy and Direction*, 103.
9 'Policy for Integration of Forces into the United Nations Command',
   n.d. AWM 114, 665/5/5.
10 Hixson and Cooling, *Combined Operations in Peace and War*, 239.
11 *ibid.*, 243.
12 Memorandum to all divisional commanders, 13 January 1951.
   Matthew B. Ridgway Papers, Eighth Army correspondence, December 1950–April 1951, box 17. Ridgway papers, USAMHI.
13 Ridgway, oral history interview by Elton and Carfield, 15–16.
   Ridgway papers, USAMHI.
14 Major General George C. Stewart, letter to the author, 8 August
   1984.
15 Correspondence between Ridgway, Van Fleet, and Major General
   Robert N. Young, commanding 2nd Infantry division, 22–26 October
   1951. CINCFE correspondence, box 19, Ridgway papers, USAMHI;
   see also Freeman oral history, 105–6, Paul L. Freeman papers,
   USAMHI. Major General George C. Stewart, letter to the author, 8
   August 1984. 'On at least one occasion [the French] fixed bayonets
   and charged a heavily fortified hill without waiting for the artillery to
   complete its work.'

16 Report, Bouchier to Chiefs of Staff, London, 3 March 1951. FO371/
92731.
17 Gaziano, *Problems in Utilization*, 13.

Chapter 3

1 Cipher message, Robertson to Minister for Defence, 7 July 1950. CRS
A5954, Box 1661, file 1.
2 Internal minute, Commonwealth Relations Office, 3 July 1950. FO371/
84088. An anonymous hand appended the observation that 'even the
Americans no longer have any illusions about the fighting qualities of
Nationalist forces, so perhaps the question will not arise.'
3 Letter, Office of the United Kingdom High Commissioner, Canberra, to
the Australian Government, 5 July 1950. CRS A462, 443/1/8 Pt 1.
4 Cipher message, Canadian Joint Staff, London, to Chiefs of Staff
Committee, Ottawa, 7 July 1950. 50069–A–40, volume 3, Historical
Section, Department of External Affairs (DEA).
5 Memorandum, Foreign Office to Secretary of State, 11 July 1950.
FO371/84091.
6 Robert O'Neill, *Strategy and Diplomacy*, 62–95, 185–200. Spender had
written to Menzies on 17 July 1950, in a phrase now famous, that 'from
Australia's long-term point of view any additional aid we can give to the
United States now, small though it may be, will repay us in the future one
hundred-fold'. CRS A462, 443/1/8 Pt 1.
7 Cable, London to Department of External Affairs, Canberra, 18 July
1950. CRS A5954, Box 1661, file 1.
8 Chiefs of Staff Committee minutes, 18 July 1950. 50069–A–40, volume
5, DEA.
9 Cable, Australian High Commission, Ottawa, to Department of External
Affairs, Canberra, 20 July 1950. CRS A1838/T184, 3123/7/7.
10 Telegram, Canadian High Commissioner, Wellington to Secretary of
State for External Affairs, Ottawa, 19 July 1950. 50069–A–40, volume 5,
DEA. The New Zealanders cited Canadian refusal to participate in the
occupation of Japan and the Berlin airlift as evidence that Canada was
becoming 'isolationist, except in the Atlantic area'.
11 Minute, DDMO(A) to CIGS, 20 July 1950. WO216/712; Minute,
Foreign Office to Prime Minister, 20 July 1950. FO371/84089.
12 Letter, Ritchie, Washington to Slim, London, 20 July 1950. WO216/712.
'It is perhaps a good lesson for them in general, for they are not used to
going backward at the beginning of a war, as we have always been brought
up to assume will almost inevitably happen when Britain takes the field!'
13 Cablegram, Australian Embassy, Washington to Department of External
Affairs, Canberra, 13 July 1950. CRS A5954, box 1661, file 2.
14 See, for example, minute of meeting between Foreign Office and officials
of US Embassy, London, 21 July 1950. FO371/84091.
15 CRS A2107, K1.07.
16 O'Neill, *Strategy and Diplomacy*, 72–6. The British were not pleased by
this turn of events, and were well aware that Spender was the principal

architect. See telegram, UK High Commission, Canberra to Ministry of Defence, London 27 July 1950. FO371/84150.

17 I.C. McGibbon, 'New Zealand and the Korean War', unpublished paper delivered to the Pacific Coast Branch of the American Historical Association's 79th Annual Meeting, Hawaii, August 1986, 28–9. Copy courtesy of the author.

18 Cable, Australian High Commission, Wellington to Department of External Affairs, Canberra, 24 July 1950. CRS A1838/T184, 3123/7/7.

19 Mansergh, *The Commonwealth Experience*, Weidenfeld and Nicolson, London, 1969, 218–20.

20 Minutes of the Chiefs of Staff Committee, 28 July 1950. 50069–A–40, volume 6, DEA.

21 Cable, Fadden, Canberra to Menzies, Washington, 27 July 1950. CRS A462, 443/1/8 Pt 1.

22 Cabinet submission 38, Fifth Menzies Ministry. CRS A4905/XMI; for Rowell's advocacy see CRS MP742, 100/1/22.

23 Robert Eaddy. New Zealand in the Korean War: The First Year. A Study of Official Government Policy. Unpublished Masters thesis, University of Otago, 1983, 84, n. 18. General Lord Freyberg, the Governor-General, was also critical of the government's policy. In a letter to Slim he wrote that in his opinion 'they should send an infantry brigade group to be incorporated in either a Commonwealth force or as part of a USA division. I am averse to the despatch of a small separate detached force. If a detached unit is sent it will be either lost completely or thrust into every bad situation that crops up.' Freyberg to Slim, 28 July 1950. WO216/820.

24 Kenneth O. Morgan, *Labour in Power 1945–1951*, Clarendon Press, Oxford, 1984, 65.

25 Minute, Directorate of Manpower Planning, 28 July 1950. WO216/344 and WO216/820.

26 WO216/344. A type C volunteer was one who gave a gentleman's agreement that he would extend his period of full-time national service by six months at the end of his eighteen months. A type K volunteer ceased to be a national serviceman upon commencement of his 18 month engagement. Both types were to be sent to Korea from the outset.

27 WO216/820.

28 A few of these men had been POWs in the Second World War, and one unfortunate was actually incarcerated by the Chinese in the same cave system where the Japanese had held him during his previous stint as a prisoner.

29 Telegram, Foreign Office to British delegation to United Nations, 29 July 1950. FO371/84159. On Rowell's thinking, see also cipher message, Rowell to Robertson, 3 August 1950. CRS A2107, K1.07. Part of this message has been censored by the Australian Archives.

30 Memorandum, no author, no recipient (Privy Council?), 1 August 1950. RG2 Privy Council Office, 18, Volume 146, D–19–21, volume 1, PAC.

31 Telegram, Canadian Department of External Affairs to Department of Defence, Melbourne, 7 August 1950. CRS A5954, box 1661.

Transcript of BBC news item, 8 August 1950. CRS A1838/T184, 3123/7/7. Canadian ambivalence to a Korean commitment is evident in St. Laurent's statement that the brigade would 'carry out Canada's obligation under the UN charter or the North Atlantic Pact.' It was possible, therefore, that the brigade, once raised, would be sent to Germany instead. This suggests that belief that the fighting in Korea might be a prelude to a Soviet assault in Europe was not confined to Washington.

32 Herbert Fairlie Wood, *Strange Battleground. The Operations in Korea and their Effects on the Defence policy of Canada*, Ministry of National Defence, Ottawa, 1966, 30.

33 Dennis Stairs, *The Diplomacy of Constraint: Canada, the Korean War and the United States*, University of Toronto Press, Toronto, 1974, 184–5. The figures for the same period in the Great War and the Second World War were 7 percent and 12 percent respectively.

34 Signal, Robertson to Rowell, 4 August 1950. CRS A5954, box 1661, file 2.

35 Signal, Robertson to Army Headquarters, Melbourne, 11 August 1950, CRS A5954, box 1661, file 2.

36 Letter, VCIGS to A/DMO, 13 August 1950, WO216/712.

37 Telegram, VCIGS to Harding, FARELF, 15 August 1950. Box 1, FELF (Korea) 1950/2. Material held by Ministry of Defence, London, 'although no final decision has yet been taken, you may assume that national service will be extended to two years with effect from 14 September.' I am grateful to General Sir Anthony Farrar-Hockley, official historian of Britain in the Korean War, for access to this material.

38 Cipher message, Lord Tedder, Washington to Chiefs of Staff, London, 16 August 1950, FO371/84159.

39 Minute, Directorate of Staff Duties to VCIGS, 21 August 1950. WO216/344.

40 Cipher message, Ministry of Defence, London to Bouchier, Tokyo, 22 August 1950. FO371/84160

41 Letter, Minister for the Army, Josiah Francis to R.G. Menzies, 20 September 1950. CRS A462, 443/1/8 Pt 1.

42 Minute, Adjutant-General to Secretary of State for War, 12 February 1951. WO32/14307.

43 Minute, no author, no recipient, n.d. (early 1951), 'Overseas Tours in Korea for Regulars'. WO32/1440.

44 Note, Slim to VCIGS, 29 March 1951. WO216/728.

45 Report, Bouchier to Chiefs of Staff, 23 March 1951. FO371/92734. 'This is the best position in which the American divisions have ever been.'

46 WO32/14307.

47 Rhodesia did offer 100 men for service in either Korea or Malaya. They were accepted for use 'in the Malayan Scouts'. Telegram Salisbury to CRO, 24 August 1950. FO371/84160.

Chapter 4

1 For the initial strength of the occupation forces in Japan, Lieutenant-General Robert L. Eichelberger, *Jungle Road to Tokyo*, Odhams, London, 1951, 270.

2 Published literature on BCOF is scant, in large measure due to the closure of British government records until 1984. See in particular Roger Buckley, *Occupation Diplomacy, Britain, the United States and Japan 1945–1952*, Cambridge University Press, Cambridge, 1982; Robert O'Neill, *Strategy and Diplomacy*, 32–3. Other than an account of the origins of the force in D.M. Horner, *High Command*, 410–33, the following deal with aspects of BCOF, mostly inadequately: F.C. Hutley, 'Our Occupation of Japan. A Memoir', *Quadrant*, January–February 1984, 19–25; Major-General R.N.L. Hopkins, 'History of the Australian Occupation in Japan, 1946–50', *Journal of the Royal Australian Historical Society*, XL, 1954, 93–116; Major J.M. Walsh, 'British Participation in the Occupation of Japan', *Army Quarterly*, October 1948, 72–81; Lt-Col F.J.C. Piggott, 'Occupying Japan', *Army Quarterly*, April 1947, 109–117. Of much greater value is Rajendra Singh, *Official History of the Indian Armed Forces in the Second World War, 1939–45. Post-War Occupation Forces: Japan and South-East Asia*, Combined Inter-Services Historical Section, Kanpur, 1958. Buckley's chapter, while good, only covers the force to the withdrawal of the British element in early 1947.

3 Horner, *High Command*, 420–1

4 *Ibid.*, 421

5 Buckley, *Occupation Diplomacy*, 89.

6 Morgan, *Labour in Power*, 194.

7 Buckley, *Occupation Diplomacy*, 92.

8 Ronald Hopkins, 'Lieutenant-General Sir Horace Robertson: Commander-in-Chief British Commonwealth Occupation Force', D.M. Horner (ed) *The Commanders*, 282–90. As with many senior Australian soldiers, there is no biography of Robertson.

9 O'Neill, *Strategy and Diplomacy*, 253; G.D. Solomon, *A Poor Sort of Memory*, Roebuck, Canberra, 1978, 84–5, also 37, 87; F. Kingsley Norris, *No Memory for Pain*, Heinemann, Sydney, 1970, 244.

10 Buckley, *Occupation Diplomacy*, 98.

11 Just how marginal to British thinking BCOF was is well illustrated in a recent article, in which all the manpower arguments are shown to have been couched in terms of requirements in the Middle East. Frank Myers, 'Conscription and the Politics of Military Strategy in the Attlee Government', *The Journal of Strategic Studies*, 7, 1, March 1984, 55–73.

12 New Zealand's role in the occupation can be followed in an excellent compilation of official documents. Robin Kay (ed), *Documents on New Zealand External Relations. Volume II. The Surrender and Occupation of Japan*, Government Printer, Wellington, 1982.

13 Robertson, History of BCOF, unpublished MS, 63.

14 *ibid.*, 40. For difficulties with Cowan, Major-General R.N.L. Hopkins, letter to the author, 3 June 1985.

15 Singh, *Post-War Occupation Forces*, 55

16 Roger Buckley, 'Working with MacArthur: Sir Alvery Gascoigne, UKLIM, and British Policy towards Occupied Japan, 1945–52', Ian Nish (ed), *Aspects of the Allied Occupation of Japan*, International Studies, 1986/4, 3.

17 Prime Minister Peter Fraser considered that BCOF served 'no sufficient purpose in Japan ... where the Australians rule the roost anyhow and ride roughshod over the members of the British Commonwealth force'. Buckley, *Occupation Diplomacy*, 237, n. 59. Gairdner later became a governor of Western Australia, and even in the 1970s was given to stating that the dominions could not govern their own affairs without guidance from Britain. Information from D.M. Horner.

18 Buckley, *Occupation Diplomacy*, 102.

19 Defence Committee Minute, 29 June 1950. CRS A2031; Chiefs of Staff Committee Minute, 3 July 1950. CRS A5954, Box 1659.

20 Defence Committee Agenda 1950/89. CRS A5799.

21 Signal, Commander-in-Chief, BCOF to Chiefs of Staff, Melbourne, 14 July 1950. See also Chiefs of Staff Committee minute, 10 July 1950. Both at CRS A5954, Box 1661, file 1.

22 Cipher message, Robertson to Chiefs of Staff, 17 July 1950. CRS A5954, Box 1661, file 2.

23 Signal, Robertson to Chiefs of Staff, 4 August 1950. CRS A5954, Box 1688, unnumbered file 'Assistance to United Nations in Korea'.

24 Letter, Gascoigne to Foreign Office, 14 July 1950. PREM 8/1175.

25 Minute, Foreign Office to Prime Minister, 20 July 1950. PREM 8/1175.

26 Robertson, untitled, unpublished MS, [operations in Korea], 16.

27 Signal, Robertson to CGS, Melbourne, 27 August 1950. CRS A5954, box 1661, file 2.

28 Cipher message, Robertson to CGS, Melbourne, 31 August 1950. CRS A5954, box 1661, file 2.

29 Cipher message, Rowell, Melbourne, to CIGS, 31 August 1950. CRS A5954, box 1661, file 2.

30 Cipher messages. CIGS to Rowell, 2 September and 3 September 1950. CRS A5954, box 1661, file 2.

31 Telegram, Bouchier, Tokyo to Ministry of Defence, London, 21 August 1950. FO371/84160.

32 Telegram, Gascoigne, Tokyo to Strang, London, 21 August 1950. FO371/84161. Gascoigne stated that he intended to stay clear of any brawl between the two. This did not prevent him from commenting on it in detail, and including Robertson's report that MacArthur's chief of staff, Major-General Ned Almond, had stated that he was prepared to risk heavy casualties among the British if they were rushed to Korea early 'because if they did more reinforcements would be made available.'

33 Minute, R.H. Scott to Sir Pierson Dixon and Sir William Strang, 19 October 1950. FO371/84108. Scott wrote that he doubted that MacArthur was always candid with Bouchier, and that he 'is not in my view the possessor of a very sound judgement and. . .lends himself too readily to echoing the General.' Bouchier's information was valuable to the Foreign Office, however, because SCAP refused military briefings to civilian members of the Liaison Missions.
34 Defence Committee Minute, 17 August 1950. CRS A2031, 137/1950.
35 'Report on visit to Japan and Korea by. . .Chairman,' Appendix 'A' to JAPC Report 4/1950. CRS A5954, box 1661, file 2.
36 Signal, Robertson to Chiefs of Staff, Melbourne, 12 September 1950. CRS A816, 19/323/15 Pt 3.
37 Minute, Rowell to Secretary, Defence Committee, 3 October 1950. CRS A5799, 50/107.
38 Signal, War Office to Army Headquarters, Melbourne, 24 October 1950. CRS A2107. K14.2.
39 Daily report, Bouchier to Chiefs of Staff, London, 10 October 1950. FO371/84069. 'Had dinner and chat with General Robertson last night. He is very happy about the new BCOF arrangements. . .'
40 Daily report, Bouchier to Chiefs of Staff, London, 24 October 1950. FO371/84070.
41 Defence Committee Minute, 13 October 1950. CRS A2031, 191/1950.
42 Minute, Chief Liaison Officer, United Kingdom Service Liaison Staff, to Department of Defence, Melbourne, 23 October 1950. CRS A5799, 50/148.
43 Defence Committee Minute, 26 October 1950. CRS A2031, 202/1950.
44 Telegram, Cassels, Melbourne to Ministry of Defence, London, 26 October 1950. FO371/84162.
45 *ibid.*
46 Letter, Sir Percival Liesching, Commonwealth Relations Office to E.J. Williams, United Kingdom High Commissioner, Canberra, 18 November 1950. FO371/84162. The CRO was particularly keen to get the High Commissioner's views on 'this tiresome business'.
47 Letter, Williams to Liesching, 29 November 1950. FO371/84162. 'I am afraid this indicates the degree of interest the Prime Minister had taken in the matter.'
48 *ibid.*
49 T.B. Millar, *Australia in Peace and War*, 175n.
50 Horner (ed), *The Commanders*, 293.

Chapter 5

1 Major-General William F. Dean, *General Dean's Story*, Weidenfeld and Nicolson, London, 1954, 8.
2 Major-General B.A. Coad, 'The Land Campaign in Korea', *The Journal of the Royal United Service Institution*, XCVII, 585, February 1952, 3–4.
3 Roy E. Appleman, *South to the Naktong, North to the Yalu, US Army in the Korean War*, Office of the Chief of Military History, Washington DC,

1960, 542–72. Of value also are Lynn Montrose and Captain Nicholas A. Canzona, *The Inchon-Seoul Operation, US Marine Operations in Korea*, Washington DC, 1955, and Robert Debs Heinl, Jr, *Victory at High Tide, The Inchon-Seoul Campaign*, Nautical and Aviation Publishing Company, Washington DC, Third Edition, 1979.

4   Brigadier B.A. Coad, 'Report on the Operations of 27 Bde, 29 Aug 50–31 Mar 51', 1–5., Coad Collection, Department of Documents, Imperial War Museum.

5   Accounts of this action can be followed in Coad, 'The Land Campaign in Korea' and 'Report on Operations', Brigadier C.N. Barclay, *The First Commonwealth Division*, Gale and Polden, Aldershot, 1954, 19–21, Tim Carew, *Korea. The Commonwealth at War*, Cassell, London, 1967, 79–95. Carew notes the withdrawal of the artillery, Barclay mentions their presence in support but not the fact of their withdrawal at a vital moment.

6   Coad, 'Report on Operations', 6.

7   Omar Bradley, quoted in Max Hastings, *Overlord, D-Day and the Battle for Normandy 1944*, Michael Joseph, London, 1984, 318. Hastings discusses this problem, solely in relation to Normandy, in 'The limits of air power', 312–24.

8   Richard H. Kohn and Joseph P. Harahan (eds), *Air Superiority in World War II and Korea*, USAF Warrior Studies, Washington DC, 1983, 66.

9   *ibid.*, 72.

10 Paul L. Freeman oral history, section 2, 13. Freeman papers, USAMHI. The description of tactical air current at the time ran as follows: If you want it, you can't get it; if you can get it, it can't find you; if it can find you, it can't identify the target, if it can identify the target, it can't hit it; but if it does hit the target, it doesn't do a great deal of damage anyway.

11 Frederick A. Bergerson, *The Army Gets an Air Force, Tactics of Insurgent Bureaucratic Politics*, Johns Hopkins Press, Baltimore, 1978, 29–38, 52–54.

12 War diary, 27th Brigade, 30 September 1950. WO281/709.

13 Cipher messages, Robertson to Chiefs of Staff, Melbourne, 6 October 1950 and 13 October 1950. CRS A5954, box 1659.

14 Headquarters, 27th British Commonwealth Brigade, situation report, 20 October 1950. CRS MP729/8, 36/431/54: 'the Brigade was finding it more and more difficult to get on the road and once on to stay on it.'

15 The Universal, or Bren gun, carrier was unpopular with the crews because the configuration of the vehicle requires the driver to sit at the very front of the carrier, with the engine at the rear. If the carrier went over a mine, the driver took the full force of the blast. Jeeps were more popular because it was believed that the engine block provided some cover.

16 War diary, 27th Brigade, 14 October 1950. WO281/709.

17 War diary, 1st Battalion, Argyll and Sutherland Highlanders, 5 December 1950. Ministry of Defence, London; Coad, 'Report on operations', 8; War diary, 27th Brigade, 27 and 29 November 1950.

'Again there were difficulties of insufficient transport and no supporting arms which factors were being constantly stressed to higher formations.

18 Signal, Coad to Robertson, 12 December 1950. CRS A2107, K1.05.

19 Signal, General Harding, FARELF, to Coad, 12 December 1950; Signal, Harding to Robertson, 12 December 1950 WO216/821.

20 Signal, Robertson to War Office, 17 December 1950. CRS A2107, K14.2.

21 Cipher message, British Commonwealth Forward Base, Korea [Britcom, Korea] to Robertson, 24 December 1950. CRS A2107, K2.05.

22 Cipher message, Robertson to Britcom, Korea, 26 December 1950. *ibid.* Robertson quickly conceded the point, noting that '27 bde has always been an improvisation' in any case and that he had full confidence in Coad and had 'never been perturbed by this situation.'

23 Note of interview, Major-General J.M. Rockingham and Colonel Herbert Fairlie Wood, official historian, March 1960, 112.3H1.001 (D13). Directorate of History, Department of National Defence (D HIST).

24 War Diary, 2 PPCLI, 6 January 1951, 7 January 1951 RG24, C17, box 18317, PAC.

25 Cable, Clutton, UK Liaison Mission, Tokyo to Shattock, Foreign Office, 19 December 1950. FO371/84162; Telegram, Arthur Menzies, Canadian Liaison Mission, Tokyo to Under-Secretary of State for External Affairs, Ottawa, 21 December 1950. 50069-B-40, vol 1 DEA.

26 Notes from interview, Rockingham and Wood, March 1960. 112.3H1.001 (D13), D HIST.

27 Report, Bouchier to Chiefs of Staff, 30 November 1950. FO371/84075. 'Great things are expected of this brigade'.

28 A good general account is Robert O'Neill, 'The Chongchon River', 289–303.

29 Professor B.H. Gandevia, letter to the author, 27 June 1985. The brigade war diary noted that 'No artillery or mortar fire could be used by 3 RAR as the positions of US Airborne troops were uncertain. 3 RAR was, however, shelled with a few rounds from the Airborne Regt.' Entry for 22 October 1950. WO281/709. Brigadier Coad noted the same incident in his report.

30 Coad, 'Report on operations', 19–20. See also 21–23. 'The A & SH were given no less than three different roles during the day, all of which were cancelled, which gives some idea of the confusion reigning at Corps HQ.'

31 War diary, 1st Battalion, the Middlesex Regiment, 30 November 1950. Ministry of Defence, London.

32 War diary, 27th Brigade, 30 November 1950. WO281/709.

33 Cable, T.W. Eckersley, Head of Australian Liaison Mission, Tokyo to Department of External Affairs, Canberra, 23 December 1950. CRS MP729/8, 49/431/245. See similar report, Eckersley to Canberra, 20 January 1951. *ibid.*

34 Telegram, Clutton to Foreign Office, 3 December 1950. FO371/
    84073. A Foreign Office official noted elsewhere that 'This is a
    realistic and sobering background against which to consider paper
    projects for an 'International UN Force' etc.' FO371/84152.
35 Report, Bouchier to Chiefs of Staff, 5 January 1951. FO371/92729.
36 Report, Spey, Singapore to Foreign Office, 26 January 1951, FO371/
    92729. The Report noted 'the increasing tendency of Tommy to
    despise his US opposite number, and to allow his feelings to show so
    plainly that they fan the ever-latent American conviction that all
    Britons high-hat them.'
37 Coad, 'Report on operations', 23, The brigade war diary entry for 2
    December noted that 'certain units are giving false information in
    order to extract from commands and staffs permission or even orders
    for premature and quite unjustified withdrawals. It was just this type
    of excitable dishonesty which caused some unnecessary and expensive
    withdrawals in France in 1940.'
38 Report, Major W.R.L. Turp, Military Attaché, Korea to War Office,
    19 February 1951. FO371/92733. See also signal, VCIGS to
    Harding, FARELF, 19 January 1951. WO216/833.
39 Report, Bouchier to Chiefs of Staff, 1 March 1951. FO371/92731.
40 Letter, Brigadier A.K. Ferguson, Tokyo to War Office, 12 March
    1951. WO216/728. See also letter, Major de Clermont, 8 Hussars,
    Korea to Canadian Ambassador, Ankara, 7 April 1951. 50069-A-40,
    vol 23, DEA.
41 Notes on an address by Lieutenant-Colonel J.R. Stone, 5 June 1951.
    681.011 (D3), D HIST.
42 Report, Bouchier to Chiefs of Staff, 23 March 1951. FO371/92734.
    For accounts of a typical relief operation mounted by 27th Brigade
    during this period see A. Argent, 'Armoured Operations in Korea.
    Task Force 'Crombez' at Chipyong-ni', *Australian Army Journal*, 35,
    April 1952, 5–9. Also Raymond T. Cassidy, 'Wonju and Chipyong-
    ni', *Infantry*, July-August 1983, 24–28.
43 Robert O'Neill, *Australia in the Korean War, 1950–53*. volume II.
    Combat Operations, Australian War Memorial, Canberra, 1985,
    131–160; Barclay, *The Commonwealth Division*, 58–70; Robert O.
    Holles, *Now Thrive the Armourers*, Harrap, London, 1952; General
    Sir Anthony Farrar-Hockley, *The Edge of the Sword*, W.H. Allen,
    London, 1981, 11–70; Carew, *Korea*, 173–230. O'Neill's must be
    judged the best account of Kapyong, while the definitive account of
    the Imjin battle will appear in the British official history by Farrar-
    Hockley, who took part in it.
44 War diary, 27th Brigade, 23 April 1951. WO281/710.
45 Carew, *Korea*, 222.
46 Ridgway, letter to the author, 21 March 1985.
47 Matthew B. Ridgway, *The Korean War*, Preface to the British Edition,
    London, 1968, xii.
48 Signal, Van Fleet to Ridgway, 11 May 1951. Box 19, CINCFE
    Correspondence, Jan 1951-June 1952. Ridgway papers, USAMHI.

49   Report on US Impressions of the British Army in Korea, 6 November
      1950. WO216/820. Of the Australian part in the battle for Yongyu,
      for example, Appleman wrote that 'they went into it with a dash that
      brought forth admiration from all who witnessed it.' Appleman,
      South to the Naktong, 660.
50   Johnson oral history, section III, 51. Harold K. Johnson Papers,
      USAMHI.
51   War diary, 27th Brigade, 24 April 1951. WO281/710.
52   Interview, Lieutenant-General Sir Richard Webb, Wellington, 16
      February 1984.
53   Fox, *Inter-Allied Cooperation During Combat Operations.*
54   Barclay, *The First Commonwealth Division,* 48.
55   Ridgway, *The Korean War,* 86–7; J. Lawton Collins. *War in
      Peacetime. The History and Lessons of Korea,* Houghton Mifflin,
      Boston, 1969, 240–1. Collins had made a number of visits to Korea
      on behalf of the JCS and therefore possessed first-hand knowledge of
      conditions. Unfortunately the volume of the official history series, *US
      Army in the Korean War,* dealing with the period from November
      1950 to June 1951, has still not been published.

Chapter 6

 1   Cablegram, New Zealand Government to Australian Department of
      External Affairs, Canberra, 17 July 1950. CRS A5954, Box 1661, file
      2.
 2   Cablegram, Menzies to Fadden, 31 July 1950. CRS A5954, Box
      1661, file 2.
 3   Defence Committee Minute, 1 August 1950. CRS A2031, 126/1950.
 4   Cablegram, Australian Government to New Zealand Government, 2
      August 1950. CRS A462. 443/1/8 Pt 1.
 5   Cablegram, Australian High Commissioner, Wellington, to Depart-
      ment of External Affairs, 2 August 1950. CRS A5954, Box 1661, file
      2. Cutler had won the Victoria Cross, and lost a leg, in Syria during
      the Second World War. He was later the longest-serving Governor of
      New South Wales.
 6   Cablegram, Fadden to Menzies, 10 August 1950. CRS A462, 443/1/8
      Pt 1.
 7   D.M. Horner, *High Command,* 425–33.
 8   Notes on discussion with CGS (Aust), CGS (NZ), CLO UKSLS,
      Melbourne, 8 August 1950. CRS A571, 57/1915.
 9   Robert Eaddy, New Zealand in the Korean War, 80.
10   Brigadier Sir Frederick Chilton, letter to the author, 23 January 1984.
11   Cablegram, Australian Government to Canadian Government, 8
      August 1950. CRS A5954, Box 1661, file 2.
12   CRS A5954, Box 1661, file 2. In a preliminary response to the
      Canadian document, one official of the Foreign Office expressed the
      view that the suggestion of incorporating the Turkish contingent into
      the Commonwealth force would cause 'difficulty with Australia and

New Zealand, on account of memories of Gallipoli'. Cable, Canadian High Commissioner, London, to Secretary of State for External Affairs, Ottawa, 28 August 1950. 112.3HI.009 (D66), D HIST.

13 Dennis Stairs, *The Diplomacy of Constraint,* 199; telegram, Secretary of State for External Affairs, Ottawa to Canadian High Commisioner, London, 24 August 1950. 112.3HI.009(D65), D HIST.

14 Cablegram, Prime Minister Attlee to Acting Prime Minister Fadden, 19 August 1950. CRS A5954, Box 1661, file 2.

15 Telegram, Secretary of State for Commonwealth Relations to High Commissioner for the United Kingdom, Canberra, 16 September 1950. CRS A5954, Box 1661, file 2.

16 United Kingdom aide memoire, 5 October 1950. CRS A5954, Box 1661, file 2. A copy of the document was provided to Menzies on 13 October. Air Vice Marshal Bouchier also though the addition of the Turks to the Commonwealth force would be a good idea. Report, Bouchier to Chiefs of Staff, 16 November 1950. FO371/84072.

17 Herbert Fairlie Wood, *Strange Battleground,* 44.

18 John English and Norman Hillmer, 'Canada's Alliances', *Revue Internationale d'Histoire Militaire,* No 51, Edition Canadienne, Ottawa, 1982, 38.

19 Kenneth Taylor, 'The Challenge of the Eighties', 198.

20 Lieutenant-General F.J. Fleury, letter to the author, 23 April 1984.

21 Telegram, Secretary, Department of Defence, Melbourne, to Department of External Affairs, Canberra, 3 November 1950. CRS A1838/T184, 3123/7/13. It is not clear why only Australia's agreement was sought, perhaps because at this stage Canada had postponed the despatch of the 25th Brigade to Korea.

22 Letter, Cantlie to Robertson, 9 November 1950. CRS A2107, K1.10. The problem of finding sufficient Urdu-speaking officers may be explained by the fact that most officers of the old Indian Army were retired after partition and independence in 1947, or stayed on in the armies of the successor states.

23 Cablegram, Robertson to Cantlie, 26 November 1950. CRS A2107, K1.10.

24 Cipher message, CGS, Indian Army to Robertson, 23 November 1950 and reply 22 December 1950. CRS A2107, K1.10.

25 Cipher message, Robertson to CGS, Melbourne, CGS, Wellington, CIGS, London, 15 November 1950. CRS A5799, 50/182.

26 Signal, Robertson to War Office, 24 November 1950. CRS A5954, Box 1661, file 4.

27 Defence Committee Minute, 30 November 1950. CRS A2031, 239/1950; 'Note on Commonwealth Division for Korea by VCIGS, n.d. (c. 20 November 1950), WO216/341; signal, Chiefs of Staff, London to Cassels, Melbourne, 27 November 1950, FO371/84162.

28 Cipher message, Robertson to Ministry of Defence, London, 5 December 1950. CRS A5954, Box 1661, file 2. Clearly Robertson did not envisage the Australian battalion being attached singly to an American regiment.

29 Commander-in-Chief, BCOF, Weekly Report, 15 December 1950. CRS A5954, Box 1639, file 3.

30 Cipher message CIGS to Robertson, 20 December 1950. CRS A2107, K14.2. Some sections of the British Army remained steadfastly opposed to the Commonwealth division, even after the final decision to form it. Minute, VCIGS to CIGS, 7 March 1951. WO216/341.

31 Cablegram, Australian Government to Australian High Commissioners, Ottawa, London, Wellington, 26 January 1950. CRS A462, 443/1/8 Pt 1.

32 Letter, Fleury to Rowlandson, 9 March 1951, CRS A2107, K1.13; signal, Fleury to Robertson, 21 March 1951. 112.009 (D96), D HIST. 'The prospects of [a] Commonwealth Division appear brighter from this end.'

33 Cipher message, Robertson to CIGS, 12 March 1951. CRS A2107, L1.15.

34 Cipher message, Robertson to Fleury, 12 March 1951. CRS A2107, K1.15; cable, Menzies, Tokyo to Under-Secretary of State for External Affairs, Ottawa, 10 March 1951. 50069–B–40, volume 2, DEA. Menzies' observation is interesting in the light of earlier New Zealand accusations that Canada was distancing itself from the Commonwealth.

35 Letter, Major-General Bierwirth, Australian Defence Representative, London, to Australian Chiefs of Staff, 14 March 1951. CRS A5954, Box 1688, file 6; letter, Garner, Commonwealth Relations Office to Brownjohn, VCIGS, 2 March 1951. WO216/341. The 'political effect on the Americans of the formation of such a division would also be salutary.'

36 Cipher message, Robertson to CIGS, 17 March 1951, CRS A2107, K1.15.

37 Letter, Official Secretary, UK High Commission, to Secretary, Prime Ministers Department, 6 April 1951. CRS A462, 443/1/8 Pt 1; cable, Clutton, Tokyo to Foreign Office, 2 May 1951. FO371/92831.

38 Robert Eaddy, New Zealand in the Korean War, 229–30.

39 Defence Committee Minute, 16 April 1951. CRS A2031, 93/1951.

40 Wood, *Strange Battleground*, 117–8.

41 Minute, UK Army Liaison Staff Ottawa to High Commissioner's Office, 27 April 1951. 50069–B–40, volume 2 DEA; Field Marshal Sir James Cassels, letter to the author, 15 October 1983.

42 Lieutenant-General Sir Thomas Daly, interview, Sydney, 12 October 1984.

43 Colonal I.B. Ferguson, interview, Canberra, 27 March 1984. Colonel Ferguson did not recall his predecessor, Lieutenant-Colonel C.H. Green, being issued with such instructions either.

44 Cipher message, War Office to Robertson, 22 June 1951. A2107,K1.15.

45 Directive to the GOC, 1st Commonwealth Division, United Nations Forces. CRS A2107, K3.1.

46 Robertson, address to the Military Board, 21 November 1951. Military Board Proceedings, 1951, volume 1. CRS A2653.
47 Fox, *Inter-Allied Cooperation*, 50.

Chapter 7

1 Defence Committee Minute, 9 November 1950. CRS A5799, 59/194. Copies of the plan are to be found in files from the Departments of Defence, Army, Treasury, External Affairs and Prime Minister and Cabinet, as well as on BCOF files now held at the Australian War Memorial. It was probably the most widely circulated of all Commonwealth documents during the war, suggesting the concern of its authors to get matters absolutely right.
2 'Plan for the non-operational control, administration and logistic support of the British Commonwealth Forces, Korea', 1–2, 10–11. CRS A816, 19/323/77.
3 Directive to the Commander-in-Chief, British Commonwealth Occupation Force, on his responsibilities for British Commonwealth Forces employed in Korea and Japan. CRS A2107, K3.
4 Koje-do was the site of a large prison camp complex established by the Americans and South Koreans. Following serious rioting among the Chinese and North Korean POWs in 1952, the American and ROK guards were reinforced with combat units from US and UN units. The Canadians objected to the transfer of a company to Koje, and precipitated a row with the Americans and with Commonwealth headquarters in Japan.
5 Message, Moncel, London to CGS, Ottawa, 14 November 1950. 112.3M2 (D294), D HIST.
6 Minutes of CGS Conference No 103, 16 November 1950. 112.3M2 (D294), D HIST.
7 Memorandum, Brigadier, General Staff (Plans) to CGS, 30 November 1950. 412B25.016(D38), D HIST.
8 For example, 29 General Hospital arrived with the British 29th Infantry Brigade Group and was merged with the BCOF General Hospital to form the British Commonwealth General Hospital, Kure. Col C.W. Nye, ADMS, BCOF to HQ, BCOF, 27 November 1950. AWM 114, 130/1/27.
9 Cipher message, Robertson to Chiefs of Staff, Melbourne, 18 December 1950. CRS A816, 19/323/54.
10 Telegram, Vice-Quartermaster-General, War Office to Robertson, Japan, 28 November 1950. CRS A2107, K14.
11 Defence Committee Agenda 50/173. CRS A5799. This agenda item noted that Chinese intervention had caused indefinite deferral of consideration of the eventual withdrawal of Australian forces.
12 'Future Outlook – BCOF', undated, (late October 1950?). AWM 114, 130/2/15.
13 'Brief for Commander-in-Chief. Reasons which prevent the reduction of BCOF', ? December 1950. AWM 114, 130/2/15.

14 Minute, Newman, Defence Division to Secretary, Australian Treasury, 11 January 1951. CRS A571, 50/2214.
15 Signal, Rowell to Robertson, 28 March 1951. AWM 124, unnumbered file, 'Korea-Prior to Dec 1951.'
16 Signal, Robertson to Rowell, 30 March 1951. *ibid.*
17 Signal, Chiefs of Staff, Melbourne to Robertson, 29 March 1951. CRS A5799, 51/78.
18 'Report by the Joint Administrative Planning Committee No 6/1951'. CRS A5799, 51/78.
19 Signal, War Office to Defence, Melbourne, n.d. (mid–April?), and signal, Robertson to Chiefs of Staff, 25 May 1951. CRS A5799, 51/78. The War Office, possibly at Robertson's behest, had concluded with the observation that 'We therefore agree with these proposals and suggest that action should be taken to implement them.'
20 Interview, Lieutenant-General F.J. Fleury, Ottawa, 10 January 1985. Memorandum, Director Military Operations and Plans to VCGS, 18 April 1951. 112.3M2 (D318), D HIST. See also Col G.M. Urquhart, 'Diplomats and Drivers – Support in the Rear of 25 Canadian Infantry Brigade Group during the Korean War', *Canadian Defence Quarterly/ La Revue canadienne de défense,* vol 10, no 2, Autumn 1980.
21 There are numerous works dealing with MacArthur's dismissal, many highly partisan. The definitive account is D. Clayton James' *The Years of MacArthur, 1945–1964,* Houghton Mifflin, Boston, 1985. Useful insights are contained in Bernard Brodie, *War and Politics,* London, 1974, 81–91, and D. Clayton James, *Command Crisis : MacArthur and the Korean War,* Harmon Memorial Lecture Number Twenty-Four, USAF Academy, Colorado, 1982.
22 'Campaign in Korea and the Situation in Japan', 28 September 1950. FO371/83008. 'He must, henceforth, be ridden by Truman on a very severe curb. He must, and will, submit to the President's direct orders, but I doubt whether he will obey anybody else. He is flushed with success [after Inchon] and is convinced that he, and he alone, knows best'.
23 Cable, George Clutton, Tokyo to R.H. Scott, Foreign Office, 3 April 1951. FO371/92656.
24 Cable, Clutton to Scott, 10 April 1951. *ibid.*
25 Cable, Scott to Clutton, 13 April 1951. *ibid.* Of Bouchier, Scott wrote, 'we have no confidence at all in Bouchier's political judgement – any more than in MacArthur's ... Bouchier is a highly impressionable individual, with a genius for vivid journalistic reporting. These are not qualities that go with balanced judgement'.
26 Cable, Clutton to Scott, 24 April 1951. FO371/92656. 'for the days preceding MacArthur's dismissal . . . [a]ll the Mad Women of Chaillot were on the rampage and if most of them were outside my control, I felt that at least as far as Bouchier was concerned some effort ought to be made to neutralise him . . . it had no effect on the accuracy or sense of his reporting, but it did stop him expressing heterodox ideas at dinner parties.'

27 'Pendennis', *The Observer*, 15 June 1951. 'From Tokyo he has taken a consistently optimistic line, and I believe that recently the anniversary occurred of his first positive assurance that there would be a truce within a week.'

28 Report, Bouchier to Chiefs of Staff, 15 June 1950. FO371/92740.

29 Cable, Clutton to Johnston, Foreign Office, 16 April 1950. FO371/92654.

30 Cable, Clutton to Foreign Office, 2 July 1951. FO371/92654; letter, UKLS to Foreign Office, 7 May 1951. FO371/95655. 'Unlike General MacArthur, I take his professions of pro-British sentiments as being a genuine expression of what he really feels.'

31 'National Service. Outline Plan Recommended by the Defence Committee'. n.d. (July 1951?). Military Board Proceedings. CRS A2653, 1951, volume 2.

32 JAPC report 19/1951, 26 July 1951. AWM 124.

33 Minute, A.S. Brown, Secretary, Prime Minister's Department to R.G. Menzies, 14 August 1951. CRS A462, 443/1/8 Pt 2.

34 Letter, Maxwell to Secretary of Defence, Melbourne, 13 August 1951. CRS A816, 52/301/319.

35 'He was a rather flamboyant figure, a great trainer of troops and a turbulent subordinate to any senior commander.' S.F. Rowell, *Full Circle*, 105.

36 Signal, Rowell to VCIGS, 23 August 1951. CRS A816, 52/301/319.

37 Lieutenant-General F.J. Fleury, letter to the author, 23 April 1984.

38 Signal, VCIGS to Rowell, 28 August 1951. CRS A816, 52/301/319.

39 Minute, C.P. Scott, Foreign Office to Col V.W. Street, Chiefs of Staff Secretariat, 29 September 1951. FO371/92835.

40 Internal minute, Prime Minister's Department, n.d. (early October 1951?). CRS A462, 443/1/8 Pt 2.

41 Report, Bouchier to Chiefs of Staff, 6 October 1951. FO371/92747.

42 Cable, Commonwealth Relations Office to Australian Government, 14 October 1951. CRS A816, 52/301/319; Fleury to Secretary of State for External Affairs, Ottawa, 30 August 1951. 50069–B–40, volume 2 DEA.

43 Signal, Clutton to Foreign Office, 9 October 1951. FO371/92657.

44 'Minutes of conference held at BCFK on 19 October 51.' WO281/10, Appendix N. The move involved the transfer of 109 officers and 800 other ranks of the Australian Military Forces. A list of the units transferred and integrated units formed is to be found in AWM 114, 130/2/43, Appendix A.

45 Letter, Chief Liaison Officer, United Kingdom Service Liaison Staff, Melbourne to Secretary, Department of Defence, Melbourne, 2 November 1951. CRS A816, 19/304/486.

46 Text of the Treaty is to be found at CRS A816, 19/304/486.

47 Minute, Secretary, Department of Defence to P.A. McBride, 3 November 1951. *ibid.*

48 Cable, Department of External Affairs to Australian Mission, Tokyo, 25 January 1952. *ibid.*

49   O'Neill, *Strategy and Diplomacy*, 289.
50   Brodie, *War and Politics*, 107. 'During the war many in the United States criticised our allies for contributing so little [in terms of force size] . . . The allies felt they were making an important contribution that ought to be appreciated rather than condemned, and considering how they would be missed in the Vietnam experience, it was a justified attitude.'
51   Ra Jong-yil, 'Special Relationship at War : The Anglo-American Relationship during the Korean War', *Journal of Strategic Studies*, vol 7, no 3, September 1984, 313. The title of the article is a little misleading, since it does not examine the relationship much beyond the end of 1950.
52   O'Neill, *Strategy and Diplomacy*, 298–9; Walter G. Hermes, *Truce Tent and Fighting Front*, Washington DC, 1966, 323–4; James F. Schnabel and Robert J. Watson, *The History of the Joint Chiefs of Staff. The Joint Chiefs of Staff and National Policy*. volume III. *The Korean War*, Michael Glazier Inc., Wilmington, 1979, Part II, 847–8.
53   Sidney T. Matthews, 'General Clark's Decision to Drive on Rome', Kent Roberts Greenfield, (ed.) *Command Decisions*, Office of the Chief of Military History, Washington DC, 1960, 350–63; Stephen E. Ambrose, *Eisenhower*, Volume 1, *Soldier, General of the Army, President-Elect 1890–1952*, New York, 1983, 274. For a refutation of these criticisms, however, Martin Blumenson, *Mark Clark*, Jonathan Cape, London, 1985.
54   O'Neill, *Strategy and Diplomacy*, 298.
55   *ibid.*, 297.
56   'Command Arrangements in Korea'. DO35/5876.
57   Minute, W.H.A. Bishop, CRO to Pritchard, War Office, 29 May 1952. DO35/5876.
58   Schnabel and Watson, 845–7.
59   Brief, undated, CRO to Secretary of State; minute, W.H.A. Bishop to Secretary of State, 18 June 1952. Both DO35/5876.
60   Mark Clark, Oral History, Section 3, 110–11. Mark Clark Papers, USAMHI.
61   Cable, Franks, Washington to Foreign Office, 22 June 1952. FO371/99614; telegram, Secretary of State for External Affairs, Ottawa to Canadian High Commissioner, London, 28 June 1952. DO35/5876.
62   Cipher message, Dening to Foreign Office, 28 June 1952; minute, R.H. Scott to Permanent Under Secretary, 1 July 1952. Both FO371/99614.
63   Letter, Clark to Ismay, 5 July 1952. ISMAY IV/Cla/8, Liddell Hart Centre for Military Archives, Kings College, London (KQC).
64   Cable, Australian government to Australian High Commissioners in London and Ottawa and ambassadors in Washington and Tokyo, 5 July 1952. DO35/5883.
65   Brief for the Secretary of State, 15 July 1952. PDO35/5876; message, Bridgeford to Chiefs of Staff, Melbourne, 14 August 1952. CRS A2151, KB1036–7G.

66 Minute, Cabinet Defence Committee Meeting, 16 July 1952. DO35/ 5876.
67 Telegram, CRO to British High Commissioners in Canada, Australia, New Zealand, South Africa, India, 31 July 1952. DO35/5880.
68 Cipher message, Dening to Foreign Office, 18 August 1952. FO371/ 99616; Cipher message BJSM, Washington to Ministry of Defence, London, 21 July 1950. FO371/84063.
69 Letter, Foreign Office to Dening, 26 September 1952. FO371/99617. 'I am increasingly impressed by Bouchier's telegrams . . . I should let Bouchier stay a bit, if he will.' Minute, Churchill to Minister of Defence, 20 August 1952. FO371/99616.
70 Report, Group Captain R.W. McNair, Air Attache, Tokyo, 2 September 1952. 50069–K–40 volume 1, DEA.
71 Brief on Command Structure for Commonwealth Forces in Japan prepared for Chiefs of Staff by CGS, 11 February 1952. 112.3M2(D573), D HIST.
72 Signal, Chiefs of Staff, Melbourne to Bridgeford, Japan, 16 August 1952. CRS A2151, KB1251G. The British First Sea Lord cabled the Vice Chief of the Naval Staff at about this time that 'the Australians get along very well with us but are touchy and present misunderstandings are most unfortunate.' FO371/99617.
73 Cipher message, QMG, Tokyo to Foreign Office, 15 December 1952. FO371/99168.
74 Cable, Dening to Foreign Office, 30 December 1952. *ibid.*
75 Command Diary, 12 February 1953. Command Reports 1949–54. First Corps. RG407. Box 1684, Washington National Record Center, (WNRC).
76 Brigadier Morton, routine report no 12 for period 1 February to 15 February 1953. 410B25.019(D303), D HIST.
77 Letters, Lieutenant-General Guy Simons to Lieutenant-General S.F. Rowell and Lieutenant-General H. Wells, 28 May 1953. 50069–B–40 vol 5, DEA.

Chapter 8

1 'Three Years in Korea. A Brief History of I US Corps'. Prepared by Historical Section, US Army, (G3), I Corps, n.p., n.d., 4–9. USAMHI Library.
2 Russell F. Weigley, *The American Way of War. A History of United States Military Strategy and Policy,* Macmillan, New York, 1973.
3 Lieutenant-General Sir Thomas Daly, questionnaire, January 1984, 3.
4 Brigadier P.J. Jeffries, questionnaire, August 1984, 1.
5 General Sir Arthur MacDonald, questionnaire, March 1984, 1; Major-General R.L. Hughes, interview, 26 January 1984; Brigadier M. Austin, interview, 27 February 1984.
6 Letter, Adams to Shattock, 13 November 1951. FO371/92750.
7 Barclay, *First Commonwealth Division*; Wood, *Strange Battleground*, 118–20; Stairs, *The Diplomacy of Constraint*, 209–11.

8   Field Marshal Sir James Cassels, letter to the author, 15 October 1983.
9   1 Commonwealth Division Periodic Report, 2 May–15 October 1951. CRS A2107, K11.09. emphasis added.
10 *ibid.*
11 Cassels, letter to the author.
12 1 Commonwealth Division Periodic Report, 15 October 1951–15 February 1952. AD314/11/3, New Zealand Archives (NZA).
13 *ibid.* This tendency in American military operations is an old one. Justifying the unsuccessful Union assaults upon Confederate positions at Kennesaw Mountain, Sherman explained that his defeat had some virtue since 'it demonstrated to General [Joseph E.] Johnson that I would assault, and that boldly.' Grady McWhiney and Perry D. Jamieson, *Attack and Die. Civil War Military Tactics and the Southern Heritage,* University of Alabama Press, University, 1982,72.
14 Headquarters I Corps letter of Instruction, 22 July 1951. WO261/46. There is no evidence that any Commonwealth formation ever used the phrase 'sharpen your bayonets'. It did adorn all corps publications for the remainder of O'Daniel's period of command.
15 Command Reports 1949–54. First Corps. Pt 2, Book 22, Command Section. September 1951, minutes of conference. RG407, box 1564, WNRC.
16 Order of the Day, 25 December 1951. RG407, box 1585, WNRC.
17 Sir Esler Dening to R.H. Scott, 18 February 1952. FO371/99613.
18 Internal Foreign Office minute, R.J. Stratton to R.H. Scott, 7 March 1952. FO371/99613.
19 Letter, Simonds to Ridgway, 18 February 1952. Special File, Ridgway Papers, USAMHI.
20 *ibid.*
21 Cassels, letter to the author.
22 Stratton to Scott, 7 March 1952. FO371/99613.
23 Memorandum for the diary, 11 March 1952. Special File, Ridgway Papers, USAMHI.
24 First Corps Command Reports, 8 July 1952. RG 407, box 1633, WNRC.
25 1 Commonwealth Division Periodic Report, 1 November 1952–1 April 1953. AD 314/11/3, NZA.
26 Record of conversation between the Canadian ambassador, Tokyo and Lieutenant-General Bridgeford. Canadian Embassy, Tokyo to Department of External Affairs, Ottawa, 3 September 1952. 50069-B-40, volume 4, DEA.
27 Oral history, General Bruce C. Clarke, volume II, 164–6. Bruce Clarke Papers, USAMHI. There are a number of comments critical of the Commonwealth Division in the I Corps Command Reports during Kendall's period of command. cf. 14 January, 28 January, 23 February, 1953. RG 407, box 1679, WNRC.
28 Commander, Royal Engineers (CRE), 1 Commonwealth Division. Liaison Letter No. 6 (1 Dec 52–28 Feb 53). CRS A2148. The

important point that he overlooked was that the Chinese were faced with heavy allied tactical air power, and with the threat of the possible use of atomic weapons. Neither of these faced the UN forces. cf. John Allan English, *A Perspective on Infantry*, Praeger, New York, 1981, 217–27, for a discussion of the CPV soldier.

29 1 Commonwealth Division Periodic Report, 2 May–15 October 1951. AD 314/11/3, NZA.

30 CRE Liaison Letter No. 5 (1 Jul–30 Nov 52). CRS A2148.

31 1 Commonwealth Division Periodic Report, 2 May–15 October 1951. AD 314/11/3, NZA.

32 Routine Report No. 3 for the period 16 Sep 52–30 Sep 52, Canadian Military Mission, Far East to Chiefs of Staff, Ottawa. 410B25.019(D303), D HIST.

33 Oral History, Clarke, volume II, 150. Bruce C. Clarke papers, USAMHI.

34 Major Robert A. Doughty, 'The Evolution of US Army Tactical Doctrine, 1946–76', *Leavenworth Papers*, No. 1, August 1979,11.

35 Weigley, *Eisenhower's Lieutenants*, 2.

36 R.H. Scott to I.M. Hurrell, 21 January 1953. FO371/105563.

37 *The Regulars*, 555–6. Unpublished MS. Donald A. Seibert Papers, USAMHI.

38 'Strict, almost hide-bound, orders are in force regarding the briefing of patrols and any set-back, however minor, is the subject of searching enquiry – indeed the unfortunate patrol commander may even have to report to the Army commander'. 1 Commonwealth Division Periodic Report, 1 November 1952–1 April 1953. AD 314/11/3, NZA.

39 Record of conversation with CBS correspondent Mr Ed Murrow. FO371/105563.

40 'Technically and tactically this was all nonsense, because was I expected to organise this headquarters if there was an attack?' Brigadier J. Burns, interview, 18 February 1984.

41 Douglas Kinnard, *The War Managers*, University Press of New England, Hanover, 1977, 58–9.

42 War Diary, HQRA, 14 January 1952. WO281/204; War Diary Canadian Infantry Brigade, 16 October 1952. RG24, C17, box 18245, PAC; unpublished MS, 546–7, Seibert Papers, USAMHI.

43 War Diary, HQRA, 22 January 1952. WO281/204; letter, Brigadier R.J. Salmon to Dr Robert O'Neill, 7 July 1980. AWM 93, 782/90/7.

44 'Description of the British Staff organisation', undated, War Diary, 'G' Section, 1 Commonwealth Division. WO281/66; Staff list – 2 Div, War Diary, HQRA. WO281/728.

45 Lieutenant-Colonel Walden F. Woodward, 'The British Army Staff', *Military Review*, April 1952; Captain Richard B. Sheridan, 'The Commonwealth Staff', *Marine Corps Gazette*, March 1955. The latter concluded that 'Because of the high quality of soldiering they demonstrated and their excellent conduct of the Jamestown line defence, their organisation and methods seem worthy of study.'

46 Major-General J.M. Rockingham, *Recollections of Korea*, 77.

Unpublished MS, MG31 G12, PAC. For a further example, war diary, 25th Canadian Infantry Brigade, 14 February 1951. RG24, C17, box 18241, PAC.

47 Robert O'Neill, *Combat Operations*, 284.
48 Dominion naval units had of course been incorporated into Royal Navy flotillas and squadrons since the Great War.
49 O'Neill, *Combat Operations*, 286; Brigadier M. Austin, interview, 27 February 1984.
50 Brigadier M. Tebbutt, interview, 20 February 1984; Colonel E. Manders, interview, 18 February 1984.
51 Entries for 16 and 17 January. WO281/142.
52 War diary, 25th Canadian Infantry Brigade, April-May 1953. RG24. C17, Box 18250, PAC.
53 Wood, *Strange Battleground*, 210.
54 *ibid.*, 231–6; see also the comments by Brigadier J.V. Allard to the Canadian official historian concerning this action, 112.3H1.001(D7), D HIST.
55 Lieutenant-General Sir Thomas Daly, interview, 12 October 1984.
56 Cassels, letter to the author, 15 October 1983.
57 O'Neill, *Strategy and Diplomacy*, 294–6; Wood, *Strange Battleground*, 191–6.
58 Foulkes to Reid, 6 July 1951. 50069-B-40, volume 2, DEA. Ironically, he felt 'that the likelihood of any misunderstandings arising with the personalities that are there now is very remote.'
59 Minute for Chairman, Chiefs of Staff, 11 June 1951. 73/1223, unnumbered file, D HIST.
60 Simonds to Moncel, Canadian Military Mission, London, 28 May 1952. 100.009(D7), D HIST.
61 Defence liaison division to Under-Secretary, 20 June 1952. 50069-J-40, DEA.
62 Moncel to Simonds, 4 June 1952. 112.009(D92), D HIST.
63 Defence Committee Minute 142/1952, 29 May 1952. See also CRS A2107, K66.6.
64 Briefing paper, 20 June 1952. 112.3M2(573), D HIST.
65 Neither Wood nor O'Neill appears to have seen this State Department note, and the original could not be located in PAC. Fortunately, a detailed paraphrase is contained in a letter from the British embassy in Washington to the Foreign Office, dated 27 June 1952. DO35/5854.
66 Draft Cable, National Defence to External Affairs, 28 May 1952. 110.009(D7), D HIST.
67 'Connelly Career Wrecked to Save Ottawa Embarrassment'. *The* [Toronto] *Gazette*, 2 December 1952. 50069-J-40, DEA; CRS A816, 19/323/70; see also DO35/5875. Bridgeford defended his actions to his Australian superiors, stating that he had never hesitated to consult the civilian heads of mission in Tokyo on matters which affected 'the interests of the country concerned', and that he considered the Koje incident 'a purely military problem . . . having given my assurance to

General Mark Clark that the Commonwealth would cooperate to the full in guarding prisoners it appeared to be normal military practice that Headquarters Eighth Army should issue the necessary orders to the formations under its command.' Cipher message, Bridgeford to the Chiefs of Staff, Melbourne, 20 August 1952. CRS A816, 19/323/85.

68 Kinnard, *The War Managers,* 110–7, discusses these problems in Vietnam, and believes that experience in both the Second World War and Korea had much to do with them. For a brief discussion of rotation policy see Martin van Creveld, *Fighting Power. German and US Army Performance, 1939–1945,* Arms and Armour Press, London, 1983, 90–1. See also D.J. Chesler, 'Effect on Morale of Infantry Team Replacement and Individual Replacement Systems', *Sociometry,* 18, 4, August 1955, 587–97.

69 Command Reports 1949–54. First Corps, Narrative and G1 Staff Section Report. September 1952, 69. RG407, Box 1641, WNRC. An Australian report on manpower favoured individual relief as being 'more economical in manpower than unit relief.' Report, Deputy Adjutant-General to DCGS, 5 November 1953. CRS MP729/8, 37/431/139.

70 Cipher message, Cassels to Director of Military Operations, London, 28 May 1951. CRS A2107. K1.15. Robertson added in November that 'our allies can NOT and will NOT understand [our] not keeping our units to agreed strengths.' Cipher message, Robertson to War Office, 9 November 1951. CRS A2107, K2.05.

71 Letter, West to General Sir John Crocker, Adjutant-General, London, 29 October 1952. CRS A2107. K1.05 (supplement).

72 Letter, Bridgeford to Crocker, 27 November 1952. *ibid.*

73 'Note on British Manpower Deficiencies'. *ibid.*

74 Cipher message, Crocker to Bridgeford, 3 January 1953. *ibid.*

75 Arthur Menzies, Canadian Liaison Mission, Tokyo, to the Under-Secretary for External Affairs, Ottawa, 7 December 1951. 50069-B-40, volume 3, DEA.

76 Dening to Scott, 4 February 1952, and reply dated 13 February. FO371/99613.

77 VCIGS to Bridgeford, 29 February 1952; Field Marshal Slim, CIGS, to Lieutenant General S.F. Rowell, Australian CGS, 22 March 1952; minute to VCIGS, 4 May 1952. WO216/634.

78 I.M. Hurrell, internal memorandum, 26 August 1952. FO371/99613.

79 Cable, Slim to Rowell, 16 April 1952. WO216/643, The British Army was also forced to keep regulars with units in Korea anything up to six months beyond the expiration of their three year 'python' overseas tours. Although permitted under army regulations, its implementation was not greeted favourably. Minute, Adjutant-General to Secretary of State for War, 17 March 1952. WO32/15283.

80 Letter, Director of Personnel Administration to Commander-in-Chief, British Army of the Rhine, 7 May 1952. WO32/1440.

81 Minute, Director of Staff Duties to Adjutant-General, 22 October

222   *Notes to pp. 161–168*

1951. CRS MP 742, 100/1/56. The Australian battalions were requiring 160 replacements per month by the beginning of 1953. Minute, acting Director of Staff Duties, general distribution, 16 January 1953. CRS MP927, A100/1/25.

82 David Curtis Skaggs, 'The KATUSA Experiment: The Integration of Korean Nationals into the US Army, 1950–1965', *Military Affairs*, April 1974, 53.

83 'Korean Personnel – Attachment to BCFK Units'. Shedden papers. CRS A5954. Box 1688.

84 Stratton, internal minute, 25 August 1952. FO371/99616.

85 J.M. Addis, internal minute, 28 November 1952, and marginal comments by Eden. FO371/99618.

86 Cable, Department of External Affairs, Canberra, to Australian delegation, UNCURK, Pusan, 3 October 1952. CRS A571, 52/2835; Notes on Defence Committee Agendum No 163/1952. Shedden papers. CRS A5954, Box 1688; Telegram, Secretary of State for Commonwealth Relations to British High Commissioner, Ottawa, 30 November 1952, and telegram, Canadian High Commissioner, Wellington, to Department of External Affairs, Ottawa, 19 November 1952. 111.41(D14), D HIST.

87 Letter, Bogert to Simmonds, 1 December 1952. 112.009(D89), D HIST. For the attitude of the Canadian government see memorandum for the Cabinet Defence Committee, 10 November 1952. 50069-B40, volume 4, DEA.

88 Brief, 14 May 1954. 410B25.019(D267), D HIST.

89 War diary, 25th Canadian Infantry Brigade, Administrative Instruction No 8, 10 March 1953. RG24, C17, Box18248, PAC. see also war diary, 2 RAR, Administrative Instruction 10/53, 8 March 1953. AWM 85.

90 JAPC report 9/1953, 30 March 1953. Held by Archives and Historical Section, Department of Defence, Canberra.

91 General Sir Arthur MacDonald, letter to the author, 14 March 1984.

92 West to Bridgeford, 22 December 1952; Bridgeford to Chiefs of Staff, Melbourne, 27 December 1952. JAPC report 3/1953.

93 Defence Committee Agendum 13/1953, 2 March 1953. CRS A5799. See also Routine report, Commander, CMMFE, to Department of National Defence, No 14, 410B25.019(D303), D HIST; cable, Arthur Menzies, Tokyo, to Under-Secretary of State for External Affairs, Ottawa, 19 December 1952. 50069-B-40, volume 4, DEA.

94 Advanced Headquarters, BCFK, notes July 1950-July 1953. unnumbered file, 'Korea. Historical notes.' held by Ministry of Defence, London.

Chapter 9

1 S.J. Butlin and C.B. Schedvin, *War Economy 1942–1945. Australia in the War of 1939–1945*, Australian War Memorial, Canberra, 1977, 139.

2 Ronald G. Haycock, 'The 'myth' of imperial defence : Australian-Canadian bilateral military co-operation, 1942', *War & Society*, 2:1, May 1984, 65–84.
3 Butlin and Schedvin, *War Economy*, 608–12.
4 Peter Calvocoressi, *The British Experience 1945–75*, Penguin, Harmondsworth, 1979, 10–20. Convertibility had been insisted upon in the Bretton Woods agreement of 1944, along with an end to discrimination against American imports as a result of Empire preference. A demand for post-war trade liberalisation had featured in Article VII of the Lend Lease agreement with Australia also, and the Australian government had signed with some misgiving on this point.
5 Calvocoressi, *British Experience*, 17.
6 Buckley, *Occupation Diplomacy*, 92, 128–32. Buckley has characterised British economic policy towards Japan in the period 1946–48 as being one of 'enlightened economic self-interest'.
7 Major-General R.N.L. Hopkins, 'History of the Australian Occupation in Japan, 1946–50', *Journal of the Royal Australian Historical Society*, XL, part II, 1954, 100–1.
8 'British Commonwealth Occupation Force Pool Account. Main File'. CRS A571, 53/755.
9 'Policy for Integration', 8.
10 Hermes, *Truce Tent and Fighting Front*, 70. 2nd Logistical Command was a relatively lowly one-star appointment at this time.
11 Routine report, Brigadier Connelly, Canadian Military Mission, Far East to Chiefs of Staff, Ottawa, 4 August 1952. 683.023 (D1), D HIST. There is no published work dealing with Korean War logistics. The final volume of the US Army official history series is scheduled to deal with theatre logistics, but as at 1987 the volume has not yet had an author assigned to it.
12 Cable, War Office to Australian Treasury, Melbourne, 4 August 1950. CRS A571, 50/2214 Pt 1.
13 Memorandum, Robertson to Secretary, Department of Defence, Melbourne, 8 December 1950. CRS AA1970/140, FA3201 (23).
14 JAPC report 2/1951, 10 January 1951. Material held in Archives and Historical Section, Department of Defence, Canberra.
15 Memorandum, Chief Finance Officer, Department of Defence to Financial Adviser, BCOF, 24 January 1951; Memorandum, Chiefs of Staff Committee, Melbourne to Robertson, 25 January 1951. CRS AA1970/140, FA3201 (23).
16 Letter, Secretary of the Army Council, London to United Kingdon Liaison Officer, Melbourne, 23 April 1951. CRS A5799, 51/116. The latter passed this to the Australian Defence Committee and not to the Australian government as such.
17 Defence Committee Agenda, 31 May 1951. CRS A5799, 51/195.
18 Signal, War Office to British Commonwealth Forces, Japan, 16 July 1951. CRS AA1970/140, FA3201 (23); signal, Department of External Affairs, Canberra to Commonwealth Relations Office, London, 15 August 1951. CRS A1838/T184, 3123/5/12/3.

19   Telegram, Forward Maintenance Area, Taegu to BCOF, Tokyo, 20
     August 1951. CRS AA1970/140, K.86; war diary, 25th Canadian
     Infantry Brigade, appendixes 1 and 3, August 1951. RG24, volume
     18,439, PAC. At the same time heaquarters, BCFK, Tokyo was
     writing to the Canadian brigade commander that 'The only ways to
     obviate this [problem of conflicting administrative methods] are either
     for your country to join the pool . . . or else for some sort of per capita
     payment to be arranged. While we would of course prefer the former,
     this seems to have been turned down . . . We must continue to press
     our government for a broad decision since we should not have to wait
     [for] the details to be worked out before we are relieved of our
     worries.' letter, personal and confidential, Brigadier J.C. Rowlandson,
     Tokyo to Brigadier J.M. Rockingham, 4 September 1951.
     410B25.059 (D1), D HIST.
20   Letter, Brigadier B.E. Alderson, Financial Adviser, Tokyo to Mr A.H.
     Howqua, Department of the Treasury (Defence Division), Melbourne,
     10 December 1951. CRS A571, 55/291 Pt 1.
21   Cable, Australian High Commissioner, Ottawa to Australian Treas-
     ury (Defence Division), Melbourne, 22 January 1952. CRS A571,
     51/1870. See also memorandum, H.C. Newman, Defence Division, to
     Secretary, Treasury, 27 February 1952. 'I think it is essential that
     early discussions with the Canadians, at the governmental level,
     should take place.'
22   Minute of meeting between Canadian High Commisioner, Mr C.
     Fraser Elliott, and Mr H.C. Newman, 20 March 1952. CRS A816,
     19/323/77; cable, High Commissioner for Canada, Canberra to
     Secretary of State for External Affairs, Ottawa, 20 May 1952.
     50069-H-40, DEA.
23   Minute, H.C. Newman to the Secretary of the Treasury, 28 May
     1952. CRS A571, 51/1870.
24   Letter, Wheeler to the Secretary of the Treasury, 30 May 1952. CRS
     A571, 51/1870; minute, J.C. Lloyd to Wheeler, 19 June 1952. CRS
     A571, 55/291 Pt 1; cable, H.C. Newman to A.H. Howqua, 29 July
     1952. CRS A816, 19/323/77. 'It is probable . . . that Canada would
     not participate in the Pool on the same basis of dollar economy as the
     sterlng area members.'
25   Memorandum, Newman to the Secretary, Department of Defence,
     Melbourne, 29 October 1952. CRS A816, 19/323/70. See also
     memorandum for the Canadian Minister for National Defence,
     'Financial arrangements for Canadian forces stationed abroad', 21
     November 1952. 50069-H-40, DEA.
26   Fox, *Inter-Allied Cooperation,* 164.
27   Cable, Chief of the General Staff, Wellington to Chiefs of Staff,
     Melbourne, n.d.; Defence Committee Minute 93/1951, 10 May 1951;
     CRS A2103; minute, Sir Frederick Chilton to Defence Committee, 24
     April 1951, Defence Committee Agenda 51/88. CRS A5799. The
     Defence Committee noted at a later meeting that 'it is most undesir-
     able that the financial arrangements . . . should be upset at this stage

    ... We do not wish to depart from the arrangements agreed to by the British Commonwealth countries concerned.' Defence Committee Minute 116/1951. CRS A2103.

28 Minute, H.C. Newman to Treasurer, 10 August 1951. CRS A1308, 742/1/257; Official Secretary, United Kingdom High Commission to Secretary, Prime Minister's Department, Canberra, 2 August 1951. CRS A571, 50/2214 Pt 1.

29 Cable, Wheeler to Wilson, 11 January 1952. CRS A571, 55/291 Pt 1. Wheeler may also have felt that generosity had its limits. At the end of the Second World War the Australian government had voted Britain £35 million in two instalments, in recognition of the sacrifice of the British people during the war. Australia had also sold the British its entire gold production for a time to help ease Britain's dollar shortage. T.B. Millar, *Australia in Peace and War,* 174. See also Morgan, *Labour in Power,* 196–7.

30 Cable, Secretary, Department of External Affairs, Canberra to Secretary of the Treasury, London, 8 January 1952. CRS A1838/T184, 3123/5/12/3; record of discussion in cable, Treasury to Australian Embassy, Washington, 30 May 1952. CRS A571, 55/291 Pt 1. The question of dollar liability arising from the Korean War was not raised in the meeting of Commonwealth Finance Ministers in London. CAB 133/123–126. For further evidence of the Australian position see cabinet agendum 183, 3 December 1951. CRS A4905/XMI, vol. 7, and cabinet submission 216, 5 March 1952. CRS A4905/XMI, Vol 9.

31 Cable, Foreign Office to British Embassy, Washington, 18 October 1951. FO371/94224. An earlier minute noted that 'discussion followed the paper in assuming that it would be a good thing if we could dodge payment of the bill, though it was not suggested that liability should be denied.'

32 Minute, E.A. Berthoud, Foreign Office to E.G. Compton, Treasury, 24 October 1951. FO371/94224; minute, Foreign Office to Anthony Eden, 27 May 1952. PRO 371/100170.

33 Notation on file, 16 February 1954. FO371/105564.

34 'Statement of Expenditure ... 1 July 1951 to 31 May 1960'. CRS A1308, 742/390 Pt 10.

35 Canada signed the treaty with Washington on its own behalf, establishing the principle that a self-governing Dominion could enter into treaty obligations with third countries without reference to, or permission from, London. Its most profound impact was to open the way to independent Dominion control of foreign relations, but it is interesting that the Canadians chose an essentially economic treaty with which to make the point.

Chapter 10

1 Wood, *Strange Battleground,* 242–4; O'Neill, *Strategy and Diplomacy,* 374–401; O'Neill, *Combat Operations,* 533–69, 586–98.
2 O'Neill, *Strategy and Diplomacy,* 389.

3   Together with Czechoslovakia, Poland, Sweden and Switzerland. The
    chairman was Lieutenant-General K.S. Thimayya.
4   'Replacement of 60 Indian Field Ambulance in Korea', memorandum,
    Secretary, Department of Defence, Melbourne to Secretary, Prime
    Minister's Department, Canberra, 9 December 1953. CRS A462, 443/1/8
    Pt 1.
5   Internal Foreign Office minute, 6 July 1952. FO371/99614.
6   O'Neill, *Combat Operations,* 586.
7   Little more can be said about the Commonwealth forces in the
    post-armistice period until the records are released over the next few years.
8   Rainer Tamchina, 'In Search of Common Causes: The Imperial
    Conference of 1937', *Journal of Imperial and Commonwealth History,*
    1, 1, October 1972, 79.
9   *ibid.,* 100.
10 E.J. Tapp, 'Australian and New Zealand Relations (1900–1950): 1.
    Defence', *Australian Outlook,* V, September 1951, 171–2; see also Robin
    Kay (ed), *Documents on New Zealand External Relations.* volume 1. *The
    Australian New Zealand Agreement 1944,* Government Printers, Well-
    ington, 1972.
11 Hosoya Masahiro, review of Buckley, *Occupation Diplomacy, Monu-
    menta Nipponica,* XXXVIII, 3, 1983, 351.
12 S.L.A. Marshall, *Commentary on Infantry Operations and Weapons
    Usage in [the] Korea Winter of 1950–51,* John Hopkins University, Chevy
    Chase, 1952, 136.
13 Colonal E.A. Harris, Headquarters, X US Corps, quoted in Major
    William J. Fox, *Inter-Allied Cooperation.*
14 Proceedings of TEAL XXI, 9–13 October 1978; Major-General P.C.
    Gration, 'Interoperability: ABCA Operations since World War II,' *Army
    Research Development and Acquisition,* 23, January–Feburary 1982;
    General John R. Guthrie, 'Address, ADPA Combat Vehicle Section
    Conference, Fort Knox', 20 September 1979. Allied Interoperability
    papers, box 5, USAMHI.
15 JCS comments, NSF Memorandum on SE Asia, 10 November 1964.
    Glen St J. Barclay, *Friends in High Places. Australian-American diplo-
    matic relations since 1945,* Oxford University Press, Melbourne, 1985,
    145. Correlli Barnett has suggested that in Korea 'the coalition contingents
    – British, Turks, whatever – simply came under American command, just
    like the Anzacs and Canadians under British command in 1914–18'. With
    regard to the Commonwealth, at least, this is a quite misleading
    comparison. John Terraine and Correlli Barnett, 'Problems of Coalition
    War', *Journal of the Royal United Service Institution,* 126, 3, 1983, 10.
16 Watt, *Succeeding John Bull,* 148; Further discussion in Robert O'Neill,
    'The Vietnam War and the Western Alliance', paper presented to the
    Symposium on the Second Indochina War, Airlie, Virginia, 7–9 Novem-
    ber 1984. Copy courtesy of the author.
17 Dennis L. Cuddy, 'The American Role in Australia Involvement in the
    Vietnam War', *Australian Journal of Politics and History,* 28, 3, 1982,
    351. Cuddy notes that in 1966 the Australian Prime Minister, Harold

Holt, in what might almost be an echo of the JCS, criticised the governments of Western Europe for having 'coasted along on the struggle and sacrifice of the United States.' *ibid.*, 345.

18 Cooling and Hixson, *Combined Operations in Peace and War*, 352.
19 Cooling and Hixson, 'Twentieth Century Allied Interoperability', *Asian Perspective,* 6, 1, 1982, 121–2.

Bibliography

Bibliographic note

The problems associated with the research for this book will be familiar to anyone who has attempted to work in the history of the post-1945 period. The situation facing private researchers has improved considerably in the past ten years, with the 'thirty year rule' having moved through the Korean War years, and with many security classifications on American documents now lifted. The researcher wishing to study the Korean War period will still find obstacles in his or her path, however.

Aside from the obvious, but real, difficulty presented by the previous destruction of records, the most consistent problem remains one of access and clearance. The New Zealand Archives in Wellington applies the thirty year rule inconsistently, and while it is possible to read documents dating from the early 1960s in some cases, other Ministry of Defence material directly relevant to the Korean War is still retained by the Ministry and has not been accessioned by the Archives. In Australia the rule is applied strictly, and obtaining permission from the originating departments to view closed material is a long process. In this connection I wish to record my appreciation to Mr Pat Galvin, Secretary of the Department of Home Affairs and Environment, for granting access to the papers of the Australian official historian, Dr Robert O'Neill, and to the Honourable John Dawkins, MP, then Minister for Finance, for overruling his department and opening records originating with the Defence Division of the Australian Treasury.

At the Public Record Office, Kew, some War Office records are still retained by the Ministry of Defence, while certain files, especially those relating to Commonwealth prisoners-of-war, are embargoed for 100 years. As this latter material is freely available at the Australian Archives in Canberra this is not as much of a barrier to the researcher as might otherwise be the case. In Canada, many policy files created within the Departments of National Defense and External Affairs are retained by the historical sections of those departments. Both exhibit a very positive attitude to non-government historians, and access and cooperation are freely given. The thirty year rule is not rigorously applied by these departments, nor by the Public Archives of Canada. The standard of these records is very high, and it is suggested that any researcher working in aspects of Commonwealth involvement in Korea, in the United Nations

Assembly or the UN Commissions on Korea, for example, would be well-advised to spend time in Ottawa.

Although access to American records is much freer than was previously the case, there are still problems. This author was denied access to the headquarters papers of the 1st United States Marine Division, held by the Washington National Record Center, while granted access to the head-quarters papers of the US Army's I Corps by the same body. State Department papers relating to the last eighteen months of the war were still closed pending completion of the publication of the series *Foreign Relations of the United States* for the years 1952–54. Access to State Department and National Security Council papers was applied for under the Freedom of Information Act at the beginning of 1985, but two years later some of these still awaited processing and clearance. No obstacles were encountered in working in the considerable collection of personal papers held by the United States Army Military History Institute at Carlisle, Pennsylvania.

Personal papers generally present another area of difficulty. As a rule, relevant institutions such as the Imperial War Museum, London or the Australian War Memorial, Canberra have made little or no effort to collect and preserve the papers or recollections of individuals with Korean War service. While I was fortunate to locate the papers of important individuals such as Generals West and Coad, other figures, such as Air Vice Marshal Bouchier, would appear to have left nothing. A comprehensive search of the correspondence files at the Liddell Hart Centre for Military Archives at Kings College, London, and at the Royal Commission for Historical Manuscripts, revealed that others' efforts to locate important sets of papers have been equally fruitless. Finally, recourse was had to correspondence and interview in an effort to fill some of the gaps in the documentary record, and many individuals gave generously of their time and recollections.

The bibliographic listing of secondary sources is selective in the sense that some works cited in the notes have not been listed here if they have provided merely confirmatory or minor points not directly related to consideration of the Korean War itself. Other works not dealing directly with the Korean War but which were of particular use in understanding the background to events or in formulating the overall approach have been included, however. No attempt has been made to provide a definitive listing of Korean War literature.

Australia

Australian Archives, Mitchell, ACT

CA3, Cabinet Secretariat.
  A4907. Fifth Menzies Ministry – folders of Minutes of Cabinet Meetings, 1951–1954.
CA 12, Prime Minister's Department, Central Office (1911–1971).
  A462. Correspondence Files, multiple number series, 1950–1956.
CA 18, Department of External Affairs (II), Central Office, 1948–1970.

A1838/T184. Correspondence files, multiple number series, 1948–.
CA 46, Department of Defence III, (1942–).
A816. Department of Defence, Correspondence files, multiple number series, 1935–1957.
AA1970/140. Selected records relating to BCOF, Japan and the Korean War, c.1945–1957.
A2031. Defence Committee Minutes, 1929–.
A2107. Correspondence files, 'K' series (Korean Operations), 1950–1953.
A2111. Correspondence files, FA (Financial Adviser's Office) series, 1950–1953.
A2112. British POW (Prisoner of War) dossiers, 1951–1953.
A2148. CRE (Commander, Royal Engineers) 1 Commonwealth Division, liaison letters, 1950–1954.
A2149. Daily operations reports – Commander-in-Chief, BCFK, 1950–1953.
A2151. Correspondence files, KB series (HQ, BCFK – General Staff branch), 1953–1956.
A2653. Volumes of Military Board proceedings, 1905–1976.
A5799. Defence Committee agenda, 1932 –.
A5954. Defence records collected by Sir Frederick Shedden, 1937–1971. (formerly located at MP 1217).
CA 68, Treasury, Defence Division.
A649. Correspondence files, multiple number series, 1942–1962.
A1308. Correspondence (Classified), 1941–1963.
CA2141, Department of the Treasury.
A571. Correspondence files, annual single number series, 1901–1976.

Australian Archives, Brighton, Victoria

CA 36, Department of the Army, 1939–1974.
MP729/8. Classified correspondence files, 1945–1957.
MP742. Correspondence files, multiple number series, 1943–1951.
MP927. Correspondence files, multiple number series, 1952–1962.
MP1131. Correspondence files, multiple number series with 'A' prefix, 1952–1962.

Australian War Memorial, Canberra, ACT

AWM 85. War Diaries, Japan and Korea. 1950–54.
AWM 89. Robert O'Neill Papers. Papers of the official historian of Australia in the Korean War.
AWM 114. Written Records, Japan (BCOF) and Korea.
AWM 123. 'Special Collection II', Defence Committee Records, 1939–1957.
AWM 124. Naval Historical Collection. 'Korea' Files.

Archives and Historical Section, Department of Defence, Russell, ACT

Joint Administrative Planning Committee minutes and reports, 1950–53.
Joint Administrative Planning Committee agenda, 1950–53.

New Zealand

New Zealand Archives, Wellington

AD Series. Army Department records relating to 'Kay Force'.
DAK Series 1. War Diaries and supplementary material.

United Kingdom

Public Record Office, Kew

Cabinet Office.
   CAB 21. Registered Files.
   CAB 133. Commonwealth and International Conferences from 1945.
Dominions Office.
   DO 35. Dominions Office and Commonwealth Relations Office –
      Correspondence, Original.
Foreign Office.
   FO 371. General Correspondence:Political.
Prime Minister's Office.
   PREM 8. Correspondence and Papers, 1945–1951.
War Office.
   WO 32. Registered Papers: General Series.
   WO 208. Directorate of Military Intelligence.
   WO 216. Chief of the Imperial General Staff. Papers.
   WO 281. Korean War: War Diaries.

Imperial War Museum, London

Major-General B.A. Coad Collection.
General Sir Michael West Collection.

Liddell Hart Centre for Military Archives, Kings College, London (KQC)

Papers of General Lord Ismay.

National Army Museum, Chelsea

Miscellaneous Documents of Colonel J.L. Maxwell, 1921–1959.
Papers and Maps of Lieutenant-Colonel C.J.G. Meade, 1940–1967.

Canada

Public Archives of Canada, Ottawa

RG 2. Privy Council Office. Series 18. Central Registry Files.
RG 24. National Defence. C. Army 1870–1965.
  1. Army Headquarters Records. Registry Systems 1903–1965.
  17. Army. War Diaries 1939–1967.
RG 25. External Affairs.
  A 12. Canada House, London. Secret and Confidential Files, 1936–1955.
  B 3. Washington Embassy 1927–1970.
  G 2, Central Registry Files, Originals 1940–1963.
MG 31. Manuscript Collection.
  G 12. Recollections of Korea by Major-General J.M. Rockingham.

Directorate of History, Department of National Defence, and Historical Section, Department of External Affairs, Ottawa

A large number of policy and correspondence files relating to Canadian involvement in Korea are held by these sections, awaiting transfer to the custody of Public Archives of Canada. They are not at present organised on a record group basis, and are controlled by departmental registries.

United States of America

National Archives and Record Service, Washington DC

RG 273. Records of the National Security Council 'P' Papers.

Washington National Record Centre, Suitland, Maryland

RG 407. Command Reports 1949–1954. First Corps.

Dwight D. Eisenhower Presidential Library, Abilene, Kansas

Office of the Special Assistant for National Security Affairs; NSC Series; Briefing Notes Sub-series.

United States Army Military History Institute, Carlisle, Pennsylvania

Allied Interoperability Papers. (Cooling-Hixson Study).
Edward M. Almond Papers.
Haydon L. Boatner Papers.
Mark W. Clark Papers.
Bruce C. Clarke Papers.
Julian J. Ewell Papers.
Paul L. Freeman Papers.
Harold K. Johnson Papers.
S.L.A. Marshall Papers. Korean War.
Office of the Chief of Military History. Korean War Interviews.

John W. O'Daniel Papers.
Matthew B. Ridgway Papers.
Donald A. Siebert Papers.
Maxwell D. Taylor Papers.

Miscellaneous unpublished papers and manuscripts

Lieutenant-General Sir William Bridgeford, papers and photographs. National Library of Australia.
Buckley, Roger, 'San Francisco and After: The United States, the Pacific Powers and the Evolution of the Japanese Peace Settlements, 1945–1955'. Copy courtesy of the author.
McGibbon, I.C., 'New Zealand and the Korean War'. Copy courtesy of the author.
Lieutenant-General Sir John Northcott Papers. Mitchell Library, Sydney, MSS 1431/26, 1431/28.
Lieutenant-General Sir Horace Robertson. Two unpublished MSS, copies in the possession of the author.
Colonel P.M. Victory, 'The Royal Artillery in Korea', unpublished MS prepared for the Royal Artillery library, Woolwich. Copy courtesy of the author.
General Sir John Wilton Papers. Currently held by Mr Ian McNeill and intended for deposit in the Australian War Memorial.

Interviews

The late Brigadier M. Austin, Commanding Officer, 1st Battalion, Royal Australian Regiment, 1952–53. Canberra, 27 February 1984.
Major-General D.M. Butler, ADC to Lieutenant-General Sir Horace Robertson, 1950–51. Canberra, 26 July 1985.
Brigadier J. Burns, Commanding Officer, 16 Field Regiment, 1953–54 and Colonel E. Manders, Battery Commander, 16 Field Regiment, 1952–53. Wellington, 18 February 1984.
Lieutenant-General Sir Thomas Daly, Commanding Officer, 28th Commonwealth Infantry Brigade, 1952–53. Sydney, 12 October 1984.
Colonel I.B. Ferguson, Commanding Officer, 3rd Battalion, Royal Australian Regiment, 1950–51. Canberra, 27 March 1984.
General Sir Anthony Farrar-Hockley, Adjutant, 1st Battalion, The Gloucestershire Regiment and POW, 1950–53. London, 10 December 1984.
Lieutenant-General Frank J. Fleury, Head, Canadian Military Mission, Far East, 1950–51. Ottawa, 10 January 1985.
Major General R.L. Hughes, Commanding Officer, 3rd Battalion, Royal Australian Regiment, 1952–53. Canberra, 26 January 1984.
Lieutenant-Colonel J.W. Moodie, Commanding Officer, 16 Field Regiment, 1950–51. Dunedin, 27 February 1984.
Lieutenant-General Sir William Pike, CRA 1 Commonwealth Division, 1951–52 and Colonel P.M. Victory, BMRA 1 Commonwealth Division, 1951–52. Bentley, Surrey, 13 December 1984.

Major-General B.M. Poananga, GSO III, 1 Commonwealth Division, 1952–53. Taupo, 23 February 1984.
Colonel R.K.G. Porter, Adjutant, 16 Field Regiment, 1950–51. Auckland, 20 February 1984.
Brigadier M. Tebbutt, GSO III, 1 Commonwealth Division, 1953–54. Auckland, 20 February 1984.
Lieutenant-General Sir Richard Webb, 2ic, 16 Field Regiment, 1950–51. Wellington, 16 February 1984.

Correspondence

Lieutenant-Colonel Roy E. Appleman, US Army official historian. 19 July 1985.
Major-General M.P. Bogert, Commanding Officer, 25th Canadian Infantry Brigade, 1952–53. 30 January 1984.
Major-General T. Brodie, Commanding Officer, 29th British Infantry Brigade, 1950–51. 10 February 1984.
Professor Roger Buckley, Department of International Relations, International University of Japan. 18 July 1985.
Field Marshal Sir A. James H. Cassels, General Officer Commanding, 1 ˚Commonwealth Division, 1951–52. 15 October 1983.
Brigadier Sir Frederick Chilton, Deputy Secretary, Australian Department of Defence, 1950–58. 23 January 1984.
Lieutenant-General Sir Thomas Daly, Commanding Officer, 28th Commonwealth Infantry Brigade, 1952–53. 27 January 1984.
Colonel J.A. Fletcher, DAQ, 1 Commonwealth Division, 1952–53. 17 December 1984.
Lieutenant-General Frank J. Fleury, Head, Canadian Military Mission, Far East, 1950–51. 23 April 1984.
Professor B.H. Gandevia, RMO, 3rd Battalion, Royal Australian Regiment, 1950. 27 June 1985.
Colonel Rupert D. Graves, Chief of Staff, US 2nd Infantry Division, 1951. 10 August 1984.
Major-General R.N.L. Hopkins, Officer Commanding Australian Military Forces Component, British Commonwealth Occupation Force, 1946–48. 3 June, 14 July 1985.
Brigadier P.J. Jeffries, Commanding Officer, 1st Battalion, The Durham Light Infantry, 1952–53. 25 August 1984.
The late Brigadier G.F. Larkin, Commanding Officer, 2nd Battalion, Royal Australian Regiment, 1953–54. 10 February 1984.
Professor Peter Lowe, Department of History, Manchester University. 18 July 1985.
General Sir Arthur MacDonald, Commanding Officer, 3rd Battalion, Royal Australian Regiment, 1953–54. 14 March 1984.
General Charles D. Palmer, Commanding General, US 1st Cavalry Division, 1951. 18 August 1984.
General Matthew B. Ridgway, Commanding General, EUSAK and Supreme Commander, UNC, 1951–52. 21 March 1985.

Major-General J.M. Rockingham, Commanding Officer, 25th Canadian Infantry Brigade, 1951–52. 22 January 1984.

Colonel G.R. Stevens, Commanding Officer, 1st Battalion, Royal Fusiliers, 1952–53. 24 January 1984.

Major-General George C. Stewart, Commanding General, US 2nd Infantry Division, 1951. 8 August 1984.

Colonel Maurice D. Stratta, Chief of Staff, US 2nd Infantry Division, 1952. 24 August 1984.

Brigadier K.R.S. Trevor, Brigade Major, 29th British Infantry Brigade, 1950–51. 10 February 1984.

Lieutenant-General Sir Richard Webb, 2ic, 16 Field Regiment, 1950–51. 19 March 1984.

Major-General Richard W. Whitney, Chief of Staff, US 25th Infantry Division, 1951. 3 August 1984.

Official histories

Australia

O'Neill, Robert, *Australia in the Korean War, 1950–53. Volume I: Strategy and Diplomacy*, Australian War Memorial and the Australian Government Publishing Service, Canberra, 1981.

——*Australia in the Korean War, 1950–53. Volume II:Combat Operations*, Australian War Memorial and the Australian Government Publishing Service, Canberra, 1985.

Canada

Wood, Herbert Fairlie, *Official History of the Canadian Army. Strange Battleground. The Operations in Korea and Their Effects on the Defence Policy of Canada*, Ministry of National Defence, Ottawa, 1966.

India

Singh, Rajendra, *Official History of the Indian Armed Forces in the Second World War, 1939–1945. Post-War Occupation Forces:Japan and South-East Asia*, Combined Inter-Services Historical Section, Kanpur, 1958.

Republic of Korea

The History of the United Nations Forces in the Korean War, Volume II, The War History Compilation Committee, The Ministry of National Defence, Seoul, 1973.

United States of America

The United States Army in the Korean War

Appleman, Roy E., *South to the Naktong, North to the Yalu*, United States

Government Printing Office for the Office of the Chief of Military History, United States Army, Washington DC, 1961.

Hermes, Walter G., *Truce Tent and Fighting Front*, United States Government Printing Office for the Office of the Chief of Military History, United States Army, Washington DC, 1966.

Schnabel, James F., *Policy and Direction: The First Year*, United States Government Printing Office for the Office of the Chief of Military History, United States Army, Washington DC, 1972.

The history of the Joint Chiefs of Staff

Schnabel, James F. and Watson, Robert J., *The Joint Chiefs of Staff and National Policy. Volume III, The Korean War*, (2 parts), Michael Glazier Inc., Wilmington, 1979.

US Marine operations in Korea 1950–1953

Meid, Pat and Yingling, James M., *Volume V. Operations in West Korea*, Historical Division, Headquarters, US Marine Corps, Washington DC. 1972.

Unpublished official studies

Fox, Major William J., *History of the Korean War. Inter-Allied Cooperation During Combat Operations*, volume III, part 2, section B, Far East Command Headquarters, Military History Section, 1952.

Gaziano, Major Sam, *Problems in Utilization of United Nations Forces*, US Far East Command Headquarters, Military History Section, 1952.

Hixson, Lieutenant-Colonel John A. and Cooling, Dr Benjamin Franklin, *Combined Operations in Peace and War*, US Army Military History Institute, Carlisle Barracks, Pennsylvania, 1982.

Odgers, George, *Australian Experience in Joint Armed Service Activities*, Historical Monograph No. 10, Department of Defence, Canberra, 1976.

Secondary Sources

Books

Barclay, Brigadier C.N., *The First Commonwealth Division. The Story of British Commonwealth Land Forces in Korea, 1950–53*, Gale and Polden, Aldershot, 1954.

Barker, A.J., *Fortune Favours the Brave. The Battle of the Hook, Korea 1953*, Leo Cooper, London, 1974.

Bartlett, Norman, *With the Australians in Korea*, Australian War Memorial, Canberra, 1954.

Biderman, Albert D., *March to Calumny. The Story of the American POWs in Korea*, Macmillan, New York, 1963.

Bidwell, Shelford, *Modern Warfare. A Study of Men, Weapons and Theories*, Allen Lane, London, 1973.

Brodie, Bernard, *War and Politics*, Cassell, London, 1973.

Buckley, Roger, *Occupation Diplomacy. Britain, the United States and*

Japan 1945–1952, Cambridge University Press, Cambridge, 1982.

Calvocoressi, Peter, *The British Experience, 1945–1975*, Penguin, Harmondsworth, 1979.

Carew, Tim, *Korea. The Commonwealth at War*, Cassell, London, 1967.

Carver, Michael, *War Since 1945*, G.P. Putnam's Sons, New York, 1981.

Conroy, Hilary, *The Japanese Seizure of Korea 1868–1910. A Study of Realism and Idealism in International Relations*, University of Pennsylvania Press, Philadelphia, 1974.

Cumings, Bruce (ed), *Child of Conflict. The Korean-American Relationship. 1943–1953*, University of Washington Press, Seattle, 1983.

Dean, Major-General William F., *General Dean's Story*, Weidenfeld and Nicolson, London, 1954.

Donovan, Robert J., *Nemesis. Truman and Johnson in the Coils of War in Asia*, St Martin's Marek, New York, 1984.

Doughty, Major Robert A., *The Evolution of US Army Tactical Doctrine. 1946–76. Leavenworth Papers*, no. 1, Fort Leavenworth, 1979.

Duncan, David Douglas, *This is War! A Photo-Narrative in Three Parts*, Harper, New York, 1951.

Eayrs, James, *In Defence of Canada*. vol. 3, *Peacemaking and Deterrence*, University of Toronto Press, Toronto, 1972.

——, *In Defence of Canada*. vol. 4, *Growing Up Allied*, University of Toronto Press, Toronto, 1980.

Farrar-Hockley, General Sir Anthony, *The Edge of the Sword*, W.H. Allen, London, 1981.

Gray, Brigadier T.I.G., *The Imperial Defence College and the Royal College of Defence Studies 1927–1977*, Her Majesty's Stationary Office, Edinburgh, 1977.

Greenfield, Kent Roberts, *Command Decisions*, Office of the Chief of Military History, Washington DC, 1960.

Heinl, Jr., Colonel Robert Debs, *Victory at High Tide. The Inchon-Seoul Campaign*, Nautical and Aviation Publishing Company, Washington DC, 1979.

Holles, Robert O., *Now Thrive the Armourers. A Story of Action with the Gloucesters in Korea (November 1950–April 1951)*, Harrap, London, 1953.

Horner, D.M., *High Command. Australia and Allied Strategy 1939–1945*, George Allen and Unwin, Sydney, 1982.

Kay, Robin (ed), *Documents on New Zealand External Relations. Volume II. The Surrender and Occupation of Japan*, Government Printer, Wellington, 1982.

Kinkead, Eugene, *Why They Collaborated*, Longmans, London, 1960.

Kinnard, Douglas, *The War Managers*, University Press of New England, Hanover, 1977.

Kohn, Richard H. and Harahan, Joseph P. (eds), *Air Superiority in World War II and Korea*, USAF Warrior Studies, Washington DC, 1983.

Leckie, Robert, *Conflict. The History of the Korean War*, Hearst Corporation, New York, 1962.

Lewin, Ronald, *Slim:The Standardbearer*, Leo Cooper, London, 1976.

Lowe, Peter, *The Origins of the Korean War*, Longmans, London, 1986.
Mansergh, Nicholas, *The Commonwealth Experience*, Weidenfeld and Nicolson, London, 1969.
May, Ernest R., *'Lessons' of the Past. The Use and Misuse of History in American Foreign Policy*, Oxford University Press, Oxford, 1973.
McCormack, Gavan, *Cold War Hot War. An Australian Perspective on the Korean War*, Hale and Iremonger, Sydney, 1983.
Millar, T.B., *The Commonwealth and the United Nations*, Sydney University Press, Sydney, 1967.
—— *Australia in Peace and War*, Australian National University Press, Canberra, 1978.
Millet, Alan R. and Maslowski, Peter, *For the Common Defence. A Military History of the United States of America*, Free Press, New York, 1984.
Morgan, Kenneth O., *Labour in Power 1945–1951*, Clarendon Press, Oxford, 1984.
Nish, Ian (ed). *Aspects of the Occupation of Japan*, International Studies, London, 1986.
Pictorial Korea 1951–1952, International Publicity League of Korea, Seoul, 1952.
Preston, Richard A., *Canada and 'Imperial Defence'. A study of the origins of the British Commonwealth's defense organisation 1867–1919*, Duke University Press, Durham, 1967.
Ridgway, Matthew B., *The Korean War*, Doubleday, New York, 1967.
The Royal Ulster Rifles in Korea, The Regimental Association, Belfast, 1953.
Rowell, S.F., *Full Circle*, Melbourne University Press, Melbourne, 1974.
Russ, Martin, *The Last Parallel. A Marine's War Journal*, Rinehart, New York, 1957.
Shipster, Colonel J.N., *The Die-Hards in Korea*, The Regimental Association, Middlesex, 1979.
Srivastava, M.P., *The Korean Conflict. Search for Unification*, Prentice-Hall of India, New Delhi, 1982.
Stairs, Dennis, *The Diplomacy of Constraint: Canada, the Korean War and the United States*, University of Toronto Press, Toronto, 1974.
Thompson, Reginald, *Cry Korea*, MacDonald and Co., London, 1951.
Weigley, Russell F., *The American Way of War. A History of United States Military Strategy and Policy*, Macmillan, New York, 1973.
—— *Eisenhower's Lieutenants. The Campaigns of France and Germany. 1944–1945*, Sidgwick and Jackson, London, 1981.

Articles

Anderton, Colonel G., 'The Birth of the British Commonwealth Division', *Journal of the Royal Army Medical Corps*, vol. 99, no. 2, January 1953.
Argent, Lieutenant A., 'Armoured Operations in Korea. Task Force "Crombez" at Chipyong-ni', *Australian Army Journal*, no. 35, April 1952.
—— 'A Battalion Prepares for War', *Infantry Journal*, vol. XVII, no.2, May–June 1972.
Asada, Sadao, 'Recent Works on the American Occupation of Japan: The

State of the Art', *The Japanese Journal of American Studies*, no. 1, (1981).

Bernstein, Barton J., 'New Light on the Korean War', *The International History Review*, III, 2, April 1981.

Boatner, Major Mark M., 'The French Battalion at Arrowhead (Korea – October 1952)', *Revue Historique de l'Armee*, Special Issue, 1954.

Buckley, Roger, 'Joining the Club: The Japanese Question and Anglo-American Peace Diplomacy, 1950–1951', *Modern Asian Studies*, 19,2, (1985).

Cassels, Major-General Sir A. James H., 'The Commonwealth Division in Korea', *Journal of the Royal United Service Institution*, XCVIII, April 1953.

Cassidy, Raymond T., 'Wonju and Chipyong-ni', *Infantry*, July–August 1983.

Chesler, David J., et al, 'Effect on Morale of Infantry Team Replacement and Individual Replacement Systems', *Sociometry*, vol. 18, no. 4, August 1955

Coad, Major-General B.A., 'The Land Campaign in Korea', *Journal of the Royal United Service Institution*, vol. XCVII, February 1952.

Cooling, B. Franklin, 'Allied Interoperability in the Korean War', *Military Review*, LXIII. 6, June 1983.

——, and Hixson, John A., 'Twentieth Century Allied Interoperability', *Asian Perspective*, vol. 6, (Spring-Summer 1982).

Crerar, Lieutenant-Colonel H.D.G., 'The Development of Closer Relations Between the Military Forces of the British Empire', *Journal of the Royal United Service Institution*, LXII, August 1926.

DeVaney, Lieutenant-Colonel Carl N., 'Know your Allies', *Military Review*, XXXII. 12 March 1953.

Dockrill, M.L. 'The Foreign Office, Anglo-American Relations and the Korean War', *International Affairs*, 1986.

English, John and Hillmer, Norman, 'Canada's Alliances', *Revue Internationale D'histoire Militaire*, no. 51, Editione Canadienne, Ottawa, 1982.

Farrar, Peter N., 'Britain's Proposals for a Buffer Zone South of the Yalu in November 1950: Was it a Neglected Opportunity to End the Fighting in Korea?'. *Journal of Contemporary History*, vol.18, (1983).

Farrar-Hockley, Anthony, 'A Reminiscence of the Chinese People's Volunteers in the Korean War', *China Quarterly*, 98, June 1984.

Foot Rosemary J. 'Anglo-American Relations in the Korean Crisis:The British Effort to Avert an Expanded War, December 1950–January 1951', *Diplomatic History*, January 1986.

Gration, Major-General P.C., 'Interoperability: ABCA Operations since World War II', *Army Research, Development and Aquisition*, 23, (January–February 1982).

Gupta, Karunakar, 'How Did the Korean War Begin?', *China Quarterly*, 52, 1972, and replies to Gupta, *China Quarterly*, 54, 1973.

Hetzel, Frederick A. and Hitchens, Harold L., 'An Interview wth General Matthew B. Ridgway', *The Western Pennsylvania Historical Magazine*, vol. 65, no. 4, October 1982.

Hopkins, Major-General R.N.L., 'History of the Australian Occupation of Japan, 1946–50', *Journal of the Royal Australian Historical Society*, XL, part II. 1954.

Hopkins, Major L.I., 'Maintenance of the Australian Infantry Battalion in

Korea', *Australian Army Journal*, No. 24, May 1951.

Horner, Major D.M., 'High Command – The Australian Experience', *Defence Force Journal*, no. 48, September/October 1984.

Hutley, F.C., 'Our Occupation of Japan. A Memoir', *Quadrant*, January-February 1984.

James, D. Clayton, 'Command Crisis:MacArthur and the Korean War', *The Harmon Memorial Lectures in Military History*, no. 24, USAFA, Colorado, 1982.

Kennedy, Paul, 'Military Coalitions and Coalition Warfare over the Past Century', in Keith Nelson and Roy A. Prete (eds.), *Coalition Warfare. An Uneasy Accord*, Wilfred Laurier University Press, Waterloo, 1983.

Leopold, Richard W., 'The Korean War:The Historian's Task', in Francis H. Heller (ed), *The Korean War: A 25 Year Perspective*, The Regents Press of Kansas, Lawrence, 1977.

Lowe, Peter, 'Great Britain, Japan and the Korean War, 1950–51', John Chapman and David Steed (eds), *Proceedings of the British Association for Japanese Studies*, IX, 1984.

Marshall, S.L.A., 'Communication with our Allies', in S.L.A. Marshall, *Commentary on Infantry Operations and Weapons Usage in [the] Korea Winter of 1950–51*, Johns Hopkins University, Chevy Chase, 1952.

Mueller, John E., 'Trends in Popular Support for the Wars in Korea and Vietnam', *The American Political Science Review*, vol. 65, (1971).

Myers, Frank, 'Conscription and the Politics of Military Strategy in the Attlee Government', *The Journal of Strategic Studies*, 7, 1, March 1984.

Nagai, Yonosuke, 'The Korean War:An Interpretative Essay', *The Japanese Journal of American Studies*, no. 1. (1981).

O'Neill, Robert, 'The Chongchon River', in Noble Frankland and Christopher Dowling (eds), *Decisive Battles of the Twentieth Century*, Sidgwick and Jackson, London, 1976.

Piggot, Lieutenant-Colonel F.J.C., 'Occupying Japan', *Army Quarterly*, LIV, 1, April 1947.

Preston, Richard A., 'The Cost of Palimony: Canada's Military Dependence on the United States', *War & Society*, 1:2, (September 1983).

—— 'The Military Structure of the Old Commonwealth', *International Journal*, vol. XVII, no. 2, Spring 1962.

Ra, Jong-yil, 'Special Relationship at War:The Anglo-American Relationship During the Korean War', *The Journal of Strategic Studies*, 7,3, September 1984.

Rennie, Lieutenant C.G., 'Mobilisation for War:Canadian Army Recruiting and the Korean War', *Canadian Defence Quarterly/La Revue canadienne de defense*, vol. 15, no. 1, Summer 1985.

Schaller, Michael, 'MacArthur's Japan:The View from Washington', *Diplomatic History*, January 1986.

Seymour-Ure, Colin, 'British "War Cabinets" in Limited Wars: Korea, Suez and the Falklands', *Public Administration*, 62, Summer 1984.

Sheridan, Captain Richard B., 'The Commonwealth Staff', *Marine Corps*

Gazette, 39, 3, March 1955.

Shy, John, 'The American Military Experience:History and Learning', *Journal of Interdisciplinary History*, 1,2, Winter 1971.

Simmons, Robert R., 'The Communist Side: An Exploratory Sketch', in Francis H. Heller (ed), *The Korean War: A 25-Year Perspective*, Kansas, 1977.

Skaggs, David Curtis, 'The KATUSA Experiment: The Integration of Korean Nationals into the US Army, 1950–1965', *Military Affairs*, XXXVIII, 2, April 1974.

Soward, F.H. 'The Korean Crisis and the Commonwealth', *Pacific Affairs*, XXIV, 2, June 1951.

Tamchina, Rainer, 'In Search of Common Causes:The Imperial Conference of 1937', *Journal of Imperial and Commonwealth History*, 1,1, October 1972.

Tapp, E.J., 'Australian and New Zealand Relations (1900–1950):1. Defence', *Australian Outlook*, v, September 1951.

Terraine, John and Barnett, Correlli, 'Problems of Coalition War', *Journal of the Royal United Service Institution*, 126, 3, 1981.

Thomas, R.C.W., 'The First Commonwealth Division in Korea', *Army Quarterly*, April 1952.

—— 'Some Impressions of Life in the Commonwealth Division in Korea', *Army Quarterly*, October 1953.

Urquhart, Colonel G.M., 'Diplomats and Drivers – Support in the Rear of 25 Canadian Infantry Brigade Group During the Korean War', *Canadian Defence Quarterly/La Revue canadienne de defense*, vol. 10, no. 2, Autumn 1980.

Walsh, Major J.M., 'British Participation in the Occupation of Japan', *Army Quarterly*, LVII, 1, October 1948.

Warner, Geoffrey, 'Books:The Korean War', *International Affairs*, 56, 1, January 1980.

Watt, D.C., 'The Historians Tasks and Responsibilities', in Yonosuke Nagai and Akira Iriye (eds), *The Origins of the Cold War in Asia*, Tokyo, 1977.

Williams, J.A., 'Korea and the Malayan Emergency – the Strategic Priorities', *Journal of the Royal United Services Institute*, 118 (2), 1973.

Wood, F.L.W., 'The Anzac Dilemma', *International Affairs*, 24, 2, April 1953.

Woodward, Lieutenant-Colonel Walden F., 'The British Army Staff', *Military Review*, XXXII, 1, April 1952.

Theses

Clemow, C.W.A., New Zealand, the Commonwealth and the Korean War. A Study in Government Policy and Unofficial Opinion. MA Thesis, University of Auckland, 1967.

Eaddy, Robert, New Zealand in the Korean War:The First Year. A Study in Official Government Policy. MA Thesis, University of Otago, 1983.

McDonald, Jr., James A., The Problems of US Marine Corps Prisoners of War in Korea. MA Thesis, University of Maryland, 1961.

Index